�֍ TORAH AND GOSPEL

Torah and Gospel

Jewish and Catholic Theology in Dialogue ✹ ✹

EDITED BY *Philip Scharper*

SHEED AND WARD: NEW YORK

Editor's Preface

This book grew out of a symposium of Jewish and Catholic theologians held in January, 1965, at St. Vincent's Archabbey, Latrobe, Pennsylvania.

In most instances, an editor would take pains to remove from a book like this all traces of its origin. In *Torah and Gospel* just the opposite has been done, and the reader may well be entitled to an explanation of why the following pages so often show that this book began in a live interchange between contributors rather than in the library of each writer.

To begin, the meeting at St. Vincent's was a symposium in the literal sense. The participants lived together for three days, and gathered about the dining (and refreshment) tables as well as the conference table. The interchange of ideas was thus almost constant, and one was often reminded not only of Plato's description of a symposium, but of meetings recorded in the Scriptures as well. Each participant seemed to feel that he had recognized his brothers in the breaking of the bread.

We have, then, attempted to convey to the reader of this volume something of the warmth as well as the wisdom of this symposium. Thus, we have printed Bishop William G. Connare's welcome to the participants as the introduction to *Torah and Gospel*, and have received Rabbi Arthur Gilbert's permission to print the remarks by which he brought the symposium to a close. Each stresses the importance of the climate of comradeship which made this symposium not merely an academic exercise but a shared religious experience.

The papers delivered at the meeting are printed here as they were given, with one exception. Rabbi Agus read an abridgement of the rather lengthy paper he had prepared. Given the value of his longer exposition of "Israel as Idea and Reality," I suggested to Rabbi Agus that his paper be published in the full form in which it appears in these pages.

Perhaps one last comment may be permitted, much as it may embarrass the contributors to and participants in the Latrobe meeting. Each came to represent his own tradition. Yet each did more: he re-presented his tradition, at its finest, in his own person. The pages that follow show, within the limits of language, how well each expressed some aspect of Judaic or Catholic tradition. These pages could not reveal, however, the degree to which each of these men exhibited that spirit of creative love which lies at the heart of both Judaism and Christianity.

—PHILIP SCHARPER

Contents

An Introduction

I receive you into a very old monastery in a very young Diocese. In each we like to think of hospitality as one of the hallmarks of our respective families.

When Benedict wrote the rule for his monks in 529, he stressed the importance of hospitality, equating every guest with his Divine Master, and deserving of attention in accord with this equation. When Boniface Wimmer, one of Benedict's more illustrious sons, in 1847 built the very first American foundation of the Benedictines on this very spot, he irrevocably committed Saint Vincent's to the continuation of this same tradition. I daresay that you have already sensed the depth and the warmth of the monks, who have asked you to tarry with them for a few days.

When one day "in a desert place apart" the Divine Master "saw a large crowd, out of compassion for them He cured their sick." When evening came on, and there was no food available, He multiplied "five loaves and two fishes . . . and all ate and were satisfied (Matthew 14:13–21). This He did, among other reasons, to emphasize the place of hospitality in His gospel.

When Hugh L. Lamb, my predecessor and the founding Bishop of this Diocese of Greensburg, a mere dozen years ago, executed the apostolic mandate erecting this Diocese, he irrevocably committed the Church in this area to this same gospel of hospitality.

Emphasis on this note of hospitality, I believe, will clarify the purposes and set the tone of our gathering. First of all, it will make clear why we have not gathered. Then, on the positive side it will show why we have come together, as friends among friends, anxious to probe the depths which unite rather than the differences which divide us.

As to the first, we can easily take a cue from the Second Vatican Council speaking on the important subject of ecumenism in its historic *Decree on Ecumenism*. We have not gathered, as the sacred Council advises, to argue the validity of our respective positions. Nothing constructive could be hoped for, if we take a strictly polemical approach to the discussions of these days. As friends engaged in friendly discussion, we are not concerned with showing either side as wrong or right.

Nor do we gather with thoughts of proselytizing or conversion on our minds. Again, we can take a cue from the Second Vatican Council, speaking in its moving *Declaration on the Relationship of the Church to Non-Christian Religions*. With frank and charitable candor the Declaration simply states that in the select company of the ancient prophets like *Sophonias (3, 9)* and *Isaiah (66, 23)*, the *Psalmist (65, 4)*, and the Apostle Paul *Romans (11, 11–32)* the Church "awaits that day, known to God alone, on which all peoples will address the Lord in a single voice and 'serve Him shoulder to shoulder.'" This, the current mood of the Church, similar I am sure to that of the Synagogue, leaves the eschatalogical hope of the human family, where ultimately it must be placed, if we are to be realistic, in the mysterious mind of God. Without prejudice to our respective convictions we can certainly pray with all men of good will, so that all will be ready to meet their Lord on "that day, known to God alone," the day of divine reckoning.

On the positive side, the spirit of our gathering, then, clearly becomes the probing of our common roots. (Constructively we must seek in the language of our respective traditions identical answers to the age-old questions, which have always bothered man in the deepest recesses of his soul, and have ultimately shaped the course of human destiny.)

In beautifully measured language the afore-mentioned *Declaration* of the Vatican Council synthesizes this work we undertake this evening. "Men expect from the various religions," the Council states, "answers to the unsolved riddles of man's condition, riddles that move the hearts of men today, as deeply as they did in olden times: What is man? What is the meaning, what the purpose of our lives? What is the moral good, what is sin? Which is the road to true happiness? What are death, judgment and retribution after death? What, finally, is that ultimate inexpressible mystery, which, encompassing our existence, is its source as well as its destiny?"

In this introduction, purposely brief, it would be difficult and indeed highly improper for me to attempt an answer to these questions in any detailed fashion. This, I believe, in essence is the continuing work of all who will subsequently participate in this Jewish-Catholic Colloquy.

May I express the hope, however, that somehow through the hours of these days we can run the gamut of that glorious symphony of words, which literally jump from every page of the *Old Testament*. This is the Testament, in which we find our common roots. Its simple theme is a sense of God's abiding presence and providence in our lives. In moving fashion it catches the many moods of this divine presence in daily life, now praising, now thanking, now imploring the God of mercy for the many needs, which press heavily upon us and our families.

For instance, where in all the literature of the world can we find words to match the 99th Psalm as it gives praise and thanks to the good God:

Sing joyfully to the Lord, all you lands; serve the Lord with gladness; Come before Him with joyful song.

Know that the Lord is God; He made us, His we are; His people, the flock He tends.

Enter His gates with thanksgiving, His courts with praise; give thanks to Him; bless His name,

For He is good: the Lord Whose kindness endures forever, and His faithfulness to all generations.

I think we could all quickly agree that the radical loss of faith on the part of millions of people is the major phenomenon of the modern world. In each of our respective traditions, I dare say, there are hundreds of tragic souls of our own acquaintance, who have lost their sense of God.

This may well be the big subject behind all the little subjects, which tantalize and torture these unfortunate souls, and twist and turn the details of their daily existence. Until they capture again "that ultimate inexpressible mystery," which is both the source and the destiny of their very being, they will continue to flounder. Until they discover that "that ultimate inexpressible mystery" is the God who dearly loves them, and anxiously provides for their every need, they will continue to drift.

May the God of Abraham, the God of Isaac and the God of Jacob carefully guide our deliberations these days, that from our common roots in Him we will succeed in some small measure in finding answers for and relieving the confusion of these unfortunate minds of our times. If we do, the hours of this colloquy will indeed be richly blessed.

In the language dear to you and your father may I say:

E-lef	kaba-lot pa-neem	l'chul-chem
A thousand	welcomes	to all of you
A-chai	ha-ahu-veem	bay-lo-heem
My brothers	beloved	in God.
Y'va-raych	elo-hay	Av-ra-ham
May bless	the God of	Abraham

elo-hay	Yits-chak	vay-lo-hay
the god of	Isaac	and the God of

Ya-a-kov et	ha-ya-meem	ha-ay-le
Jacob	days	these

v'yaf-re et	see-cho-tay-hem	l'so-fo.
and make fruitful	their discussions	to His end.

Shalom.   Shalom.

—✝ WILLIAM G. CONNARE
Bishop of Greensburg

✿ TORAH AND GOSPEL

1

✿ Evaluating the Past

RABBI SOLOMON GRAYZEL

Evaluating the Past in Christian-Jewish Relations

DR. SOLOMON GRAYZEL *has been Editor of the Jewish Publication Society of America for the past twenty-five years. Ordained at the Jewish Theological Seminary in New York, he received his Ph.D. in philosophy from the Dropsie College in Philadelphia. Author of several volumes, among which are* The Church and the Jews in the 13th Century, A History of the Jews *(Jewish Publication Society), and, most recently, the popular paperback* A History of the Contemporary Jews *(Meridian, 1961), Rabbi Grayzel is currently Secretary to the Committee engaged in preparing a new translation of the Bible of which the* Torah *has thus far appeared.*

Our Teacher Moses offered history as a guide: "Remember the days of old; consider the ages past . . . ." A modern teacher, George Santayana, offered history as a warning: "They who do not know their history are destined to repeat it." No doubt both views are right: There are trends in the past that should be followed, and others that should be avoided. The trouble begins when you have to decide which is which. No one argues any longer that history is a science; and, since it is an art, differences of interpretation are to be expected.

For almost two thousand years, Judaism and Christianity have

5

lived side by side. We may consider the religions divine in origin, but we must assume that their institutions have been and must continue to be human; otherwise they would not have histories. As a matter of fact, the Jewish and the Christian peoples not only have separate histories, but also a joint history, since each religious group has continuously affected the other. It is only proper, therefore, that their contacts should be historically evaluated, that we may know what is to be avoided and what encouraged in their relationship in the days that lie ahead.

At what point may one set the beginning of Christian-Jewish relations? It is a mistake to set it at the Crucifixion, for to do so is to assume that in any ordinary course of events Jesus would not eventually have found a place among the Jewish teachers of ethics. Nor is it possible to set it at a time loosely called "The Parting of the Ways"; for the phrase is too vague and describes a process rather than a date. The beginning of that process, and the beginning of the relationship, is best set about the year 50 A.D., at the Council of Jerusalem.

Read simply and without regard to complicating exegesis, Chapter 15 of the Book of Acts describes not so much a compromise as a policy; and chapter 2 of Galatians tells of the failure of this policy. The question placed before the gathering at Jerusalem involved a redefinition of the term "Covenant." Did man live up to the Covenant between God and Israel through the symbol of circumcision, followed by a life of observing the commandments, or had Jesus replaced the Covenant, so that faith in him was enough to transform personality? James, unwilling to reject the Gentiles and unable to break with the Covenant of Jewish tradition, suggested a way out of the difficulty. He would let Jews, whether they believed in Jesus or not, continue to obey the old Covenant, while Gentiles who believed in Jesus would be expected to begin with the Noachide commandments and the Promise. The view of the possibility of two covenants living peacefully side by side,[1] expressed at this precursor of all ecumenical councils, bears at least a resemblance to the doctrine of religious freedom discussed at Vatican II.

The situation, as it developed, soon created a breach between the two attitudes and widened it beyond repair. There were misunderstandings between the party of Paul and the party of James. The letter to the Galatians strikes one as an answer to charges leveled against Paul by the group which was laying the foundations for a Judeo-Christianity. The latter group would not agree that the Covenant with Abraham was a temporary one.

Events in the next generation strengthened Gentile Christianity. The destruction of the Temple, the failure of several other attempts to throw off the Roman yoke, the appeal which Paul's view of Jesus made to the pagans and to the Fearers of the Lord— these steps in the process of separation are well-known and require no elaboration here. Before long, both sides broke off friendly relations. John's biography of Jesus shows how much anti-Jewish feeling had crept into Christian society. The introduction of an anti-Christian prayer into the synagogue ritual shows how resentful the Jews had become over the pro-Roman attitude of the Christians and over their acceptance of Jesus as a supernatural Messiah. The Christians, moreover, were developing a literature of their own which was progressively replacing the reading of the Torah and the Prophets. The Hebrew Scriptures were used mainly as a source of proof texts, and the use of these astounded the Jews. The dialogue between Justin and Trypho, probably based on an actual encounter, reveals Trypho's polite astonishment at Justin's interpretations.[2]

The rivalry between the two groups grew increasingly sharp and bitter. By the middle of the second century, Christianity was denying the three essentials of Judaism: the unity of God as the Jews understood it, the uniqueness of Israel, and the immutability of Scripture. It claimed for itself the Election and the Promise, that is, the sacred ideas and the basic hopes which

Judaism had developed and which, the Christians asserted, they had never really understood.

Perhaps, if the Jews had had the power, they would have tried to suppress Christianity. But they did not have the power. Perhaps the Christians would have resorted to physical measures if they could. But they could not; Rome even considered them a subversive element and persecuted them. There is no clear contemporary evidence that the Jews had a hand in whatever persecutions the early Christians suffered.[3] Some of the better-placed and therefore more conservative-minded Diaspora Jews must have looked upon the Christians as troublemakers; but there is no proof that they encouraged their persecution. The relations were strained, even unfriendly, but their expression was largely verbal. It is possible that *Toledot Yeshu,* a contemptuous counter-gospel, had its beginnings among the Jews, about this time. Free from any sort of compulsion, the increasing number of Christians indulged themselves in the syncretistic religious attitude which had long prevailed in the Roman Empire. The Jews enjoyed social standing, and even the Christian teachers admitted that Jewish tradition and literature were divinely inspired. It is not hard to see why a considerable number of Christians, surely not of the lower classes, visited the synagogues and adopted a number of Jewish observances.[4] The leaders of the Church could do nothing about this so long as Christianity was not the religion of the State.

The situation changed when the Church became allied with the State. Thereafter it became necessary to explain not why there were periodic attacks on the Jews, but why Judaism was not entirely uprooted. Roman respect for tradition has been offered as the reason for this moderation. Possibly this vaunted Roman habit of mind played a part, but it could hardly have been the sole or even the most important reason for Jewish survival. Had it been so important, Bishop Cyril of Alexandria, for example, would have been punished severely for inciting the mob to destroy the Jewish community of Alexandria early in the fifth century, whereas, in reality, his action evoked no particular condemnation. History and legend refer to similar riotous actions in various parts of the Empire. Neither Theodosius nor Justinian hesitated to interfere in Jewish affairs and change well-established customs. Neither the Emperor Heraclius in the seventh century nor Leo III in the eighth felt restricted by Roman tradition when they attempted to convert the Jews of the eastern empire by force.[5] As a matter of fact, respect for the tradition of Roman law was more widespread in the western than in the eastern empire—and understandably, since at that time the ties between Church and State were weaker in the eastern empire. Theodoric the Ostrogoth invoked the Roman tradition of toleration in his attitude to the Jews, and the same spirit found expression in Pope Gregory I's principle that their traditional rights must not be violated.[6] Yet the same Pope, as saintly a head as guided the Church during the first millennium, commended King Reccared of Visigothic Spain on his efforts to force Christianity on nonbelievers.

A more potent reason than the Roman tradition of toleration must be found to explain the survival of Judaism during the early centuries of Christian alliance with the State. The reason appears to have been the economic one. Numerically and commercially, the Jews were especially significant in the larger centers of population in the eastern Mediterranean lands. It was one thing to have one or another community hurt by a riot. It was quite another matter to destroy by death or exile, or to disrupt by forced conversion entire communities whose members contributed to the prosperity of the realm. State reasons, dangers from without, rather than religious zeal alone explain the actions of Heraclius and Leo III.

For whatever reason or combination of reasons, a Jewish people survived, and its survival demanded theological explanation. St. Augustine gave it a form destined to be repeated frequently thereafter. Psalm 59, 12(11) reads: "Slay them not, lest my people forget; scatter them by Thy power and cast them down." In his comment on this, St. Augustine drew the conclusion that it was not intended for the Jews to be killed, but that their dispersion and degradation were punishment enough.[7]

In western Europe the situation was different, but the forces operating in the Christian-Jewish relationship were the same. The story must be told in terms of Church and State, of economic developments, and inevitably also in terms of the characters and personalities that stood at the head of the religious and secular institutions.

Despite their experience in Visigothic Spain in the seventh century and other occasional attacks and ephemeral persecutions, the Jews found Christianized western Europe a peaceful haven for some five hundred years, down to the period of the Crusades. Local Church councils kept urging the Christian population not to have contact with or respect for their Jewish neighbors. Occasionally, a zealous Churchman like Bishop Agobard of Lyons fulminated against them.[8] Generally, however, the few centuries following the barbarian invasions were happy ones for the Jews of Italy, France, and the Rhineland. The explanation lies close at hand.

The barbarians had reduced Roman civilization to ashes. The cities had all but disappeared; the economy became primitive, and politics was the expression of the whims and ambitions of the local nobility. The Jews could not fit into the agricultural organization of society at that time. They could not be the local nobleman's fighting men or his serfs. Nor could they have any extensive landholdings, because early Church regulations prevented them from having Christian slaves or even pagan slaves who might express a desire to become Christians. Jews were driven either out of agriculture or out of Judaism. In time, they therefore took over the economically risky and personally dangerous occupation of trading. They attached themselves to monastaries or to the residences of the strong men of some district. Then, through their connections with other Jews in distant lands, they provided whatever their patrons needed above the absolute necessities of life. This simplified description of the economic history of the Jews in the early Middle Ages helps explain why the Jews became affluent, influential, and comparatively free.[9] Kings and nobles made use of their talents in government and finance; and the Jews looked upon themselves as little lower than the nobility in political status. They certainly did not consider themselves serfs.

The political and economic status of Jews at this time was possible, however, only because the economic needs of society synchronized with a period of weakness in the Church organization. The internal problems of the Papacy, the weak religious discipline among the lower clergy, and the State's control of the upper clergy made it difficult for the Church to enforce its authority. The theory of the Church on its relations to the Jews remained dormant. Reassertion of that theory and its vigorous implementation had to wait until the internal reforms of the Church were achieved in the eleventh and twelfth centuries and until the struggle for Church supremacy against the State was at least temporarily won under Innocent III.

Several aspects of the Jewish situation also help explain the Christians' attitude toward them which came to the fore during the eleventh to fourteenth century. There was considerable fear of the influence of Judaism. There is little direct proof that the Jews in the West influenced their pagan slaves or their Christian domestics to become converts to Judaism; but it appears reasonable to assume that they sometimes did. Repeated conciliar objections to intermarriage between Jews and Christians indicate that such unions occurred and that they sometimes resulted in a loss to Christianity. Every so often, there is a reference to conversion to Judaism of a more or less prominent Christian. Best known is the case of Bodo, a deacon connected with the court of Louis the Fair, Charlemagne's son.[10] It may be surmised, moreover, that where contacts were frequent, religious discussions were equally so. In such private or semipublic disputations, the average Christian of those days was not adequately prepared to counter the Jewish interpretations of the Bible. Later the Church forbade ill-prepared Christians, including the clergy, from disputing freely with Jews. But during those centuries, the outspoken Jew may not have persuaded the deeply committed Christian of the truth of Judaism, but he did persuade him of the danger from its free expression.[11]

Worst of all was the dilemma of the simple parish priest, trying hard to impress his flock with the teaching that the Christian life was the good life which God rewards. He could not help but see the possibility that the prosperity of a good Jewish neighbor might raise doubts in the minds of his parishioners. It is hardly surprising, therefore, that these parishioners were made to see the connection between the Jews and the devil.[12] The Church in those days lived in constant dread of heresy; and it is no wonder that the Albigensians in the twelfth and thirteenth centuries, like the Lutherans several centuries later, were called Judaizers.

Given this fear and suspicion of Jews and Judaism, the events of the crusading era follow naturally. Poorly organized and even more poorly led, the peasant armies which entered upon the First Crusade found the Jewish communities on their line of march too defenseless and too tempting to overlook. Few royal officials came to their aid, and fewer Churchmen raised their voices against the attacks made upon them. During the Second Crusade the saintly Bernard of Clairvaux spoke out in warning, and the attacks against the Jews were, in fact, fewer and less bloody. The Jews also obtained letters of protection from the Pope, on the one hand, and from the Emperor, on the other. But what was gained in this way was lost, because, by this time, a Christian middle class had come into being. It looked upon the Jews as possible competitors whose removal was desirable, especially where the Jews were their creditors.[13] Then and thereafter the characteristic business of the Jews ceased to be commerce and became moneylending.

From this point on, the Jewish situation deteriorated rapidly. The State—whether emperors, kings, dukes, or autonomous cities —had only moderate need of them. Each of these rulers was ready to sacrifice or defend his Jews as the policy of the moment demanded. Yet, when sacrificing them, whether to satisfy the clamors of the Christian middle class or to solve personal need of funds, pious claims were never wanting. Religion was employed as a protective coloration.

It is here significant that two myths about the Jews first appeared in the twelfth century. One was the story of the wandering Jew, which portrayed and justified the sense of Jewish rootlessness. The second was the infinitely uglier and more dangerous charge of ritual murder. Refuted by popes and emperors, time and again disproved, the charge was nonetheless raised countless times. It led to literally hundreds of massacres and caused an untold number of unofficial and judicial murders.[14]

If, economically, the European Jew was now expendable, religiously he was now negligible as a danger to Christianity. Conversion to Judaism was exceedingly rare. Except for a corner of the Iberian peninsula, Europe was fully Christianized. Nevertheless, the very able Pope Innocent III hewed strictly to the theological line set forth by St. Augustine eight centuries earlier. In an explanatory statement introducing the Bull of Protection which he issued early in his reign, Innocent argued that the Jews must not be killed because, by their very existence, Jews offer proof of Christian truth. In other communications, Innocent accused Jews of blindness and blasphemy, of plotting and arrogance. He submitted to the Twelfth Ecumenical Council, the Fourth Lateran in 1215, a series of laws, climaxed by the imposition of a Jewish badge which was intended for separation and

degradation.[15] Innocent III it was who set the tone and the
methods for anti-Jewish legislation by the Church from which
the Jews of Europe were not to free themselves till modern
times.

One possible explanation for the heightened anti-Jewishness
at this time is that the attempt further to weaken the Jews was
part of the struggle between Church and State. If the State, especially the Empire, by its new theory of Jewish servitude claimed
control over the Jews and their property, the Church in effect
countered by asserting its spiritual authority to assign them a
low place in Christian society and to reduce their economic
potential. Basically, however, the Church-State struggle represented a revival of the old conflict which had its origins soon
after the Council of Jerusalem. One of two religions claiming
the same divine origin now had the opportunity of defeating the
other, and it proceeded to do so. It was to be a theological and
physical (if not a religious) triumph; but the religious justification could come later. The Church's hope of converting the Jews
grew with its power, and the efforts it made toward that end were
truly extraordinary. The advice of good Pope Gregory I was not
heeded, and force was used much more widely and more frequently than suasion.[16] In the spiritual climate of the Middle
Ages, it is understandable that the Church urged secular rulers
not to put Jews in positions of authority over Christians; it was
the incitement to riot by local clergy and the preaching of hate
by clerical orators that clashed with the ideals of Christianity.[17]

The attitude of the Jews toward the Christians is far more
difficult to document than that of the Christians toward the Jews,
since Christian attitudes were expressed in action by organized
civil and religious institutions. But one may take it for granted
that there was a sense of outrage among the Jews over the ever-
present threat of violence. There was fear, distrust, and possibly
contempt. *The Book of the Pious,* for example, a thirteenth-
century work intended for the masses of Jews rather than for

scholars and intellectuals, still speaks of Christians as idolators and assumes as quite natural that Jews would accept martyrdom "for the sanctification of the Holy Name." Yet Maimonides a generation earlier had spoken of Christianity and Islam as preparations for Judaism. Manahem haMeiri, at the beginning of the fourteenth century, mentions Christianity and Islam as "within the confines of religious understanding," as opposed to paganism which is outside such confines.[18] Within another century, Joseph Albo, who lost a son in the Spanish riots of 1391, spoke of Christianity and Judaism as trunks stemming from the same roots. Clearly, the two religions, as expressed on their highest intellectual and spiritual levels, were not inherently inimical to one another.

The details of the relationship during the next few centuries —the pressures, the compulsory disputations, the attacks on the Talmud, the Inquisition, the expulsions, the ghettos—are either well-known or too tedious to recount. What is historically germane to our subject as well as instructive is that the relationship between Jews and Christians during the centuries following the thirteenth was affected by the extent of the powers of the Church, the nature of its leaders, and the cultural climate of any given period. In the fourteenth century, during the Babylonian Captivity of the Church and the schism which followed, the popes had little to say about the Jews, and what they did say was, on the whole, of a protective nature.[19]

During the fifteenth century, the so-called Conciliar period, the members of the ecumenical councils were more anti-Jewish than the popes, except, of course, for the anti-Pope Benedict XIII (Peter de Luna), who set out to curry the favor of the Conciliarists.[20] These were Churchmen who, having despaired of the popes' ability to reform the Church, tried to take authority into their own hands and impose upon the Church the will of the majority of prelates. It was a democratic movement in the sense of being more directly representative of public opinion among the Chris-

tians of western Europe. The Jews now became pawns in the
diplomatic game among the popes who were eager to restore their
independence, the Conciliarists who were determined to rule the
Church, and emperors and kings who were playing for their
private advantage. Generally speaking, in the course of the fifteenth century, the German and North Italian rulers wanted
their Jews to enjoy a certain amount of economic freedom. The
Spanish rulers, beginning with the middle of the century, wanted
to consolidate their power through the clergy, the lower nobility,
and the middle class in the towns, and insisted on establishing an
inquisition. The popes of that day found themselves under the
necessity of agreeing with both sets of rulers. In their own states
they were quite liberal, though when conciliar pressures became
strong, they would revoke temporarily what privileges they had
granted. The popes who were under the influence of the spirit of
the Renaissance, such as Alexander VI (Borgia) and Leo X
(Medici), were not at all inclined to make life any harder for
their Jews than they absolutely had to make it.[21]

Had the Renaissance influence lasted longer, spread more
widely, and penetrated more deeply than the mind and manners
of an upper class, the goals of the Christian attitude toward the
Jews might have been affected, or at least the method of attaining
them modified. Unfortunately, the Rennaisance as a movement
was short-lived, killed by the bitterness of the Catholic-Protestant
conflict. The reaction which followed was social as well as theological. Hostility to Jews and Judaism became a test of Christian zeal, and Protestant in this respect vied with Catholic. The
contents of Pope Paul IV's terribly repressive Bull *Cum nimis
absurdum* of 1555[22] were no harsher than what Luther had said
about the Jews and Judaism after he discovered that his brand
of Christianity had found no followers among Jews. Conversionary
efforts were made in both Catholic and Protestant States; ghettos
were established in both; and both segments of Christendom saw
Jews expelled or readmitted for reasons that were basically eco-

nomic. If it took longer for the Catholic countries to readmit Jews, the reason was that the northern, Protestant States were the first to experience the economic revolution which eventually spread to all countries and brought a change of attitude all over western and central Europe.

Even the three hundred years between the Council of Trent and Vatican I, among the dreariest centuries in Catholic-Jewish relations, are instructive from the viewpoint of the Church's responsiveness to the winds of change. The Tridentine attitude of unflinching intransigeance with respect to established principles and methods was breached occasionally in the matter of Jewish policy. One notable example was Pope Clement XIII's sending of Cardinal Ganganelli to Poland in the 1760's to investigate the ritual murder accusations over which there was a flurry at the time.[23] The report was, of course, a complete exoneration of the Jews. Yet the lower clergy of Poland did not discourage this resort to terror and ugliness, even though Ganganelli himself soon became Pope Clement XIV. A second example, closer to our own day, was the readiness of Pope Pius IX to abolish the Roman ghetto in 1848. Unfortunately, a revolutionary upheaval in Rome soon after drove the Pope into temporary exile. Pius IX returned from that exile, persuaded that a policy of conservatism was best. Emanicipation for the Jews of Rome came only in the wake of Italian unification.[24]

The Jews had not sought segregation; the ghetto was imposed upon them. Life was hard within its walls, largely because the ghetto was an economic as well as a spiritual prison. But hard as it was, life was not the dreary thing modern sociologists and historians suppose; it was brightened by the religious round of the year and by the intellectual devotion to religious study. The ghetto walls did, however, emphasize the existence of an enemy population outside, a population that could be easily brutalized. The ghetto inhabitants could easily, therefore, adopt the attitude that Christianity as a religion was hardly worth their notice.

Again, however, rabbis like Loew of Prague in the sixteenth century and Moses Rivkes of Vilna in the seventeenth tried to explain that Christianity, believing in a divine Creator, was not paganism, that to help Christians was a religious obligation, that to do business with them was not sinful. It remained, of course, for the eighteenth and the nineteenth centuries, when more or less peaceful, social and business contacts were reestablished, to see new attitudes prevail on both sides—along with an entirely new set of problems.

What has been said above appears to lead to a number of conclusions in broad, historical terms.

1. A policy of repression and physical efforts at conversion of the Jews may have been inherent (but not inevitable) in a situation which brought together two religions, each of which denied the premises of the other. When Christianity was a minority religion in the second century, Tertullian argued that religion cannot be forced on the unwilling (*non est religionis cogere religionem*). With the attainment of majority status and power by Christianity, a policy of active suppression proved irresistible. Nevertheless, every so often in the centuries that followed, the sentiment of toleration was repeated with sincerity by the most deeply religious spirits, such as Pope Gregory I and Thomas Aquinas.

2. The policy of suppression was raised almost to a principle during the Middle Ages, as a result of the fear of Judaism on the part of the lower clergy. Members of the lower clergy were not very well prepared for their tasks, and they considered the persistence of the Jews a direct challenge to their life and preachments. Injuries to Christianity were discovered and propagated in order to justify this fear.

3. The papacy, generally speaking, was more tolerant than the lower clergy. The Jews sometimes served as an instrument of policy, sometimes as a means of proving zeal; but popes were always susceptible to the spiritual climate about them. This

showed itself in the attitude toward the Jews which changed from age to age. Anti-Jewishness was not a dogma, but a matter of policy.

4. The State protected the Jews when the latter were useful or played a substantial part in the economy of the country. Sometimes protection was extended even when it went contrary to the plans of the Church; but it was never extended if it went contrary to the personal advantage or to the political aggrandizement of the head of the State.

5. The attitude of the Jews toward Christians and Christianity varied from age to age in accordance with both Jewish experience and intellectual status. But there was always an awareness of the Jews' minority status and of the danger from the majority.

It is clear, therefore, that the relationship between Judaism and Christianity has fluctuated in accordance with the interplay of a number of forces. Within the limits of our experience, Judaism and Christianity—these two interpretations of God's relationship to man—are inseparably joined. One of the most scholarly books dealing with this subject to have appeared in fairly recent years was written by the late Peter Browe, S.J.; it tries to assess the effectiveness of the methods used to convert the Jews.[25] After reviewing the various methods that have been used to achieve the conversion of the Jews, Father Browe concluded with the question, "Why did all these efforts fail?" He answered sadly, but wisely, by saying, in effect, "Because God so willed it."

Perhaps the conclusion of the Council of Jerusalem was the correct one after all. God does not want the type of ecumenicity which is implied in uniformity, in complete like-mindedness, but rather in cooperation in the midst of friendly disagreement, even on the most fundamental elements of our faiths. Our common business in this world is not to attack or undermine one another, but to convert the pagans in our midst.

NOTES

1 The trends within the earliest Christian community, which eventually led to the formation of a Judeo-Christian attitude, as opposed to a Gentile-Christian attitude, are discussed by Hans Joachim Schoeps, *Theologie u. Geschichte des Juden Christentums* (Tubingen, 1949). See especially pp. 258 ff. Compare James Parkes' interesting little book, *Jesus, Paul, and the Jews* (London, 1936), pp. 144 ff. and Joseph Klausner, *From Jesus to Paul* (New York, The Macmillan Company, 1943), pp. 366 ff.

2 Trypho's politeness emerges even from the brief discussion of the encounter in A. Lukyn-Williams, *Adversus Judaeos* (New York, Cambridge University Press, 1936), pp. 31 ff.

3 See Marcel Simon, *Verus Israel* (Paris, 1948), pp. 151 ff.

4 For early councils and popes that dealt with the subject, see C.-J. Hefele and H. Lecherque, *Histoire des Counciles*, I, pt. 1, pp. 145–152.

5 See S. W. Baron, *A Social and Religious History of the Jews*, II and III (New York, Columbia University Press, 1952, and Philadelphia, Jewish Publication Society, 1957), *passim*.

6 S. Grayzel, "The Papal Bull *Sicut Judaeis*," in *Studies and Essays in Honor of Abraham A. Neuman* (Philadelphia, Dropsie College, 1962), pp. 246 n, and 247.

7 See Bernhard Blumenkranz, *Die Judenpredigt Augustins* (Basel, 1946), pp. 186 ff.

8 See Idem, *Les Auteurs chrétiens latins sur les Juifs et le Judaisme* (Paris, 1963), pp. 152–168.

9 A discussion of the part the Jews played is presented by Irving A. Agus in his *Urban Civilization in Pre-Crusade Europe*, 2 vols. (New York, Yeshiva University Press, 1965).

10 See Blumenkranz, *op. cit.*, pp. 184–191.

11 Peter Browe, *Die Judenmission im Mittelalter und die Paepste, Miscellanea Historiae Purtificiae*, VI (Rome, 1942), p. 88.

12 See Joshua Trachtenberg, *The Devil and the Jews* (New Haven, 1943), especially pp. 14–15, and Guido Kisch, *The Jews in Medieval Germany* (Chicago, 1949), pp. 323–327.

13 Kisch, *ibid.*, pp. 316–322, 327–333.

14 See Cecil Roth, *The Ritual-Murder Libel and the Jew: The Report of Cardinal Lorenzo Ganganelli* (London, 1935), and M. Stern, *Paepstliche Bullen ueber die Blutbeschuldigung* (Munich, 1900).

15 S. Grayzel, *The Church and the Jews in the 13th Century* (Philadelphia, Dropsie College, 1933), no. 5 (Bull by Innocent III, 1199), nos. X, XI (decrees of Lateran IV, 1215).

16 Browe, *op. cit.*, pp. 220 ff., also pp. 13–48 on conversionary preaching.

17 On February 20, 1422, Pope Martin V gave the Jews of Central Europe a

Bull of Protection in which he denied charges raised against them by incendiary preaching; presumably John Capistrano was the person meant. See M. Stern, *Urkundliche Beitraege ueber die Stellung der Paepste zu den Juden* (Kiel, 1893), no. 21.

[18] Jacob Katz, *Exclusiveness and Tolerance: Studies in Jewish-Gentile Relations in Medieval and Modern Times* (New York, Oxford University Press, 1961), *passim*, especially chap. X, "Men of Enlightenment," pp. 114 ff.

[19] Grayzel, in *Abraham A. Neuman.*

[20] For the Bull of anti-Pope Benedict XIII and the attitude of the Conciliarist party, see Max Simonsohn, *Die Kirchliche Judengesetzgebung in Zeitdlter der Reform-Konzilien von Konstanz und Basel* (Breslau, 1912).

[21] See Cecil Roth, *The History of the Jews of Italy* (Philadelphia, 1946), pp. 197, 206. For these and other popes of the Renaissance age, see Attilio Milano, *Storia degli Ebrei in Italia* (Turin, 1963), pp. 236 ff.

[22] Coquelines, *Bull. Romanum*, IV, pt. 1, pp. 321 f.

[23] Roth, *The Ritual-Murder Libel*, and Stern, *Paepstliche Bullen.*

[24] Roth, *Italy*, pp. 459–473.

[25] Browe, *Die Judenmission.*

REVEREND JOHN B. SHEERIN, C.S.P.

Evaluating the Past in Catholic-Jewish Relations: Lessons for Today from the Pain of the Past

REV. JOHN B. SHEERIN, C.S.P., *was ordained in July, 1937, and has been Editor of* The Catholic World *(the oldest Catholic magazine in the United States) since 1947. He received a Bachelor of Law degree at Fordham Law School in 1930, and was admitted to the bar in 1932. He was licensed to practice before the Supreme Court of the United States in 1938. Father Sheerin received a Master's degree in English from the Catholic University of America and taught at St. Paul's College, Washington, D.C., between 1938–44. He founded the Paulist Information Center in Boston, Mass., and served there for two years before becoming Associate Editor of* The Catholic World, *and later, Editor-in-Chief. In 1957, Father Sheerin was one of two Catholic observers at the World Council of Churches' North American Faith and Order Conference and their Central Committee Meeting in 1962. This was the first time that the Vatican has sent official observers to the Central Committee meeting. He was again an observer in 1963.*

After serving on the American Bishops' Press Panel at the Second Vatican Council in 1962, Father Sheerin was appointed moderator for the 1963 session. He also attended the 1964 session. Author of many articles for such publications as Commonweal, Guide, The Ecumenist, Jubilee, *and* The Catholic Lawyer, *his syndicated column,* Sum and

Substance, *is published in more than twenty Catholic newspapers. He contributed monthly to* The Homiletic and Pastoral Review *between 1944–56, and authored* The Sacrament of Freedom *(Bruce, 1961).*

Pope John had no desire to indict the past as a means of promoting the unity of Christians: "We do not intend," he said, "to conduct a trial of the past, we do not want to prove who was right and who was wrong. All we want to say is 'Let us come together. Let us make an end of our divisions.' "[26] It seems to me that we might apply the same rule in approaching the problem of Catholic-Jewish relations in the past. This is a dark page in Catholic history, but I feel that it serves no useful purpose to point an accusing finger at this Pope or that Crusader. It suffices that we Catholics make a general act of contrition for our treatment of the Jews in the same spirit in which Pope Paul at the Second Vatican Council begged forgiveness for any Catholic culpability in the division of Christianity. In fact, the Council declaration on the Jews is an act of contrition.

To be effective, an act of contrition must include a firm purpose of amendment, and our amendment could begin with a resolve to do what we can to dissipate the multitudinous misconceptions and the lying fables that Christians have often used in the past to justify their harsh treatment of the Jews. Traditionally the most damaging canard has been the charge that the Jews are guilty of *deicide,* the killing of the incarnate Son of God, Jesus Christ.

The Second Vatican Council's statement on the Jews rebuts this charge and insists that the Jewish people should never be represented as a people "rejected, cursed or guilty of deicide." What happened to Christ in his Passion cannot be attributed to the whole Jewish people of his day, much less to the Jews of today. A phobia, however, cannot be dispelled merely by a Council declaration. What is needed is a wide-ranging study of the origins of this charge that has resulted in so much hatred and contempt, so much anguish and tragedy for the Jews. At what point in the history of Christianity did this indictment first appear? Today, the Roman Catholic Church is engaged in renewing its inner life by returning to the pure sources of doctrine, and the Gospels are the vehicles that convey the pure doctrine. Yet a study of these Gospels fails to reveal any antagonism toward the Jewish people as a people, much less any sweeping arraignment of them as "Christ-killers." With evangelical simplicity, the Gospels name names and implicate certain individual Jewish leaders as accomplices in the travesty of justice perpetrated by Pontius Pilate, but the sacred books do not condemn the Jewish people. Moreover, in his report introducing the statement on the Jews at the third Council session, Cardinal Bea asserted that the Jewish leaders did not fully understand the divinity of Christ in such a way that they could be formally called *deicides*. He supported this assertion with Christ's words on the cross: "Father, forgive them for they know not what they do."

In denying any anti-Jewish bias in the Gospels, I do not mean to dismiss in cavalier fashion the contention of scholars such as Jules Isaac. This great humanist and warm-hearted historian has written with affection about Christ in his *Jesus et Israel,* paying tribute to the love which Jesus had for his own people. Nevertheless, Isaac claims that some of the authors of the Gospels engaged in unfair polemics in order to discredit the Jews. After reading this volume. Father Gregory Baum, O.S.A., made a close study of the Gospels to test Isaac's thesis. For the book moved Father Baum profoundly and profoundly disturbed him as he shared Isaac's anguish over anti-Semitism. Baum's conclusion, as contained in *The Jews and the Gospel,* is that nowhere in the Gospels can one find evidence of hostility to the Jewish people, not even in St. John. Father Baum affirms, "I have tried to examine carefully the teaching of the Gospels and the letters of St. Paul on the relationship of the Jews to the new community of salvation and I believe that I have been able to show that there is no foundation for the accusation that a seed of contempt and hatred for the Jews can be found in the New Testament."[27] Baum, however, does agree that Christian literature of later centuries exploited the Gospels to create a weapon for the struggle against Judaism. "Christian authors have covered the mystery of Israel with theological embroidery which has contributed to the contempt and debasement of the Jewish people, and these theories have become so much entangled with the Church's teaching that they have formed the mentality of generations, of whole centuries, even to our day."[28]

This distortion of the truth by Christian writers and preachers can serve as a warning to Catholic apologists today. These early Christians were undoubtedly men of devotion and integrity, but in the heat of the polemic fray they succumbed to the usual temptations besetting debaters. Anxious to score a victory over his opponent, a debater is tempted to touch up a dull argument with a dash of color, dramatize a weak point, quote a word out of context, or read into a sentence the meaning he would like to find there. This anti-Jewish apologetic, more visceral than spiritual, assumed major proportions in the fourth century. Constantine the Great became Emperor in 312 A.D., permitted Christians to practice their religion, and in 313 A.D. granted them a preferential position in the Empire.

Rejoicing in their new freedom and prestige, the Christians encountered the intransigent resistance of the Jews who conscientiously refused to accept the case for Christianity. The natural reaction of the Christian apologists was to attempt to discredit the Jews, and so we find what Jules Isaac has described as "the teaching of contempt" in his volume that bears that same title.[29] Isaac makes it clear, however, that this Christian anti-Semitism did not involve any essential Christian teaching. "It must be clearly understood that to oppose the teaching of contempt is not to oppose a doctrine essential to the Christian faith. On the contrary, the object of our attack is a tradition, time-honored and therefore all the more powerful, influential, and destructive, but in no way normative from the religious point of view."

What were the main themes of this Christian teaching of contempt for the Jews? They were, first, the claim that the dispersion of the Jews in 70 A.D. was a divine punishment of the Jews for the crucifixion of Christ; second, the myth that Judaism was in a degenerate state at the time of Christ and the Jews therefore were unable, through their own fault, to recognize Christ as the Messiah; third, that the Jews are a *deicide* people.

Some say that these myths were more common in Europe in past centuries than is so in the United States of 1965. That may well be the fact. I have inquired of American Catholics here and at Rome whether they were taught at school or at home that the Jews are a *deicide* people, and the answer has been that they never received such a teaching. Yet there is unquestionably a latent anti-Semitism in many Catholic circles in the United States. It bears no resemblance to the anti-Semitism of the Nazis, as this was an anti-Christian movement as hostile to Jesus as it was to the Jews. According to experts of the stature of Charles Journet and Henri deLubac, Hitlerian anti-Semitism had no roots in Christian preaching or teaching. With this opinion Father Baum agrees, but he adds that Christian preaching has created a type of Jew whose image has entered the Christian subconscious, producing a psychological mechanism of which pagan hate can take possession.

Anti-Semitism among American Catholics has its psychological core in a false stereotype of the Jew that is a composite of Scriptural and theological errors as well as of civic, social, and economic half-truths. The precise relation between religious feeling and these nonreligious factors is hard to discover, for sometimes the least devout are the most anti-Semitic. There is no doubt, however, that some anti-Semitism exists among us and we can take a cue from the bishops at the Second Vatican Council in facing the problem with courage and integrity. It would have been very easy for them to dismiss anti-Semitism as a problem freighted with political implications. Cardinal Bea, in introducing the statement on the Jews, admitted the bishops ran the risk of being suspect of political involvement if they approved the statement, but insisted that the reform of Catholic attitudes was important enough to justify the risk.

In reexamining our attitude toward the Jews, we may consider the Jew either as a member of the Jewish faith or as an American citizen. It is in the latter role that the Jew presents a highly complex challenge to the American Catholic.

First, the Christian anti-Semite is hostile to the Jew because of his religious faith. Anti-Semitism is a mélange of many factors, but what complicates any diagnosis of anti-Semitism is that the anti-Semite usually does not consciously know why he dislikes the Jews. Tending to project his own fears and frustrations upon a target outside of himself and his social group, the anti-Semite rationalizes his attitude by substituting respectable motives for his true motives. In short, the anti-Semite who is a Catholic discriminates against the Jew for many motives, and one of these is certainly the Jew's religion.

To eliminate religious bias will be a task of great magnitude. The first step is to try to refute the theological myths about the Jews that are cited in Isaac's *Teaching of Contempt*. The second and more important enterprise, however, is to make a positive presentation of the Gospel teaching on the Jews. This is to be found at its best in St. Paul's Epistle to the Romans, Chapter 11, in which the Apostle shows how the Jews remain a people set apart for God and how they remain, in spite of the Passion, the People of God's predilection in a very true sense. As Father Baum comments on this Pauline theme, "I am convinced, like the majority of modern commentators, that this is the clear and unambiguous teaching of *Romans*."[30] At the very beginning of Chapter 11, Paul asks, "Hath God cast away his people?" Then he answers, "By no means." According to Paul, the Jews are "very dear" to God precisely because they have been divinely called, and God's calling is "without repentance."

Father Baum does not go so far as certain Protestant theologians who see the Jews as the only visible People of God, and therefore claim that Christians cannot unite in a single, historical community so long as the People of God's choice remain aloof. He does agree, however, that we are justified in speaking of "the mystery of Israel," for the Jews are in a position that can be understood only by the man of faith, not by the historian or sociologist. "The Jewish people," he says, "will accompany the Church like a cloud, a symbol to all Christians of the gratuity of divine grace and the boundless measure of divine fidelity."[31]

This reeducation of the Christian anti-Semite in the New Testament concept of the Jew may seem like a hopelessly utopian dream. Yet a century ago, it probably seemed equally as utopian to talk about reeducating the average Catholic to a theologically correct concept of the Protestant.

The second task is to improve the Catholic attitude toward the Jew as an American citizen. This is a thorny problem that promises to become aggravated with the passing years. Eugene Lipman and Albert Vorspan, in *A Tale of Ten Cities* (a report published in 1962 by the Union of American Hebrew Synagogues), comment on the current scene: "Our ten studies of American cities demonstrates clearly that religious tensions and conflicts are widespread in America today . . . Careful analysis is required of the question: why, in a more mature America, are interreligious conflicts apparently sharpening?"[32] The fundamental problem as it pertains to Jews is that in case after case arising in State courts and ending in the United States Supreme Court, Catholics are found supporting manifestations of religion in public life, whereas Jews are on the other side. Many American Jews have demanded, for instance, that Bible reading, prayers, and religious celebrations be eliminated from the public schools.

I feel that the Council speeches on the topic of religious liberty will develop among Catholics a more sympathetic understanding of the position of Jews in this controversy over religion in public life. Bishop after bishop stood up in St. Peter's Basilica to insist unequivocally that every man has a right to practice his religion publicly as well as privately, that no man is to be coerced into acting against his conscience or restrained from acting according to his conscience. They affirmed that it was unlawful for the State to discriminate against religion and, on the contrary, that it has the duty to protect and promote religious liberty. I think we may expect the American Catholic, therefore, to be reluctant to impose his religious convictions on public policy and legislation.

In post-Reformation Europe, the Jew in Catholic countries usually fared better in his religious life than did the Protestant, the usual explanation being that a Protestant was a heretic, that he was a baptized Catholic who could be forced to live up to his baptismal obligations. The principle was found, even in St. Thomas. To the question, "Should unbelievers be forced to accept the faith?" the answer was that heretics and apostates are to be forced, physically if need be, to fulfill the promises made in baptism, but that those who never were Catholics must not be compelled to embrace the Faith. Nevertheless, the Jew's lot was not a happy one. The ghetto was not the scene of misery and human degradation some historians have made it out to be, but the Jew was isolated from the main currents of European life. In the sixteenth century, moreover, nationalism arose and rabid nationalists often fixed upon old wives' tales of Jewish ritual murder as a pretext for pogroms, expulsions, and massacres of Jews.

Today in the United States, our law makes no distinction between Christians and Jews, between the baptized or the unbaptized. The First Amendment says simply, "Congress shall make no law respecting an establishment of religion or restricting the free exercise thereof." The framers of the First Amendment at least intended to forbid to the national government any show of favoritism toward a particular religious group. In recent decisions, however, the Supreme Court has broadened the interpretation to prohibit not only aid to sectarian religion, but even preferential aid for religion in general over nonreligion. Justice Douglas, for instance, in the *Zorach* case in 1952 stated that, in adjusting the schedule of public events to sectarian needs and in encouraging religious instruction, our government follows "the best of our traditions." But in a later opinion (*Engel* v. *Vitale*, 1962), Judge Douglas went so far as to say that our whole system of State and Federal government is "honeycombed" with unconstitutional aid to religion, and he condemned even the traditional custom of providing paid chaplains for the military forces.

The prospect is that there will be constant friction between Catholics and Jews in the future over these Church-State problems because Catholics generally object to a ban on aid to religion in public life, whereas many Jews uphold such a prohibition, allowing aid to religious bodies only in cases in which a secular benefit is evident. (I use the term "many Jews" advisedly because Jews are far from unanimous on this point.) The result of this difference of opinion is that Jews often find themselves on the same side with atheists and secularists in Church-State cases, and Catholics therefore tend to regard them as a threat to the traditional American way of life. In this disaffection we have a breeding ground of anti-Semitism.

The American Catholic, however, would do well, in accord with the Council's declaration on Religious Liberty, to show respect for the Jewish conscience and its right to freedom. For the Jew feels that these religious symbols in American public life are not only psychologically harmful to his children, but constitute also an infringement of his religious liberty. In some cases, he is being coerced into acting against his conscience. They may be only minor intrusions, this recitation of the Lord's Prayer or that Christmas celebration, but the Jew often looks at them in the light of his own history and fears that they cast a shadow over his future religious liberty. He looks back at history and sees that the Catholic Church often collaborated in the punitive measures meted out by government to the Jews; indeed Catholic Churchmen sometimes inflamed the passions of the mobs that launched the pogroms. On the other hand, the Jew remembers that it was the Enlightenment that emancipated the Jew and guaranteed him equality in democratic society, and it was the Enlightenment that brought about a salutary separation of Church and State. In brief, many Jews feel that the Enlightenment, with its secular humanism, has been the friend of the Jew, whereas official Christianity has been his enemy. When he looks with suspicion on governmental aid to religion it is because he fears religion will take the form of Christian religion, and he remembers what official Christianity has done to him in the past.

Rabbi Arthur Hertzberg says that the State in medieval Europe was apt to be neutral to Jews when its ruler was not influenced by Christian prelates. "All the centuries of pain add up to two points that are relevant to our present concerns. In the hard school of suffering, Jews have learned almost instinctively that their freedom is safest—indeed that they can achieve freedom— only in society in which the Church is blunted in its dominance of public life."[33] Speaking of anti-Semitism, Hertzberg goes on to say, "The West has produced too many pogroms, auto-da-fe's and Auschwitz's for the Jews to believe, with Olympian calm, that this is an accidental feature of European civilization and that it will go away some day. The Jews must diagnose the Western tradition as not merely prone to the virus of anti-Semitism but as endemically ill with the disease. Therefore, for their own safety and for the lives of their children, Jews must look for a radical change in the very foundations of Christian civilization so that it should not spawn future assaults on themselves."[34]

The argument advanced by many Jews for taking religion out of public life is persuasive. We can understand why the Jew can be uneasy about his future when he remembers that his past in Christian civilization has been soaked in his own blood. On the other hand, the defenders of the traditional position find themselves in an embarrassing situation. The "radical right" are stalwart supporters of "religion in American life." With such friends, religion needs no enemies. Yet I feel that a valid case can be made out for the retention of certain religious symbols and customs, lest the total secularization of American public life lead to religious indifference and the notion that religion is irrelevant to the great problems of the modern world.

However, the important consideration for American Catholics vis-à-vis American Jews is that we keep our eyes fixed on the freedom of the Jewish conscience. We live in an era of unprecedented violence and we find it hard to erase from our memories the vision of that dreadful act when our President was assassinated. The role of the servants of the Lord, be they Catholic or Jewish, is to renounce anything that smacks of violence and to resolve to discuss the burning issues of our time with careful deliberation, sweet reasonableness, and genuine compassion. Yes, there will be conflicts between Catholics and Jews over the First Amendment's guarantees of religious liberty, but if we have mutual respect for each other's freedom of conscience and if we conduct our discussions in irenic fashion, these conflicts can become creative and constructive.

Bishop deSmedt of Bruges, in a notable speech at the Second Vatican Council, said that the authentic, ecumenical tone means that we must know what our partner in dialogue believes, what he thinks we believe, what he thinks he is missing from our belief, and that we must speak a language he understands and not resort to polemics. The ecumenical tone is just as necessary in discussing civic questions as in dealing with questions in theology. The ecumenical tone is a lesson we have learned from the pain of the past and I feel that it will be an immense help in removing the anti-Semitism that casts a dark cloud over the future.

NOTES

26 Quoted by Bernard Leeming, S.J., in *America*, Jan. 14, 1961, p. 465.

27 Gregory Baum, O.S.A., *The Jews and the Gospel* (Westminster, Md., The Newman Press, 1961), pp. 4–5.

28 *Ibid.*, Introduction, p. 5.

29 Jules Isaac, *The Teaching of Contempt* (New York, Holt, Rinehart, and Winston, Inc., 1964), p. 34.

30 Baum, *op. cit.*, p. 261.

31 *Ibid.*, p. 262.

32 *Ibid.*, p. 292.

33 Arthur Hertzberg and Joseph Moody, *The Outbursts That Await Us* (New York, The Macmillan Company, 1964), p. 153.

34 *Ibid.*, p. 155.

2

✪ The Bond of Worship

RABBI SOLOMON B. FREEHOF

The Bond of Worship

RABBI SOLOMON FREEHOF *has been Rabbi of Rodef Shalom Congregation, Pittsburgh, Pennsylvania, since 1934. Ordained at the Hebrew Union College, Cincinnati, Ohio, Rabbi Freehof served thereafter for nine years as a member of its faculty. A Past President of the Central Conference of American Rabbis and the immediate Past President of the World Union for Progressive Judaism, Rabbi Freehof is also a member of the Executive Board of the Union of American Hebrew Congregations. He is known widely as the author of many books (including commentaries on the book of Job) and widely read volumes dealing with Jewish liturgy, Jewish preaching, and Reform Jewish practice.*

Saul of Tarsus, the great Apostle to the Gentiles, had strong, controversial opinions and drew sharp distinctions between the religion which he had been taught and the form of religion which he was now proclaiming. Yet, in spite of his controversial mood, he never permitted his Gentile audience to forget that the two religions were in essence, or at least in origin, forever one. Paul expressed this basic unity in the Epistle to the Romans where he explained the relationship between the new teaching and the old by using the traditional metaphor of the olive tree. He described the new converts who had come from paganism as being shoots or branches from a wild, unproductive olive tree which was now grafted onto the fruitful olive tree (namely, Judaism); and he warned them in these words: "Thou bearest not the root, but the root beareth thee."

The newly grafted branches drew life from the old Jewish roots. This became increasingly clear when the Church Fathers finally overcame the heresy of Marcion. The Marcionites taught that the God of the Old Testament was an entirely different God from the God of the New Testament. In fact, deeming the God of the Old Testament a sort of a demon, the Marcionites urged that the Old Testament be rejected entirely by Christians. With the suppression of this heresy by the Church, the Old Testament remained forever the root of the Christian tree. Both Judaism and Christianity were nourished and grew on God's word speaking through the Hebrew Scriptures.

This Scriptural bond was not merely literary. It was a living experience in both Christianity and Judaism, for the Bible was not confined to scholars, rabbis, bishops, and priests. It was taught to all the people because it was part of daily worship. The record of the earliest Christian worship, found in the eighth book of the Apostolic Constitution (the Clementine Liturgy), describes the regular readings from the Old and the New Testament as being part of the Christian worship in the same way as the readings from the Law and the Prophets were an ancient part of Jewish worship. If Christianity had not developed this type of worship, the Bible would never have grown to be the fertile common ground between the two faiths. Today, when we are earnestly concerned with the obligations of religious comradeship, we must take a more careful look at the older Jewish and Christian services. As we do so, we shall discover not only that the liturgy was a channel for the stream of the common Biblical interest in Judaism and Christianity, but that the liturgy itself and the mood of worship at the basic level constituted a unique bond between the two religions, greater even than that of the Bible itself.

Because of the frequent mention of the synagogue and its

services in the Gospels and in the Acts of the Apostles, there always has been a strong feeling among Christian scholars that Christian worship must have been originally modeled on Jewish worship in the synagogue. Some study has been made of this early relationship. Oesterley writing on *The Jewish Background of Christian Liturgy,* Gavin on *Jewish Antecedents of Christian Sacraments,* and Cresswell on "The Clementine" all devoted much technical scholarship to a study of the earliest Christian liturgy. These studies, chiefly confined either to similarity of texts between Jewish and Christian worship or to analogies of liturgical arrangements, are all valuable. But our concern in this chapter is not the detailed matter of similarity of texts or arrangements of the service, but rather the total concept of synagogue worship itself. The Synagogue, as such, was unique as a socio-spiritual institution in the history of human religion. In turn, this uniqueness was taken over by the Church which became, aside from its theology, a unique socio-spiritual institution in the Roman world. This uniqueness in the concept of congregational worship was the unspoken but living bond between Church and Synagogue, and perhaps one of the chief reasons for and evidences of their living strength.

The socio-spiritual uniqueness of synagogue worship, and therefore of church worship, becomes clear when we contrast its special characteristics with those of all developed religions in the pre-synagogue past. What was worship like, for example, in the Temple in Jerusalem at the time of Isaiah? On the Day of Atonement the high priest conducted the entire service and, except for uttering a pious phrase at a certain point in the service, the people who crowded the Temple took no active part at all. Ancient Judaism and, in fact, every ancient religion was a spectator religion. Whether the people came or not was immaterial to the service. They were not worshipers; they were audience.

The synagogue service offers a unique contrast to the entire past in that it was the first truly democratic, participatory service:

the synagogue did not have the hereditary priesthood, nor was it essential; the worship could be conducted by anyone from any family. The locale was no longer important: the old priestly, sacrificial Temple had to be on Mount Zion; the synagogues, on the other hand, could be in any village. No longer did the service consist of animal sacrifices which only the priests were elibigle to make; worship now consisted primarily of prayer, song, and preachment in which all were participants. In the synagogue was found the world's first democratic, spiritual, mobile worship, characteristics which the early Christian Church was to embrace in its own highly participatory services. Its priesthoods, as they developed, were never hereditary. Its worship consisted no longer of animal sacrifice, but largely of prayer, song, and sermon. The modern changes in the Catholic Church with regard to the Mass, stressing the vernacular and the increased participation of the people—the whole democratic tendency—may seem radical to some. In reality, however, these changes merely reemphasize the democratic spirit of worship in the early Church and in the synagogue. The Church, in its worship, is not a descendant of the Temple of Mount Zion so much as it is the child of the democratic, popular, prayer-worshipping synagogue.

The very character of early Christian worship is one reason why the Church outlived the Roman persecutions. Rome was full of non-Roman religions, many of them encouraged by the Government. Each religion had its own regular priesthood and its own sacred place of worship. Whenever governmental favor was taken away from any of these foreign cults, however, its temples were destroyed, its priests scattered, and the cult eventually died out. Fortunately, however, the Christian Church was not, in the old sense, a temple; it was a synagogue and did not need the imperial approval. Driven from the streets of Rome, it went into the catacombs. Driven from the city, it went into the forest. Wherever the Christians gathered, there was a church-synagogue. As Scripture says (Exodus 20, 24), "Wherever I will cause My name to be mentioned, I will come to thee and bless thee." Thus, being actually a synagogue, democratic and ubiquitous, the Church could come back from catacomb and forest and establish itself as a permanent part of human history.

The origin of the synagogue is lost in antiquity. The period in which it developed, the five centuries between the Babylonian Exile and the destruction of the Commonwealth by the Romans, was a highly creative period, but it is full of uncertainty. Therefore, most of the original creations of the period cannot be chronologically fixed. The completion of parts of the Bible, the rise and development of the Pharisees, Essenes, and so forth, and the development of the synagogue and its worship can be discussed only in a general way. As for the synagogue, it seems certain that it found its first life spark in the Babylonian Captivity, a fact that in itself may explain one characteristic element of its mode of worship.

The Babylonian Exile itself presents a historical puzzle. In ancient times, all conquered peoples were carried away into exile, since labor was the chief form of wealth. Conquered peoples, exiled, died in exile; the East is a cemetery of dead nations and forgotten languages. It was only the Jewish people that did not die; they lived to return and continue their national and religious life. This historical exception was largely due to the preachments of the prophets. Other conquered peoples believed that the defeat of their nation meant the defeat of their gods. Therefore, as this people was taken into exile, so the gods, too, were taken into exile and became part of the growing pantheon of the conqueror. But the prophets had taught that the punishment of defeat and the exile of the people was not a defeat of the God of Israel, but a vindication of His word. Furthermore, the prophetic teaching that the whole earth is full of God's glory made it possible for the Jewish people to continue worshipping the God of their fathers, even in an alien land. So the people in Babylon gathered around the exiled Prophet Ezekiel, as he himself tells us, and he became their honored guide.

When the Jewish people continued such informal gatherings on their return to Israel, the spirit of the vindicated prophet now guided them. Of course, they rebuilt the Temple of Sacrifice on the Holy Mountain as Scripture required, but they also established meeting places in every little village. The fair presumption is that the spirit of the prophet dominated these meetings, and that therefore the oldest element in the slowly developing synagogue service was the regular reading from the Prophets and then from other parts of Scripture. So it was in the early Christian service, too. Sometimes it was the Reading from the Law and the Reading from the Prophets; sometimes it was Gospel and Epistle; sometimes it was all four, but always it was the reading of Scripture. The reading was not merely reading; it was the basis of interpretation and of preaching, since, after all, the original prophetic impulse was an expression of religious oratory. Thus the prophetic eloquence lived through the Scriptural reading. Sometimes by the fire of the words themselves, sometimes in the additional preachment—in one way or another, the living word of God became a permanent part of the worship both of synagogue and of church.

It is to be noted that whenever there was a creative change in synagogue or church, it managed to express itself in the prophetic manner and brought about a new flowering of preaching. We may say that the earliest and the continuous, creative vehicle of inspiration of synagogue and church was the prophetic method of uniting eternal truth with daily experience, merging the timely into the timeless. Thus, not merely are the prophets, as Biblical treasure, our common spiritual possession, but the living prophetic technique of the preaching word is also a permanent part of the liturgy and the life of Judaism and Christianity.

During the Second Commonwealth, when the synagogue grew,

the Biblical Book of Psalms was finally developed and completed, and it is logical to conclude that the development of the synagogue and the development of the Book of Psalms constituted a continuous interaction. There were, of course, many psalms which belonged to the older, priestly Temple on Mount Zion and were part of the Levitical Temple music, but the scores and scores of personal psalms, of lyric psalms, psalms of doubt and of pain, of fear and of hope, could not have belonged to the formal atmosphere of the ancient Temple. They belonged to, and in all likelihood were written for, the humble synagogue assemblies scattered in the villages throughout the land. That this was so is further confirmed by the fact that to this day the bulk of the content of the synagogue service comes from the Book of Psalms, as well as by the fact that in the early Christian service every deacon was required to know the psalms by heart. These psalms were essentially prayer, communion between the individual and God. They must be counted as the devotional creativity of the Synagogue and the Church, the source of its hymnology and of its prayers. Through the Biblical reading and preaching, God spoke to the people. In the psalms, and in the prayers developed from them, the people spoke to God. The preachment was edificatory. The psalms and prayers were devotional.

Looking back over history, it seems strange that an institution like the Synagogue, democratic and spiritual, could ever have developed at all. In fact, one might say it is quite non-Scriptural. The Biblical picture of a place of worship was the Temple in Jerusalem, with its hereditary priesthood and its animal sacrifices. Except for the nature of God worshipped in it, this ancient, sacrificial Temple was otherwise in its outer form much like the temples of all the other religions, and, as in them, the people were merely nonparticipating spectators. This type of temple is the only one authorized in Scripture, and the status of its priests, the minutiae of its various sacrifices, and the very details of its architecture occupy a large part of the Bible text. Except for one vague reference in Psalm 74, 8, there is not a single reference to the worship-synagogue in all of Scripture. How, then, could such a non-Scriptural institution as the Synagogue ever have arisen and grown strong enough not only to be deemed, eventually, an adequate substitute for the Temple (after the Temple had been destroyed), but strong enough also to transfer itself to Christianity in the form of church service?

Part of the reason was, of course, that the prophets had deprecated the complete reliance upon the sacrificial cult as being the full, true worship of God. Interestingly enough, as the synagogue readings from Law and Prophet became fixed, this prophetic deprecation of the ritual was carefully emphasized. In readings from the Torah, especially in Leviticus where the details of the sacrificial cult are given, accompanying Readings from the Prophets emphasized the ethical obligation and undervalued the priestly ritual. Thus, the right of a popular-worship institution justified itself. Of course, the synagogue could never have been established as a *substitute* for the Temple, for the Temple alone was Biblical; it had become a substitute only as a result of history: the destruction of the Temple and the scattering of the children of Israel throughout the world. But it could not be *established* as a substitute. The Temple itself was rebuilt as soon as the people returned from the exile, and it stood as long as the Roman Empire permitted it to stand. And, as the Bible required, the Temple remained a center of worship and a center of regular pilgrimage.

Yet the democratic spirit which developed the worship-synagogue also began to influence the classic Temple itself to the extent that this was possible under Biblical restriction. The people, now accustomed to the synagogue in which the worship was democratic, developed a system of committees (twenty-four of them from twenty-four districts of the country) whose members stood by the sacrificial worship and thus participated. A synagogue was established within the Temple precincts itself. At the hour when the committee from a certain district stood by the sacrifices in Jerusalem, the people at home conducted their synagogue services at the same hour. Thus the hours of the regular sacrifices in the Temple became the hours of the services in the various synagogues—the morning service for the morning sacrifice, the afternoon service for the afternoon sacrifice. All this was expressed in the dictum which said that the services of worship were in place of the Temple services of sacrifice (Berachos 26b), and the synagogue worship was called *"Avodah Shebelev,"* "the sacrificial ritual in the heart." If, therefore, certain parts of Christianity, especially Catholic Christianity, think of their worship as rather analogous to the worship in the Temple in Jerusalem, with a priesthood, an altar, and with what might be called a ritual of sacrifice, it is because the structure of temple worship was carried over into the synagogue and hence into the church.

Thus the historic, Biblical Temple influenced the synagogue in a unique way: it gave to the synagogue regularity and continuity. Without the Temple influence, the worship-synagogue might have been merely occasional, taking place only on Sabbaths or on fast days; but because the Temple in Jerusalem was daily, fixed, and regular, the synagogue became daily, fixed, and regular. In this way, the spiritual bond of prayer and preachment became in Judaism and in Christianity an unbroken, daily communion between man and God—between *every* man and God. Through the synagogue and the church a new contact was established between the soul of man and the Soul of the Universe, never again to be broken completely.

When, therefore, Paul the Apostle described Judaism as the root of the olive tree which nourishes the Gentile branches grafted onto it, he did not refer only to the treasure of Biblical morality and spirituality which was its common possession. He meant also the synagogue mode of worship which was the unique discovery and creation of post-Exilic Judaism, and which occurred at the time in which he grew up. The unique, democratic institution, in which average men and women poured out their hearts in prayer, lifted up their voices in song, meditated on the deeper meaning of sacred Scripture, this institution which could be established on any spot of this earth's surface and would exist wherever the faithful maintained it became the living, socio-spiritual instrumentality for the permanence of root and branch, Judaism and Christianity. For both derive from it what no other religion could give—the living word of God through preachment: the heartfelt worship through prayer and the constant communion of living day by day, all through life, in the presence of God, our Eternal Father.

REVEREND AIDAN KAVANAGH, O.S.B.

The Tradition of Judaeo-Christian Worship: Our Debt to Each Other

REV. AIDAN KAVANAGH, O.S.B., *has been Professor of Liturgy and Sacramental Theology at St. Meinrad Seminary, Meinrad, Indiana, since 1963. Ordained there in 1957, he earned an S.T.D. after a year of research at Oxford and study at Theologische Fakultät Trier, Trier, Germany. Father Kavanagh published his doctoral thesis on the* Anglican Prayer Book at the Time of the Reformation. *His other publications include articles in* Exodus (Fribourg), America, *and* Worship. *He is also Associate Editor of* Worship *and holds membership in the National Liturgical Conference, Liturgical Commissions of the Archdiocese of Indianapolis and of the U.S. Benedictines.*

No modern Christian Biblical, patristic, or liturgical scholar possessed of competence in his field would judge Christianity's debt to Judaism as anything short of incalculable. Especially is this true in the area of worship. The more closely we examine the origins of Christian worship, the more we see them begin to merge into Jewish tradition both in structure and in detail.[1] Moreover, the very originality of Christian liturgical tradition depends far more on developments it has made out of the Jewish tradition than on some break with it, even if the break was creative.[2]

Too often, Christians have assumed uncritically that their tradition of worship took form as an essentially unconditioned beginning. They have pointed to the vast contrast between the Pentateuchal code of worship and that of the Gospels. Against the ritual details of Exodus, Leviticus, and Deuteronomy they have cited Jesus' words that his followers are to worship in spirit and in truth, and they see his "cleansing of the Temple" as a rejection of its liturgy. But to assume that the full meaning of God's saving acts (and still less a tradition of worship flowing from contemplation of them) sprang into being fully formed in time, without development, is naive, to say the least. In both the Jewish and Christian traditions of worship, what confronts us is a far more complex reality than discrete, self-explanatory instants of divine revelation. Because *men* are involved socially as time-conditioned recipients of the divine activity, matters of *development* and *continuity* in the context of *liturgical assemblies* come into play.[3] Once this is grasped, the student of Judaeo-Christian worship has become sensitive to more than mere contrasts between the two traditions. He is now able to discern the main themes of continuity between them and to see the younger tradition's debt to the elder. He can now detect, for instance, the manner in which the two traditions have always been troubled with ritualism's becoming an end in itself. He can appreciate the concern of Hebrew prophet and Christian reformer (both standing fully within their own traditions), in condemning this cancerous aberration as destructive of the worshipping community on which it feeds.

It can hardly be overemphasized that the unifying keel of the Judaeo-Christian tradition is the worshipping community, the assembly of living men united in response to the divine actions in history that have made the community to be what it is. To be ignorant of the community is to be ignorant of the term of God's saving Word. For whenever God speaks to man He does so only to mold for himself a people, ". . . a man according to his heart, and it is in and for this work that He himself is gradually to be known."[4]

If this insight teaches anything, it is surely that an evaluation of the continuing life of the Judaeo-Christian worshipping community must come first in the process of giving an adequate exegesis of the literature and institutions arising out of the community. And here we are on ground that is not only holy but is also truly irenic. Texts by themselves can be used as weapons of warfare. But when we view them, not as instruments of attack, but as the remains of a community of men in response to God, we have shifted from the totalitarianism of "things" to the personalism of a living community whose core is a divine and living Person in dialogue with men. We say living, and thereby mean to indicate a dynamic continuity of growth within the community as it responds to and is formed by the living God. Growth means change, development, a deepening of awareness, and a process of maturation in response to others. And we should be dishonest as Christians if we did not frankly state our conviction that, as we have said, the very originality of our Christian liturgical tradition depends far more on developments it made out of the Jewish tradition than on some break with it.

But we hasten to add that those developments, far from being breaks of opposition as they are so often presented, appear consistently to result from *renewed meaning* being given by Jesus and the early Christian community to familiar concepts of worship. And let us further add that this process of renewed meaning did not begin with Jesus or with the Christian community. The Hebrew Bible itself discloses that the life of Israel, in response to the divine Teacher who leads gradually but surely, was constantly larger than the frameworks inherited from its past—as indeed one would expect of a community of living persons bearing an inherited but living tradition. The psalms alone exhibit such a development toward the refinement of religious sensitivity. The prophets acted as spurs toward an ever more deeply interiorized understanding of the nature of sacrificial cult, and through them came the Word of the Lord: "rend your hearts and not your garments, for what is pleasing before His sight is not the sacrifice of bulls and goats, but that of a pure and contrite heart"—a prophetic word that Jesus made his own.[5]

The Hebrew Bible, in which this developing tradition is especially enshrined, was accepted by the early Christian community as a finished whole. In addition, the community also shared in other aspects of contemporary Judaism, such as in the interpretations of the sacred texts by the various rabbinic schools, in the intense messianism that can be seen in the Qumran documents,[6] in religious movements of the time such as Essenism, in apocalyptic piety and eschatological expectation, in the rather Hellenized *gnosis* of the Diaspora, and in all else that constituted the richness of Jewish religion at the time. But in a special way, because of the type of man its founder was, Christianity partook deeply of a contemporary trend in Jewish piety that Bouyer calls "the spiritualization of the sacrificial rite or the ritualization of all existence."[7] Far from meaning to imply that the institutions in Israel were thus emptied of their religious content, Bouyer maintains that, on the contrary, this trend had as its purpose the permeation of the whole of life by this religious content.

According to the prophets, this was the heart of the Covenant, the reason for Israel's chosenness, and the criterion of its faithfulness. Exclusivism and mechanism in Judaic worship they condemned: the living God was not confined within a building to await Israel's pleasure anymore than He could be coerced by any sort of cultic act. True worship, pure and undefiled, was essentially the personal response of the People, each and all, to the living God. Thus we can detect, especially after the Exilic period, a shift in the polarity of Jewish piety away from (but not necessarily in opposition to) the objective, sacrificial worship of the Temple toward the more "personalized" worship of the synagogue. This worship consisted in meditative reading of the Law and Prophets, together with the "sacrifice of praise" uttered by the lips and hearts of men in psalm and in the blessing-thanksgiving form of prayer, the *berakah*.[8]

The *berakah* form of prayer may be described as a main liturgical result of this spiritualizing tendency, the "ritualization of all existence" we have already mentioned.[9] Praising the mighty deeds God wrought for his People throughout salvation history, the *berakah* gathered all these together in a context of blessing and offered men's thanksgiving to the source of all good things. Thus all is consecrated by thanksgiving: "We will take what is good, and requite Thee with the fruits of our lips" (Hosea 14, 2); "Everything God has created is good, and nothing need be refused, provided it is accepted with thanksgiving, for then it is consecrated by the Word of God and by prayer" (I Timothy 4, 4–5). This prayer is intimately personal: it reposes upon the community's faith-knowledge of, and its faith-commitment to the divine goodness constantly being manifested for men. In this prayer form men give themselves over completely in response to that saving will made known through God's Word and deeds in history; and this indeed is the purest form of *gnosis*. For as the great *Tefila berakah* prays, "Instruct us, O Lord our God, in the knowledge of Your ways and circumcise our heart that we may fear you."[10]

Not only was this piety shared by the first Christians, but it was also determinative of subsequent Christian liturgical development—standing until this day at the fountainhead of all orthodox Christian worship. For the content and form of the *berakah*, originating in the Biblical Word, developed within the synagogue liturgy to which the Christian synaxis of the Word (sometimes called the "Fore-Mass") owes so much. It also flowed over into the usage of the common family or fraternal meal on Sabbaths and solemn festivals. These meals were called *Chaburoth*, and their importance in contemporary piety at the time of Christi-

anity's beginnings has lately been revealed in the Qumran manu-
scripts.

If we recall what has been said of the spiritualizing movement
that gave impetus to the *berakah* sacrifice of praise, and if we
then see it in the context of a fraternal *Passover-Chaburah* meal,
we may sense that we are beginning to verge upon the purest
idea of what the Christian Eucharist was meant to be. The words
of the Mishnah on the Pasch sum up this piety in a manner impossible to improve upon:

It is therefore incumbent on every person, in all ages, that he should
consider as though he had personally gone forth from Egypt, as it is
said, "and thou shalt explain to thy son in that day, saying, 'This is
done because of what the Lord did for me in Egypt'" (Exodus 12, 27).
We are therefore in duty bound to thank, praise, adore, glorify, extol,
honor, bless, exalt, and reverence Him, who wrought all these miracles
for our ancestors and for us; for He brought us forth from bondage to
freedom, He changed our sorrow into joy, our mourning into a feast.
He led us from darkness into a great light, and from servitude to redemption—let us therefore say in His presence, "Hallelujah."[11]

With this we see into the very core of Christian worship as it is
embedded in the celebration of the Passover mystery on the eve
of Easter. At this point of deepest juncture between Judaism and
Christianity, it has been from the beginning customary for the
Christian community to celebrate, as in one great act, the birth
of itself as a People and of each of its members, the exodus of all
from bondage into freedom in the passing over of Our Lord
from death to life.

Not to understand this celebration is to misunderstand Christianity itself. But it is impossible to comprehend either the structure or the content of the rite apart from its Judaic matrix. At
every point the deep piety of the Jewish people flows mightily
into the celebration, and this we can affirm from the earliest
times. It is possible to summarize the rite in four headings.

First, there existed a period of preparation for those who were to be received into the Christian community on this night.[12] During this time (usually about three years by the third century), the whole man was formed in matters of community faith and life. In the later books of the New Testament and in early patristic writings we have remnants of this catechesis. As it begins within the Judaeo-Christian communities of Syria and Palestine, this catechesis is woven out of Old Testament typology. In this context Jesus is presented as Messiah, the Servant who fulfilled the *ebed* role of Israel so vividly proclaimed in Deutero-Isaiah and who came to serve the world by saving it through his death. This is the oldest stratum of Christology, and it is heavily Judaic. The earliest formulas of Christian liturgical prayer, which arise out of Palestine, constantly refer to Our Lord in Judaic patterns, for example, "We give Thee thanks, O our Father, for the holy vine of Thy servant David, which Thou madest known to us through Jesus Thy Servant."[13]

Second, toward the end of the catechumenate period, the preparation for a person's reception into the community became gradually more liturgical. It finally concluded in the paschal vigil itself, with baptism by immersion (Ezekiel 47, 1–12; John 7, 37–39; Apocalypse 22, 1f), anointing of the newly baptized, a signation with the mark of the cross (the Hebrew *tav,* a symbol of the Name of God),[14] and a clothing of the neophyte in a white garment and a crown of leaves—a symbol associated, it seems, with the Feast of Tabernacles and also with Essene practice.[15]

Third, the baptismal liturgy seems to have been concluded with a post-baptismal catechesis that took the form of a paschal homily. Daniélou thinks that this homily ". . . replaced the *haggadah* on the liberation of the Jewish people at the time of the Exodus, which inaugurated the Jewish Paschal meal,"[16] and a remarkable example of this is to be found in I Peter 1, 22–2:10 (to 5, 11?), a book which some scholars regard as containing the earliest paschal-baptismal rite and catechesis.[17] The same tend-

ency is found in a paschal homily of Melito of Sardis (d.c. 190),
which rises to a rhapsodic level verging on something like the
paschal *Exultet* hymn still employed in the Latin Rite Easter
Vigil.

Fourth, the rite of Christian initiation concluded with the
eucharistic meal, the introduction to which was the homiletic
haggadah as in the Passover supper. The Christian meal at this
period quickly flowed into the *berakoth* over bread and cup—
the origin of the eucharistic anaphoras used by the various Christian families of rites down to the present day as the central
prayer of the Mass. The earliest texts of the eucharistic anaphora,
such as those of Addai and Mari from eastern Syria, of Hippolytus' *Apostolic Tradition* from the West, and possibly the
eucharistic fragments in the *Didache* itself—all these bear strong
affinity to the *berakah* forms found in the Hebrew Bible, in
Seder Amram Gaon, and even in modern synagogue use. This is
not fortuitous. In the anaphoras' *haggadah*-recounting of God's
mercies shown throughout history (terminating with His last and
greatest mercy given us at the Last Supper), through its final
development of thanksgiving and prayer for God's accomplishing
His saving purposes in us now and in the future, the Christian
eucharistic anaphora is a direct development out of Judaism.[18]

This has the most salutary effects on our understanding of the
baptismal-eucharistic core of Christian worship. As we begin to
see more clearly than ever before that the most hallowed of our
traditions spring from roots deep in Judaism and are adequately
comprehensible only in that perspective, we are lifted over many
impasses that have dogged our theology, our cult, and our polity
since the "imperialization" of Christianity in the fourth century.

Our appreciation of the Eucharist in terms of *berakah,* as we
have briefly described it, has already begun to soften controversies that have until now appeared insuperable—dividing East and
West (*epiklesis* versus words of institution), dividing Catholic
and Protestant (Eucharist as "sacrifice" or as "memorial"), and

dividing Catholic theologians among themselves (the relation between the eucharistic symbols of bread and wine and the presence of Christ). We now see the whole eucharistic anaphora as *berakah,* as "the prayer" *par excellence* and a prime theological source for our understanding of the sacrifice of praise in which the unity of all the community in Christ is secured. As the great Christian memorial of the history of our salvation, we approach that divine mystery in this prayer, dedicating and offering ourselves with all our being to the Father from whom it all proceeds, as the celebrating community. In this memorial sacrifice the mystery becomes present among us for our salvation, our judgment, and our comfort, much as the rabbinical tradition viewed the *shekinah* becoming present in the assembly met to meditate liturgically on the *Torah.* Thus our concept of sacramental presence attains a far more balanced and richer perspective within the personal dynamic of the worshipping community: "Wherever two or three gather together in My Name, there am I in the midst of them."

In addition to this, our recovery of a sense of the *Word,* through a revival of Biblical studies in worship especially, is beginning to revitalize our concept of the Service of the Word or "Fore-Mass." Scriptural typology and liturgical kerygma are thus complementary sources of the renewal in catechetics which is today reshaping the formation of Christian consciences. We are in the process of rediscovering the whole prophetic dimension of the Judaeo-Christian tradition and of relearning what obedience to the living God entails.

And with all this as its necessary complement goes a whole renewal in our understanding of the nature of the Church as the People of God, as a community of service in and for the world. The highest title of the lowest Christian is that most cherished by the Bishop of Rome from time immemorial: *Servus Servorum Dei.* In the eucharistic *berakah* we have prayed for twenty centuries as we present all that we are to Him whose Son gave all

that He was for our salvation, *Nos servi tui sed et plebs tua sancta
. . . offerimus.* The problem of authority in the Church is being
seen liturgically in terms of service, and these terms are derived
from Judaism.[19]

Nothing could be farther from the truth than to dismiss this
whole process of recovery as a matter of antiquarian pedantry or
merely cultural interest. The data yielded through studies of
liturgical origins has not only deepened our understanding of the
act of Christian worship, but it has now begun to reform that act
along lines more adequately expressive of its inner content to
men of the twentieth century. In this contemporary process, perhaps the most signal restoration of liturgical reform has been a
renewed and renewing realization of the role of the worshipping
community after so many centuries of subjective individualism.
Nor is this social aspect a latecomer in the movement for liturgical renewal. It has been an explicit corollary in the movement
since the inception of its modern phase by Dom Lambert Beauduin at the beginning of this century,[20] and the father of the
liturgical movement in this country, Dom Virgil Michel of St.
John's Abbey, Collegeville, Minnesota, was the father also of the
Catholic Action movement here as well.[21] The renewal of social
and liturgical sensitivities among Catholics has developed together in a continuity that is not merely fortuitous. The liturgical
renewal, thus taken in its full dimension, has had a direct role to
play in bringing about the present situation of mutual concern
between Catholics and Jews on matters of social importance and
cooperation.

All this means that we, as Christians, are gradually but surely
beginning to learn once again what it is to celebrate in an act of
worship. As Rabbi Heschel has said,[22] celebration is an active
state of expressing with a solemn reverence that is profoundly
spiritual our debt to Him who makes all things new. It is not
to receive pleasure—even spiritual pleasure—afforded by an interesting act or a ceremonial spectacle. Rather, it is to respond

in a human way, less unworthy than any other, to the living God who makes Himself present and known to men only within the community He has always been forming for Himself. The world has learned much in two thousand years, but it may be that it has forgotten more. And all of us are part of that world. Jews and Christians have much to teach that world if we can first learn to learn from each other in humble obedience to the Word we both revere. I dare not speak for Jews, but our learning of all this as Christians is largely concomitant with our returning to the holy tradition from which we spring.

NOTES

1 Space prohibits giving an adequate bibliography of Christian studies on this matter. Summaries of the evidence, with current bibliographies, can be found in two recent works, L. Bouyer's, *The Spirituality of the New Testament and the Fathers*, History of Christian Spirituality I, translated by Mary Perkins Ryan (London, Burns and Oates, 1963), and J. Daniélou, *The Theology of Jewish Christianity*, A History of Early Christian Doctrine Before the Council of Nicaea I, translated by John A. Baker (London, Darton, Longman and Todd, 1964).

2 Here, I am agreeing with the thesis advanced by L. Bouyer, "Jewish and Christian Liturgies," in *True Worship*, edited by Lancelot Sheppard (Baltimore, Helicon Press, Inc., 1963), pp. 29–44, especially p. 33.

3 See Carroll Stuhlmueller, C. P., "Old Testament Liturgy," in *Studies in Salvation History*, edited by C. Luke Salm, F.S.C. (Englewood Cliffs, N.J., Prentice-Hall, Inc., 1964), pp. 81–91, especially pp. 82–84.

4 L. Bouyer, *Rite and Man: The Sense of the Sacral and Christian Liturgy*, translated by M. Joseph Costelloe, S.J. (Notre Dame, University of Notre Dame Press, 1963), illustrated.

5 See Hosea 6, 6; Psalms 40, 6–8; 51, 16 f.; etc.; Matthew 9, 13; 12, 7.

6 See J. Daniélou, *The Dead Sea Scrolls and Primitive Christianity*, translated by S. Attanasio (Baltimore, Helicon Press, Inc., 1958), *passim*.

7 Bouyer, *Spirituality*, p. 24.

8 Bouyer, *ibid.*, p. 23.

9 See the comments of D. Hedegard, *Seder R. Amram Gaon* (Lund, 1951), pp. xxiii f., 139 f.; J. P. Audet, "Esquisse historique du genre littéraire de la 'bénédiction' juive et de l' 'eucharistie' chrétienne," *Revue Biblique* 65, 1958, pp. 371–399; summary in Bouyer, *The Spirituality*, pp. 23–26.

10 From the most ancient text of this prayer surviving, in Hedegard, _op. cit.,_ pp. 146 f.

11 Treatise Pesachim x, 5, in _Eighteen Treatises from the Mishna,_ translated by D. A. de Sola and M. J. Raphall (London, 1843), p. 124. Quoted in Stuhlmueller, _art. cit.,_ p. 87.

12 Details of this period are forthcoming only in later documents such as Hippolytus' _Apostolic Tradition_ (c. 220); see _The Treatise on the Apostolic Tradition of St. Hippolytus of Rome,_ edited by G. Dix (London, SPCK, 1937), pp. 23–32. Allusions to a period of preparation are, however, to be seen in the _Didache,_ the _Epistle of Barnabas,_ and in the _First Apology_ of St. Justin Martyr, c. 150. Such periods were known in Jewish communities of the time, notably at Qumran: see J. Daniélou and H. Marrou, _The First Six Hundred Years,_ The Christian Centuries I, translated by Vincent Cronin (New York, McGraw-Hill, Inc., 1964), pp. 67 f

13 _Didache_ 9:2; Psalms 80:8–12. For patristic parallels see J. Quasten, _Monumenta eucharistica et liturgica vetustissima_ (Bonn, Petrus Hanstein, 1935), p. 10, note 6. Also see W. Zimmerli and J. Jeremias, _The Servant of God,_ Studies in Biblical Theology 20 (London, 1957); Bouyer, _The Spirituality,_ pp. 176–179; Daniélou and Marrou, _op. cit.,_ pp. 334–335. We have tried to give a brief summary of this matter in "The Liturgy as Service," _Worship_ 39 1965, pp. 5–11.

14 See Daniélou and Marrou, _op. cit.,_ p. 70. Also see Philippians 2:6–11, an extremely archaic remnant of what may have been an early hymn to Christ, concluding with a typical Judaic note associating the "name" with Christ. See Daniélou, _Sacramentum Futuri_ (Paris, Beauchesne et ses Fils, 1950), pp. 203–216. On the cross as symbol, see Daniélou, _Jewish Christianity,_ pp. 265–292.

15 See Daniélou, _Jewish Christianity,_ pp. 326–328.

16 Daniélou and Marrou, _op. cit.,_ p. 72.

17 See F. L. Cross, _I. Peter: A Paschal Liturgy_ (London, Mowbray, 1954); M. E. Boismard, "Une liturgie baptismale dans la Prima Petri," _Revue Biblique_ 65, 1956, pp. 182–208. For a more general discussion of the Exodus theme in early Christian, Biblical typology, see Daniélou, _Sacramentum Futuri,_ pp. 131–199, especially pp. 140–141 on I Peter; C. Stuhlmueller, C.P., "Baptism: New Life through the Blood of Jesus," _Worship_ 39, 1965, pp. 207–217.

18 For a relation of the anaphora to various forms of _berakah_—in other words, the synagogue _berakoth_ in connection with the readings and _Shema,_ and the _Tefila_ or _shemone-esre_ (whence may arise the litanaic intercessions in the eucharistic anaphora as suggested by St. Clement's _First Epistle,_ 40)— see Bouyer, "Jewish and Christian Liturgies," in _True Worship,_ pp. 40–41.

19 These terms are most explicit, even in the architectural details of the earliest Christian churches of the Syro-Palestinian area. These churches seem to have been constructed consciously along synagogue lines, with the chair of the presiding rabbi ("The Chair of Moses") becoming the bishop's _cathedra,_ and the seats for the Jewish elders becoming those for the Christian _presbyteroi._ See Bouyer, "Jewish and Christian Liturgies," _loc. cit.,_ pp. 35–38;

W. Rordorf, "La théologie du ministére dans l'Église ancienne," *Verbum Caro* 18, 1964, pp. 84–104.

20 See Beauduin's *La piété de l'Église* (Louvain, Abbaye du Mont-Cesar, 1914).

21 See Paul B. Marx, O.S.B., *Virgil Michel and the Liturgical Movement* (Collegeville, Minnesota, The Liturgical Press, 1957). Also see E. Koenker, *The Liturgical Renaissance in the Roman Catholic Church* (Chicago, University of Chicago Press, 1954), pp. 17, 125–137; A. Lichtenburger, "The Social Implications of the Liturgical Renewal," in *The Liturgical Renewal of the Church*, edited by M. H. Shepherd (New York, Oxford University Press, Inc., 1960), pp. 101–120.

22 "Idols in the Temples," in *Religious Education* 58, 1963, pp. 127–137, especially pp. 136–137.

3

✿ Biblical Scholarship: Bond or Barrier?

DR. SAMUEL SANDMEL

Jewish and Catholic Biblical Scholarship

DR. SAMUEL SANDMEL, *Provost since 1957 of the Hebrew Union College, Jewish Institute of Religion in Cincinnatti, Ohio, and Professor of Bible and Hellenistic Literature, is a specialist in the New Testament and its relation to Judaism. Ordained in 1937 at the Hebrew Union College, Rabbi Sandmel received his Ph.D. from Yale. He has served as Hillel Professor of Jewish Literature and Thought at Vanderbilt University, as Director of the Hillel Foundation at Yale University, and, in 1961, as President of the Society of Biblical Literature. A member of the Editorial Board of the* Hebrew Union College Annual *and the* Journal of Biblical Literature, *Rabbi Sandmel's books include* A Jewish Understanding of the New Testament, Philo's Place in Judaism, The Genius of Paul *(Farrar, Straus, 1958), and* The Hebrew Scriptures *(Knopf, 1963). Oxford University Press will publish his* We Jews and Jesus *in the spring of 1965. He is a member of the Central Conference of American Rabbis.*

It seems to me that our topic can possibly be approached by dividing it into four parts and then adding a conclusion. Any such division implies a neatness of separation which cannot be completely justified; yet unless our material is arranged so that its great bulk does not dismay us, I know of no way in which we can focus our attention on the topic. Moreover, I shall need to

63

spend some time on Protestant Biblical scholarship and because there I shall indicate a motif which is relatively absent from both Catholic and Jewish scholarship, I should want to make it clear that I shall be describing Protestant scholarship and not devaluating it. For my attitude toward Protestant Biblical scholarship is one of high admiration, even though I believe its initial impulse differentiates it from the Jewish and the Catholic.

My task would be easier and somewhat fresher if I thought I could assume the common possession of most of the facts, and could thereby limit myself strictly to interpretation. I do not think that I can do that. Let me assume, a little arrogantly, that my task involves the wish to try to interpret Jewish Biblical scholarship to Catholics and Catholic Biblical scholarship to Jews and to assume that, somehow or other, I have certain facts which are possessed in a number of instances only by half of the audience, so that I have to tell the other half what these facts are. To the extent that this assumption is right, then I may be possibly giving new material to some readers, material which will be at the same time not at all new to others. Also, space considerations make it impossible to deal with all the facts, and therefore I can promise you some significant omissions.

Let me begin with the first topic, which I shall label "Understanding" and the "Body of Interpretation," for herein is a chief clue to an approach among Jews and Catholics which is somewhat analogous. With this double rubric in mind, let us look first at the Jewish aspect.

I

What shall we say is the difference, if any, between understanding and interpretation? On the first level, there is this distinction, that when an ancient text is found in one language and the vernacular used by a student is in a different language, translation is first needed for simple and bare comprehension. Let us then reserve understanding to connote "bare comprehension," such as is implied by translation. Thus, when Jews in Palestine ceased to use Hebrew as their spoken language and the language of mundane affairs, they had to deal with the translation of Scripture before they could arrive at an interpretation. By interpretation, on the other hand, I would allude to that stage which comes after understanding, that stage which raises the question of the implication of that which is understood, or which causes the inferences to be drawn from that which is understood, or which transfers the understanding of the ancient by application to the contemporaneous situation.

There is an inherent, but demonstrable process in respect to a literature which is deemed sacred, whereby when understanding has developed into interpretation, then the reverse process can take place, with the consequence that interpretation thereafter comes to be the understanding. To illustrate this by an example, the half-verse Genesis 4, 26 b reads in the Hebrew, in respect to Enos whom Jews call Enosh, that "then there began the calling upon the name of the Lord." Involved in the matter of the understanding of that passage is the Hebrew word which yields the root "to begin." Identical with this root, "to begin," is another Hebrew root which means "to profane." Related to these two roots is still another Hebrew root, *yahal,* which means "to await" or "to hope." Involved in understanding the passage is the need to determine which of these three root meanings is the appropriate one for the passage, and thereafter to supply a grammatical explanation of the particular form, *huhal,* so as to buttress the understanding by the aid of the grammar. Since one cannot have a word-for-word correspondence in a translation, allow me to translate this passage into idiomatic English: "Then man began to call upon the name of the Lord." This rendering is to be found in most translations. The question then arises: Why is it that in the ancient versions the text is translated in a variety of different ways? The Aramaic translation, called the Targum, renders it,

"This one *hoped* to call on the name of God." When the rendering is "profane" or "hope," are we in the area of understanding or in the area of interpretation? It is my opinion that we are in the area of interpretation. For, although the Hebrew verse contains no difficulty in itself, its implication does contain a difficulty, since the developing, interpretive tradition, even in very early times, attributed to Father Abraham the momentous discovery of the existence of God. Our half-verse, in seeming to ascribe the discovery to Enos, stands in apparent conflict with that broadly accepted theme, and each of the two ancient translations which I have cited contains an interpretation designed to divert the sense from the natural, and to make it conform with the broad and almost universal motif of Abraham's priority. Among the traditional Jewish interpreters and commentators on this half verse, there is to be found an agreement that the verse meant literally that man profaned God's name; what I am contending is that when this conclusion arises, understanding has given way to interpretation, and interpretation in turn has come to affect understanding. That is, the Jewish understanding of the verse was the direct result of the interpretation of it.

A body of interpretive material is a conflation of the multiple instances in which a text, either uncertain or having a specific implication, comes to acquire a widely agreed upon meaning. Somewhat analogously, to cite two more well-known instances, an "eye for an eye and a tooth for a tooth" means, in the body of Jewish interpretive material, monetary punishment, not the literal, physical eye for an eye. The passage "Thou shalt not seethe the kid in its mother's milk" came to imply to Jews that they should make a dietary separation between meat dishes and milk dishes.

Once there arises a body of interpretive material which is transmitted from generation to generation, and which carried over into preaching and into the schools, then the interpretation becomes interchangeable with the understanding. In this sense the growth of a body of interpretive material becomes the clue to how a tradition understands its sacred text. But the next question must then be asked respecting this process whereby understanding becomes interpretation and interpretation becomes understanding: Wherein can there lie certain controls against caprice and against the farfetched? The answer would appear to lie in the observation that that process of making the ancient relevant to the contemporaneous carries in itself the inherent danger that the contemporaneous may distort, rather than elucidate and amplify. Accordingly, the ancient Jewish literature tells us about rules of interpretation formulated successively by Hillel and Ishmael, and then by others. These formulations not only give legitimacy to particular hermeneutic principles, but also, by giving legitimacy to particular ones, imply illegitimacy in others. We are somewhat in the dark about those which are implicitly illegitimate, but there are some stray clues to certain types of extreme interpretations in the form of allusions in rabbinic literature to "interpreters of difficult things and interpreters of closed-up things." It is conventional to explain these allusions as involving extreme allegorists and their unrestrained allegorical interpretation. The ancient Jewish rabbinic writings contain a few allegories, and Josephus, who reflects a good bit of the rabbinic interpretive material, provides us with still others; but to know the full weight of the allegorical, we must turn to Philo of Alexandria. In Philo, a very apt student of Plato and the Stoics, allegory is the interpretive device whereby Plato and the Stoics intrude into the context of Scripture. Thus, Adam is mind, Eve is sense perception, and the Serpent is pleasure, so that when mind and sense perception become bent on pleasure, they lose the the virtue of the Garden of Eden, from which four rivers flow— these four rivers being the four Stoic cardinal virtues. To cite another example, Cain is the man with poor arguments and fluent speech, and Abel the man with excellent arguments but halting speech; in this contest, the fluent always kills the halting.

So completely alien is Philo's body of allegoric interpretation
to rabbinic interpretation that scarcely one reflection of this content is to be found in rabbinic literature. One might, from the
standpoint of rabbinic interpretation, rule Philo to be illegitimate
and classify him with the disqualified interpreters. Yet Philo
himself speaks in a number of passages of "canons of allegory" as
if to imply that even in his environment certain controls were
needed. Philo, however, never directly states what these canons
were. The only regulation that seems to me to operate in his case
is this—that the allegorical quality which he ascribes to a Biblical character seems to be derived from the supposed etymology
of the Hebrew name of that character. Thus Abram, prior to the
change of his name, means "lofty father" and implies that the
patriarch, at that stage in his career, was a meteorologist—that
is to say, an astrologer; when Abraham's name is changed (in the
Greek the change of Abraham's name involves only the addition
of an *alpha*), the name *Avraham*, Abraham, means "elect father of
sound." In Philo's interpretation, "elect" has to do with the cir-
cumstantial fact that Abraham had done nothing prior to God's
call of him to justify God's call, which is to say that Abraham was
either predestined or simply chosen. As for "sound," speech is the
fallible brother of thought, and this whole allusion in Abraham's
name is to Abraham's embarkation on introspective dialectics by
means of which he moved from faulty thought to proper reason
and arrived at the discovery of the existence of God. "Father"
alludes to his capacity to order his mind and his reason. We have
the paradox in Philo, on the one hand, that apparently his allegorical ascription of qualities comes from the Hebrew meanings
of the names, and, on the other hand, he can be so elastic about
the Hebrew meanings that one wonders just what limitation he
might have seen in them!

The ancient rabbinic tradition was itself aware of modes of
interpretation, as distinct from rules, and these modes included
those in which the literal was, as it were, departed from. The four

Hebrew consonants which make up the word *Pardes,* "garden," allude to four types of exegesis. The *P* stands for *Pshat,* which means literal; the *R* for *remez,* which means that which is hinted at in the text, that is to say, an interpretation which is not devoid of some bond to the text. The *D* yields *drush,* which means that which is sought into, or possibly sought for, namely, an interpretation which would not arise immediately but which on inquiry might emerge; and the *S* stands for *sod,* which means secret, esoteric, and possibly alludes to a mystic type of interpretation. By and large, this mystic bent, insofar as it occurs in the Jewish tradition, is an embellishment of the three preceding ones, and not a substitute for them; it exists side by side, but does not supplant the textually bound interpretation.

The implication of interpretation, and of controls on interpretation, and of the transmission of the interpretations controlled in this sense, means that from its Scriptural side the rabbinic literature is a vast repository of Scriptural exegesis. That early body of Jewish lore, called the Mishnah, consists of inferences drawn from Scripture, these stated laconically; in almost all cases, the succinct statment abstains from supplying the Scriptural basis. The clarifying commentary on the Mishnah, called the Gemara, necessarily raises in its discussion the question of the Scriptural basis for the Mishnaic statement; it therefore portrays this sage or that sage in the act of suggesting what the Scriptural basis could be. Sometimes these sages, agreeing on the Mishnaic utterance, disagreed on what might be the Scriptural verse that justified it, for each could suggest what seemed to him a more likely source. So voluminous is the Gemara and so thoroughly quoted is Scripture that I would rather doubt that there are many Pentateuchal passages which do not appear in some form in the rabbinic literature. If one abstained from studying Scripture but studied only the rabbinic literature, he would coincidentally absorb a great deal of Scripture. But the Scripture that he would

absorb would be the Scripture as this growing literature interpreted it and thereby understood it.

A definition which I might, therefore, give of the Jewish Bible
is that the Jewish Bible is the Bible as understood and interpreted
by Jews throughout the ages. Although I teach a course in Philo, I
try to make it clear that Philo represents a unique instance of a
body of Jewish interpretation of a tangential nature which had no
permanent sequel in the unfolding Jewish tradition. The Jewish
Bible is the Bible, the understanding of which has sequels down
to our own time.

The Jewish Bible is, therefore, not Scripture in its pristine
meaning, but Scripture as expounded in the Jewish tradition. It is
true that in the Spanish-Jewish period there arose philologians
who made inquiries into the plain and simple meaning of Scripture; their academic achievements, perpetuated through humanism and the Christian Hebraists, make their way into the commentaries of our day that are the most complete and the most
incisive. Yet these excursions into the literal, as exemplified by
Abraham Ibn Ezra or David Kimchi, did not lead to the discard-
ing of the traditional interpretation. We see this most clearly in
the case of the French rabbi, Rashi, who composed a commentary
for virtually all of the thirty-nine books of the Hebrew Bible
(or twenty-four if you want to use the traditional Jewish count).
What is distinctive about Rashi's commentary is his ability to
give for each verse, phrase, or word in the text the quintessence
of the interpretation which lies in the voluminous rabbinic literature. Rashi is seldom original; his greatness lies in his ability to
compress the content of a tremendous range of information which
was at his fingertips to compress. In many passages Rashi simply
quotes a few Biblical words and then suggests that the literal
meaning is the plain and simple meaning; but then he goes on
to give the traditional Jewish understanding of that phrase.

Neither the Ibn Ezras nor the Kimchis nor the Rashis saw
any direct tension between the literal and the interpretive, for

the living Scripture to them was a combination of both, and especially of the latter. Side by side with the ancient rabbinic writings
called the Mishnah and Gemara, which together comprise the
Talmud, there was a body of writings called the Midrash. The
Midrash alludes to that body of traditional Jewish interpretation
arranged according to the sequence of the verses. The content of
this interpretation parallels and is often exactly identical with
Talmudic interpretation, for the distinction is preeminently
that of arrangement, and not of content. In the Talmud, the cita-
tion of the verse depends upon context; the Midrash, however,
is a verse by verse commentary, somewhat as if the Talmudic
interpretations were culled from it and arranged in the verse by
verse order, or else the Talmudic cited from the Midrash. When
we speak of the Midrash Tabbah, we ordinarily have in mind the
five exhortatory and edifying commentaries to the Pentateuch, as
distinct from older Midrashic commentaries called Halachic,
which were primarily legalistic. The Talmud and the Midrash,
then, are in a real sense the body of interpretive Jewish material
about Scripture, and they constitute the eyes though which Jews
looked at Scripture. They are the body of what I might call
"overmeanings."

Overmeaning supplants plain meaning; overmeaning implies
contemporaneity, namely, a living and growing body of interpretation. Contemporaneity might be understood as the opposite of
the pristine meaning.

II

Quite analogously, the Christian tradition developed its own
body of interpretive material. The analogues with the rabbinic
material are more those of form, naturally, than they are of content. They are also the product of the circumstance that, by and
large, Christianity ceased to use the Hebrew and instead relied
upon the Greek. The Letter of Aristeos, or as some prefer to call

it, Pseudo-Aristeos, which deals with the supposed origin of the
Septuagint, is significant in making the point that so accurate and
responsible a translation was the Greek version that it is the equal
of the Hebrew in its inspiration and in its reliability. There are,
of course, an Origen and a Jerome who, as great scholars and
academicians, make detailed inquiry into the writings to be re-
assured that the translation was equally eminent with the Hebrew
original, but there are also Clement and Origen handling New
Testament materials allegorically whenever the inner problems
seem acute enough. To a later generation, the allegorical interpretation always seems outmoded, and hence it is normal for the
allegorists of one generation to recede in significance as the
generations go on. The Christian overmeanings include elements
as diverse as the conviction about the original sense of the
Hebrew of Isaiah 7, 14, about which Jews and Christians
quarreled, and in more recent times Christians among themselves have quarreled; also included are those passages in the
Gospels in which the sisters and brothers of Jesus are interpreted
to be cousins, this latter in the interest of the perpetual virginity
of Mary. If I do not misunderstand the Christian tradition, which
henceforth for purposes of distinction I shall call Catholic, these
overmeanings take on the word "tradition," namely, the body of
continuing "Revelation inherent in the Church," a tradition
which is broader than mere Scriptural interpretation, yet also includes Scriptural interpretation. As it applies to Scriptural interpretation, tradition in this Catholic sense might be described as
that body of continuing revelation of the implications of Scripture.
To the Jewish analogue of this unfolding material the Jews gave
the name of the Oral Torah, limiting Scripture to the Written
Torah; in the Jewish conception, the Oral Torah is not only just
as valid as the Written, but the tradition holds that it was revealed either in essence or in actuality to Moses at Sinai simultaneously with the revelation of the Written. What these two
terms, the Oral Torah and the Christian "tradition," assert is that

bodies of interpretation are not simply human concoctions, but are products of the Divine.

I do not believe that in Judaism the question is ever raised that was raised in the sixteenth century after the Protestant Reformation, namely, the relative authority of Scripture and the relative authority of the Church. When the question was raised, Catholics gave the answer that it was the Church which was the teacher and guardian of Scripture, and, while the Church was not in any sense superior to Scripture, it was the Church which was responsible for the interpretation of Scripture. This was, by and large, as I understand it, a response to those Protestants who were saying that the Church was nothing and that Scripture alone was the authority. I do not know of anything comparable in any Jewish writings, for since Jews lacked authority of persons, there was no Jewish analogue to what is involved in Catholicism as the authority of the Church. For Jews, authority lay in Scripture, and it lay in the tradition which interpreted Scripture. But there was no authority of persons; there was only the authority in the tradition. Among Catholics, authority has lain in the Church as well as in Scripture, but never only in Scripture.

III

When Protestants contended that authority lay in Scripture, and Scripture alone, they began to develop those men who made contentions out of their own learning and out of their own conscience about what Scripture meant. These contentions contradicted the body of Catholic overmeaning, and the response of the Church was to designate commissions which could yield authoritative answers which would be binding on Catholics. Such took place in connection with the Council of Trent, and such took place in subsequent papal commissions, and one can say that by and large, until the past half-century, Catholic Biblical scholarship was able to operate with profundity only in those areas allowed to it in the framework of the decisions of the authorized commissions. When the Higher Criticism first arose, Catholics participated in it, but were gradually impelled to withdraw from it, with the consequence that, by and large, the Higher Criticism was, until very recent times, an almost exclusively Protestant preoccupation. This was the case not only because Protestants were interested theologically in discovering what the pristine sense of Scripture was, but also because the march of scholarship was bringing into the forefront conclusions which were completely at variance with what is found both in the Jewish Oral Torah and in the Catholic tradition. The iconoclastic nature of much of Protestant scholarship is best discerned in the upheavals within Protestantism between Modernists and Fundamentalists; while they argue with each other from the standpoint of basically different assumptions, in neither case are these assumptions based directly on some body of tradition but emerge from preconceptions about the nature of Scripture. Thus, the Fundamentalists argue on the basis of the supposed inerrancy of Scripture, and the Modernists argue that a Scriptural document should be approached just as any other ancient documents. But Fundamentalists and Modernists hold in common that it was the individual learning or the individual conscience which was the decisive factor, and not some body of material intermediary between the nineteenth century researcher and ancient Scripture.

To revert now to our words "understanding" and "interpretation," Protestant scholarship must be credited with a tremendous achievement toward the understanding of Scripture, in the form of the dictionaries, encyclopedias, handbooks, grammars of Hebrew, the cultivation of comparative linguistics, anthropology, and the like, with the result that even the Fundamentalists who want to differ with the iconoclasm of the Modernist interpreter feel called upon to utilize the grammars, dictionaries, and other tools created by these people. The Fundamentalist could be shocked by and ignore the Graf-Wellhausen hypothesis, but he could not ignore the wealth of learning called into being to support that hypothesis. He had to deal with the cumulative learning, no matter how sharply he wanted to reject its bent. All too often the Fundamentalist was caught in the vise of seeming to reject understanding as well as interpretation, and many a Fundamentalist tradition chose to ignore understanding, simply because the interpretation was distasteful.

Roman Catholics, since they had tradition, have never been Fundamentalists in the sense of Protestant Fundamentalists, and they have had no need to defend a Fundamentalist preconception. They could be disposed to disregard, really to ignore, the Protestant interpretation as wrongheaded, but when the time was to come that they felt ready to encounter it, they could often feel free to accept it or reject it on the basis of the inherent value or lack of value that they saw in it. That is to say, there was enough freedom in Catholic Biblical scholarship for Catholics to confront the iconoclastic scholarship on its merits, and not have to shy away from it, as Fundamentalists did, simply because it was inconoclastic.

IV

Respecting Jews, the fact needs to be stated openly that, by and large, Jews were represented in the modern scholarship of the nineteenth century by remarkably few people. A few, such as Heinrich Graetz, can be cited as having worked within some of the framework of the Higher Criticism, but the fact is that Jews as yet were not truly to be found in the stream of Western intellectual thought, and certainly not in Western Biblical scholarship. The German, David Hoffman, did write a book, the translation of whose title is *The Most Significant Errors of the Graf-Wellhausen Hypothesis;* his book was a rejection of the Higher Criticism not only because it was out of consonance with Jewish tradition, but also because Hoffman was among the succession of

Jews who saw, in the Higher Criticism, an animosity toward Judaism. The fact is that this animosity can be documented, especially in the case of the great Septuagint scholar, Lagarde, but in the broader perspective, the German, Protestant Higher Criticism was just as much anti-Christian as it was anti-Jewish, for it was just as iconoclastic toward the Gospels as it was towards the Law of Moses.

If that succession of iconoclastic scholars can be convicted of anything, it is that they seldom challenged their own presuppositions, and they fitted neatly either into Hegelianism or into adaptations of Darwinism which prompted them to speak of the evolution of this or that; and they often made the documents fit into a Procrustean bed. We must beware, however, in our wish to point out the inadequacies of that scholarship, not to fall into the pit of distorting it or of failing to do justice to its tremendous achievements. The time was to come when the interpretation by the nineteenth-century German Protestants was challenged by, among others, Protestants themselves, but the contribution made to the understanding is not to be underestimated. This was particularly the case as more and more Semitic languages came to be understood, the knowledge of Hebrew enriched, and as archaeology both fed the knowledge of languages and increased the understanding of the Biblical milieu. I think it can be said truthfully that in the nineteenth century Jews, like Catholics, largely held themselves aloof from the truly scientific study of Scripture, and only at the turn of the century did they begin to enter into its domain.

I suppose the most significant developments in the twentieth century have been the tremendous increase in the knowledge of the Hebrew language and of its Semitic relatives, the tremendous increase of archaeological data, and the progressive decline of the prevalence of the Graf-Wellhausen hypothesis. The limitations of time and space prevent recapitulating the whole story here. Catholics and Protestants in the twentieth century began to read each other's books, and Catholic and Protestant archaeologists began to become acquainted not only with each other's work, but with each other; Jews began to enter into the field of scientific Bible study and to read the Christian writings as well as to compose their own. The barriers here too began to fall, especially in the United States. In Palestine, in the days before it was Israel, the qualifying adjectives, Protestant, Catholic, or Jewish Biblical scholarships were beginning to disappear, their place taken by simply "Biblical scholarship." More and more individual Jews began to participate in this scholarship, sometimes with all the radicalism of the Protestant iconoclasts, and sometimes contending with the Wellhausenites on their own ground. When Palestine became Israel, Jewish Biblical scholarship, especially the archaeological, came to be enriched. While the Modernist crisis, principally connected with Alfred Loisy in 1910, slowed down Catholic Biblical scholarship, its insights nevertheless proceeded to proliferate and to deepen.

The fact needs to be faced that this new and significant development represents a joining by Catholics and by Jews in the Protestant search for the pristine meaning of Scripture. At last we are united in common academic quests, reading each other's books, and agreeing and disagreeing with each other, not on denominational lines, but in the way that scholars differ in weighing the material they deal with.

V

Lastly, we must ask the question: What, in this light, is the status of the Oral Torah and the Catholic tradition? There are, I believe, two answers that can be suggested, though I am not sure that everyone would suggest both of the answers. The first of these would be quasi-theological, namely, that the body of scholars, whether Jewish or Catholic, carrying on the work of Biblical interpretation, represent a continuity with the ante-

cedent past, and that continuity would imply the continuity of
Biblical revelation through the Biblical interpreter. If I understand the Catholic attitude correctly, the work of Catholic Biblical interpretation would represent one aspect of the continuing
revelation embodied in the Catholic concept of the Church as the
vehicle for revelation. Certainly from the Jewish standpoint there
has been the conception that the Oral Torah is unending and
hence continuous.

The second answer is nontheological and represents quite a
secular approach, derivative from the discipline called the history
of religions. Here I feel on much safer ground if I make the
assertion respecting Judaism, and then leave it to our Catholic
friends to comment on whether or not it applies to Catholicism.
The assertion is this, that the rabbinic interpretation of Scripture comprises insights and doctrines and convictions which in
themselves represent matters of significance and matters of value.
I can best illustrate this, perhaps, by alluding again to Philo. His
Biblical interpretation is farfetched, and there was no sequel in
Judaism to what he did; nevertheless, the body of Philonic material is not only itself worthy and of value, but also contains in
itself material to edify and to instruct. If this is true of the
Philonic material, which had no sequel, then how much more
is it true of the rabbinic material which has had a sequel, and
the effect of which has been of tremendous influence on unfolding
Judaism. The visible aspects of Judaism in our day, namely, synagogue and rabbi, are not Scriptural; the visible aspects of
Catholicism are comparably not directly Scriptural, for the papacy,
the hierarchy, the totality of sacraments, and the religious orders
are all developments of the ages after Scripture, however deeply
rooted in Scripture they may ultimately be. I suppose the chief
difference between Judaism and Catholicism, on the one hand,
and Protestantism on the other—this is meant again to be descriptive and not comparative—is that neither tradition embraced the

view of *sola scripura,* where as Protestantism did, at least in principle.

However much scholars, transcending denominational lines, may unite in the common search for the correct understanding of Scripture and for the consistent, restrained, and profound interpretation of it, I for one am prepared to recognize, at least respecting Jews, that the pristine meaning of Scripture is quite distinct from the meaning which Jews came to find in it. I believe it is possible to distinguish between the pristine sense of Scripture and the developed sense. The pedant in me often rebels against attributing to the pristine sense of Scripture the tremendous insights which the rabbinic tradition derived from Scripture; I like to keep these separate so as to appreciate each more. They constitute a double heritage, or perhaps it might be phrased that they constitute double aspects of a larger heritage. It is wrong in methodology and it is wrong in understanding to play them off against each other, just as it is wrong to fail to make the distinctions between them. Both are worthy. But there is no Scripture without understanding and there is no Scripture without interpretation, however valiant the efforts have been by Karaites among Jews, and Protestants among Christians, to "return" to Scripture.

When we read each other's books on Scripture, when we read each other's books on the interpretation in our traditions of Scripture, we engage in a common, religious task, and insofar as we are able to enlighten ourselves and each other, inevitably our understanding is deepened, our horizons broadened, and that which in Scripture can be of benign influence radiates the more effectively among men.

REVEREND ROLAND E. MURPHY, O. CARM.

Present Biblical Scholarship as a Bond of Understanding

REV. ROLAND E. MURPHY, O.CARM., *Professor of Old Testament at The Catholic University of America, served (1964–65) as Visiting Professor at the Pittsburgh Theological Seminary (Presbyterian). He was recently appointed coeditor with Père Benoit (of the Jerusalem Biblical School) of the biblical issue of* Concilium, *a new publication edited by experts of the Second Vatican Council.*

Father Murphy was ordained in May, 1942, in Chicago, and received an S.S.L. degree in 1958 at the Pontifical Biblical Institute in Rome. Since 1958, he has been Editor-in-Chief of the Catholic Biblical Quarterly *and has authored many articles and two books:* The Dead Sea Scrolls and the Bible *(Newman, 1956), and* Seven Books of Wisdom *(Bruce, 1960). Father Murphy taught Scripture at the Carmelite Theological Seminary, Whitefriars Hall, Washington, D.C., for several years and, on a fellowship from the American Schools of Oriental Research, conducted archeological work in Palestine. He has also been a visiting professor at the University of Notre Dame summer sessions.*

Some limits, however arbitrary, must be set to the title of this article. Present Biblical scholarship will be understood as that of the past twenty-five years, and Biblical scholarships will be limited to the Old Testament, yet will include also the pertinent and important achievements in such areas as Ugaritic literature and Biblical archaeology. One cannot do justice to so vast an area, but it is hoped that the selections will be at least representative and provocative.

One can detect a parallel between Catholic and Jewish Biblical scholarship in their relatively recent emergence. As regards Catholics, the state of siege in which the Church found itself in the face of the advance of critical scholarship and modernism was responsible for the small achievements of the late nineteenth and twentieth centuries. The "progressive" Biblical encyclical, *Divino afflante Spiritu,* appeared in 1943, and the advances made since that time are truly remarkable.[1] As regards Jews, there were various economic and social factors at work. But for them, too, the advance of Higher Criticism constituted a problem, as Robert Gordis has noted:

. . . modern Jewish research suffered from a third defect, the virtual neglect of the Bible by modern Jewish scholarship. . . . In view of these factors [the reference is to Higher Criticism], it becomes easy to understand the neglect of Biblical research by modern Jewish scholars. With only a few exceptions, even those of liberal views found it difficult to subject the Bible to this merciless type of analysis and atomization. A few traditional scholars, like the more conservative Christian scholars, attempted to refute one or another aspect of the Higher Criticism, but they were voices crying in the wilderness. Indeed, in some cases, their attack failed to discriminate between the valuable and the transitory elements of Biblical criticism. All in all, the structure was too imposing and too extensive to yield to such puny efforts. As a result, Jewish scholars either accepted the results of the Higher Criticism, as Graetz did in the first volume of his *Geschichte der Juden,* or they avoided the subject altogether. Whatever creative work was done by Jewish scholars in the field of the Bible was largely peripheral, dealing with the text, the ancient versions, and similar themes. Today there is a real possibility of substantial and creative Jewish scholarship in the field of the Bible. The valuable results of nineteenth century Biblical criticism will endure, but a widespread and wholesome reaction has set in against its excesses, induced in large measure by the important archaeological discoveries and by more sympathetic and scientific techniques of research. Contemporary scholars, Christian and Jewish alike, see the Bible within the framework of the cultural, political, and economic world in the ancient Near East. As a result, they approach the Bible with a wholesome and growing respect, not only for the exalted value of its religious and ethical teaching, but also for the essential veracity of its account of the Hebrew people and its religion. Jewish scholars today need no longer sacrifice either their scientific conscience or their love for Jewish tradition in order to participate in Biblical research.[2]

The Catholic scholar can practically make his own this judgment by Gordis. The general absence of Catholic or Jewish influence in the molding of modern, Old Testament scholarship can be seen in the recent surveys of Old Testament research by H.-J Kraus[3] and H. F. Hahn.[4] The masterful introduction to the Old Testament by Otto Eissfeldt[5] is also instructive in this regard: the advances in Biblical scholarship have been due largely to non-Jews and non-Catholics. But, at the same time, the generous recognition of recent achievements by Catholics and Jews may be seen in the latest edition of Eissfeldt.

At the present time, Biblical research by Catholics is directly influenced, in varying degrees, by the foremost Jewish scholars. Ephraim Speiser of the University of Pennsylvania has put everyone in his debt by his perceptive translation and commentary on Genesis, which inaugurated the Anchor Bible.[6] The highly personal, existential interpretations of Martin Buber and Abraham Heschel betray an awareness of the Old Testament in its historical conditioning as well as its relevance to the modern man.[7] The remarkable synthesis of Yehezkel Kaufmann, which was made available to the English-speaking world by another brilliant Jewish scholar, Moshe Greenberg, will perhaps not win general adherence because of its one-sided evaluation of Biblical data, but neither can it be safely disregarded.[8] One could continue in a similar vein regarding the studies of Julian Morgenstern, M. D.

Cassuto, Samuel Sandmel, Cyrus Gordon, Sheldon Blank, Robert
Gordis, H. L. Ginsberg, Ralph Marcus and a host of others. These
names appear consistently in the list of scholarly, interpretative
studies of the Old Testament, and anyone who neglects their
works does so to his own harm.

I

What has made possible this interchange between scholars of
all faiths is a common concern for understanding the Biblical
message in its historical perspective. This means that one must
situate a text of the Bible against its historical background, and,
if possible, in its original life-setting, such as the temple liturgy
or covenant-renewal, in order to understand exactly what the
Biblical text conveyed to ancient Israel. From this point of view,
all interpreters are equal—they must use the same tools:
philology, literary criticism, history, archaeology, and so on.[9] As
will be indicated later, the problem shifts when one attempts to
get beyond the question, "What *did* the text mean?" to "What
does the text mean?" But on the level of objective analysis,
where the text is subject to the control of historical and literary
evidence, a consensus of opinion is possible, even apart from
one's particular religious commitment.

A practical example of this is the evaluation of the evidence
supplied by archaeology and extra-Biblical literature as it pertains to the Old Testament. The work of E. Speiser teems with
allusions to concrete, historical facts which illustrate the Biblical
text and bring us closer to its historical meaning. Speiser's approach to Genesis is structured along lines that have become the
common property of all scholars today—that there are three
constituent strands in Genesis (and in the Pentateuch) that have
been woven together to form the book; these strands incorporate
early (as well as late) material which was handed down by oral
(as well as written) tradition. These conclusions are the fruit of

the literary criticism to which Genesis has been subjected over the years.[10]

Although there is doubtless less unanimity, one can speak also of a consensus concerning the valid, historical background reflected in the patriarchal narratives (Genesis 12–50).[11] By this is meant the fact that certain practices of the patriarchs have now been shown to be anchored in the social climate of Mesopotamia-Palestine in the first half of the second millennium. This evidence has to be handled carefully. It does not "prove" that Genesis 12–50 is history, but it is proof that these chapters rest on a chain of tradition that goes back to the patriarchal period. This seems undeniable, even if the factuality of many events remains questionable. Scholars are now less ready to dismiss these events as inventions or to propose hypothetical reconstructions. The documents from Nuzi and Mari have established the authentic coloring of these ancient stories, and we may single out a few examples. The wife-sister motif of Genesis 12, 10–20, even if it is employed again in 20, 1–18 and 26, 1–11 in the reinterpretation given to it by the Biblical writers, is to be associated with the Hurrian social practice whereby a wife enjoyed special status and protection when she was also recognized as her husband's sister either by adoption or in reality. Again, the transfer of the birthright and paternal blessing from Esau to Jacob (Genesis 27) reflects the Hurrian practice of a personal decision on the part of the father (despite the interpretation actually given to the episode on the part of the Biblical writer). Finally, Rachel's theft of the household gods is to be explained from the Hurrian concept of the role these played in the daughter's title to inheritance.[12]

I think it is fair to say that both Catholics and Jews are predisposed by their respective traditions to recognize valid history in the Bible. Speiser has gone on to point out that the Israelite traditions presuppose a kind of informal canon at work early in Israel's history,[13] and he has even constructed a daring apologia for the call of Abraham—that Abraham's abandonment of his home and gods fits in well with the uninspiring social and religious climate of ancient Mesopotamia. Such reasoning as this must be properly understood, however. It does not prove that Abraham was called by God; that is purely a matter of faith shared by Jews and Catholics. Not long ago the whole problem of the truth of the Bible had to be aired in connection with the assessment of the work of the Jewish archaeologist, Nelson Glueck.[14] Gleuck's achievements have been particularly significant. His surface exploration of Transjordan unearthed evidence which pointed to the thirteenth century as the date of the exodus; his exploration of the Negeb has provided evidence for associating Abraham with the Middle Bronze I occupation of the Negeb (twenty-first to the nineteenth century). But Glueck himself has indicated that one cannot "prove" the Bible; one must believe, or not believe, that it is the Word of God. On the other hand, this kind of evidence is surely welcome, just as much as the evidence that disagrees with the Biblical text (such as the results of the excavations at Old Testament Jericho and Ai).

The limitations of space prevent us from illustrating other examples of consensus which could be instanced throughout the Hebrew Bible. One could point to the studies of R. Gordis and M. H. Segal on the wisdom literature;[15] those of A. Malamat, B. Maisler (Mazar), and W. W. Hallo on Israelite history;[16] those of M. Buber, A. Heschel, and A. Neher on prophetic literature;[17] or those of E. Bickermann on the Maccabean period.[18]

II

One of the most significant discoveries of the last decades has been the literature from ancient Ugarit (modern Ras Shamra), first unearthed in 1929. Since this date the language was deciphered and discovered to be very similar to Hebrew. A whole literature of this Canaanite people has been translated: the legend of Keret, the epic of Aqhat, the cycle of Baal and Anat, and so forth. In this scholarly enterprise Jewish scholars have been among the foremost. Cyrus Gordon wrote what has become the standard grammar of the language, published (with an *imprimatur!*) through the Pontifical Biblical Institute.[19] Very important studies of the text and their contents have been forthcoming from H. L. Ginsberg, M. D. Cassuto, and T. Gaster.[20] These works have proved to be indispensable in the continuing study of the Canaanite background of Hebrew language and culture. The contributions of Ugaritic studies to our understanding of the Bible have been constantly stressed by W. F. Albright, and, even if the claims seem at times exaggerated, no one can dispute the fact that Hebrew grammar and lexicography, the structure of Old Testament poetry, and the world of thought in which Israel moved have been greatly clarified by these studies.[21]

Another area where Jewish and Christian scholars have joined forces is the study of the transmission of the Biblical text, both the *veritas Hebraica* and its daughter versions, such as the Aramaic targum, Septuagint, and so on. At the present time at the Hebrew University, a new edition of the Hebrew text is being prepared by Jewish scholars on the basis of the famous Aleppo codex, which was produced over a thousand years ago by the Massorete, Ben Asher.[22] Research on the Targum has been done by A. Sperber as well as by Father A. Diez-Macho, M.S.C., who discovered a complete Palestinian targum in the Vatican codex Neofiti I. The names of the late M. L. Margolis, Peter Katz, Harry Orlinsky, and now Father D. Barthélemy, O.P., are important in the study of the Greek translations of the Old Testament.[23]

We have already spoken of the American Jewish archaeologist, Nelson Glueck. It is perhaps unfair to choose one archaeologist out of the numerous experts in Israel, such as Y. Aharoni, N. Avigad, M. Avi-Yonah, S. Yeivin, and others.[24] But the name of Yigael Yadin merits special mention because of the monumental exploration of the Biblical Hazor, and also the recovery of ancient artifacts and manuscript fragments in the region of

Engaddi.[25] The birth of the State of Israel, with the ensuing need of building and expansion, created many problems of archaelogical investigation, and these have been handled by competent archaeologists whose studies have appeared particularly in the *Bulletin of the Jewish Israel* (since 1951), *Exploration Society* (1933), the *Israel Exploration Journal* (since 1950), and *Eretz-Israel* (since 1951).

The bond of present Biblical scholarship has been prepared and forged in these subsidiary but important areas of Biblical study. This is due simply to individual achievements of the respective scholars, and in some cases to the collaboration of Christians and Jews. Here we may recall the touching tribute to the memory of the late Alfred Pohl, S.J., by the Italian Jew, Sabatino Moscati, or the words with which Cyrus Gordon dedicated his *Introduction to Old Testament Times*: "Dedicated to my friend Pater Professor Alfred Pohl, S.J., who is doing more than any other man to further the scientific study of the Ancient Near East."[26] The collaboration of the Jesuits of the Pontifical Biblical Institute with both Protestants and Jews can hardly be improved upon.

III

This paper would be incomplete if it restricted itself to the realm of agreement between Jewish and Catholic Biblical scholars. A few questions should be raised concerning the theological exegesis of the Old Testament. In this case the Bible is approached from faith; the Word of God is heard within a tradition. And in this respect the Jewish and Catholic positions are again similar. Both approach the Old Testament from their respective beliefs which have been formed, even allowing a personalist approach on both sides, in the Talmud and rabbinical literature,[27] and in the writings of the Fathers and the Councils of the Church.[28]

It is not easy to characterize the power of these respective traditions. The Catholic position is more dogmatic and obligatory, even if there is a large area of undefined material, as has been explained above. The Jewish stance is much less dogmatic, particularly as reflected in the writings of such modern exponents as M. Buber and A. Heschel. But the fact remains that the Bible is approached in any case out of a clearly known tradition; in both cases the question is asked, "What does the Bible mean here and now?" This is faith seeking to understand.

Is dialogue possible at this level? I believe it is, if dialogue means that people of disparate beliefs speak together in order to understand one another. And a great deal of this interchange is necessary. Christian-Jewish dialogue in the past has been primarily polemical, but H.-J. Schoeps has shown in *The Jewish-Christian Argument* (New York, Holt, Rinehart and Winston Inc., 1963), how it finally became dialogue in the confrontation between K. L. Schmidt and M. Buber. It is probably significant that the attempted dialogue of J. Maritain, however sincere, did not succeed (perhaps, among other reasons, because it failed to build on whatever common understanding a Biblical basis can offer to both groups).

How does the Christian understanding of the Old Testament differ from the Jewish? The Christian understanding sees the Old Testament as preparatory, as incomplete without the fulfillment in Christ to which it is oriented. Not all Christians are at one in this, as the recent studies in C. Westermann, *Essays on Old Testament Hermeneutics* (Richmond, John Knox Press, 1963), and B. W. Anderson, *The Old Testament and Christian Faith* (New York, Harper & Row, Publishers, 1963), have shown.[29] But the Christian view does not mean that the Old Testament is to be flattened out or allegorized out of existence, as was done in some areas of medieval Christian exegesis. Modern Biblical studies have rendered this virtually impossible, as the unsuccessful efforts of W. Vischer demonstrate. Rather, the Old Testament must be

understood on its own terms before its relationship to the New
Testament can be properly appreciated. And in this effort of
understanding, Catholic theological exegesis has much to learn
from the Old Testament itself and from the Jewish understanding of it.

First and foremost, we may single out the reverence for the
majesty and transcendence of God which permeates the Biblical
record and Jewish tradition. The development of Catholic
theology has not been without its dangers. One may be seduced
by formulas because one somehow treats them as corresponding
exactly to reality. The cold and sober language of scholastic
theology may quench the liveliness of the Biblical Word. The
true category of God as "wholly other" cannot be neglected in
theology without disaster. The Old Testament itself bears witness to how Israel learned this lesson. The comfortable doctrine
of the sages had "explained" the justice of God in terms of
retribution in this life: God rewards the good and punishes the
evil (Proverbs, *passim;* Psalms 37). No matter how orthodox this
principle may be, it could be and was erected into a human law
that limited the Lord. It was in this manner that the author of
Job and Qoheleth read their contemporaries, and they both
struck a blow for divine freedom. The Lord was not to be contained within the theology of the sages. There was a certain
inevitability to this impasse which arose; the hard facts of experience spoke against the equation that wisdom (justice) equals life.
This impasse had to be reached before a breakthrough could
occur, and a fuller understanding be reached, that wisdom (justice) equals life eternal. But this new insight could be had only
after Israel's vision of the hidden God had been purified in Job
and Qoheleth. This example from the Old Testament itself serves
notice to Christian theology of the dangers inherent in rational
scholasticism. It must never lose the sense of the personal mystery
of God which permeates the Old Testament.

Secondly, we may point to the concept of the People of God

which runs through the documents issued by Vatican Council II on the liturgy, the Church, and ecumenism. This notion has underscored the fact that a legal and juridical concept of the Church must not be allowed to obscure its familial and collective character. The idea of the People of God is found in the New Testament, along with the implicitly related themes of election and covenant. But it is from the Old Testament that the children of the New can learn to deepen their sense of People—here on the broad canvas of Israel's salvation-history the life of the People is depicted, with all its glories and faults, with all its deep feeling for community and communion with God.

Finally, may we not detect on the American scene a greater sense of social ethic, a fearless criticism (and, in many Catholic circles, self-criticism) which points back to the Old Testament prophetic model? The problems which the prophets faced are perhaps not *literally* those of today. But their attitude and their voice need to be heard for the resolution of today's problems. The intense interest and great achievements of Jews in areas of social concern reflect how attuned they have been to their great prophets. May we all hear the Word as clearly.

The insights of Jewish understanding of the Old Testament are bound to be enriching and provocative for Catholics—enriching, because every insight that is theologically valid reveals an aspect of God's truth. One thinks of the Jewish stress on the corporate aspect of the Servant of Yahweh in the chapters of Deutero-Isaiah. This emphasis is as much a part of the Jewish commitment as the Christological interpretation is for the Catholic. And it is a necessary emphasis which the Catholic may not lose sight of, if he will appreciate the concrete manner of God's progressive revelation in the Bible. The Jewish contribution will be provocative because the mystery of God's ways with Israel, and so with man, is laid bare—the corporate aspect of salvation which comes from God. No complete explanation of this mystery has been reached; it is really unattainable. But much of what we may come to understand will rest upon a deeper intelligence of the Servant of the Lord.

We have indicated in the briefest way some of the advantages which Catholic scholarship and, indeed, Catholic life derive from the Old Testament and from Jewish scholarship. It would be presumptuous of me to suggest that the relationship can also be reversed. I must ask my Jewish brothers if that is possible. But it would be in the interests of dialogue for me to express some *desiderata*. Until I began writing this article, I had never before adverted to the fact that there exists no *Theology of the Old Testament* written by a Jewish scholar in the genre of those by Christian scholars such as Eichrodt, Jacob, von Rad, or van Imschoot. Perhaps such an approach involves a systematization, or conceptualization, that clashes with the concreteness native to the Judaic tradition. One must admit that a synthesis of the multifaceted encounter of God and Israel is problematical. At least one Catholic scholar has raised the question, "Is a Theology of the Old Testament possible?"[30] There is difficulty in analyzing the concept, but in practice no one would deny the success of the recent studies of Old Testament theology which we have mentioned. The point is that this development is the poorer for lacking its Jewish counterparts (and I might add, more numerous Catholic studies than have been thus far forthcoming). We should sidestep the speculative difficulties in the concept and work out a veritable theology of the Old Testament that speaks in objective but sympathetic terms to all men. This would be part of the dialogue.

A second suggestion presents itself: There is no Jewish journal which is exclusively devoted to Biblical articles. Many such articles appear in various Jewish publications (*Jewish Quarterly Review, Hebrew Union College Annual*) as well as in scholarly publications under Catholic auspices (*Biblica, Catholic Biblical Quarterly*), or in those journals published on an interdenominational basis (*Journal of Biblical Literature, Vetus Testamentum*).

This is all to the good, and even necessary; it secures worldwide and interconfessional attention. But I can only point to the advantages accruing to the Biblical movement among American Catholics from the existence of a journal like the *Catholic Biblical Quarterly* which has encouraged Catholic scholars to publish the results of their studies and in many instances to enrich the understanding of the Bible out of the Catholic tradition. This does not involve a narrow confessionalism, nor does it restrict publication in other journals. Rather, it offers a new and distinctive voice for the academic world to hear. I believe that this world would hear more accurately, and to its own profit, a distinctively Jewish interpretation of the Old Testament.

NOTES

[1] The most adequate treatment of the changes in the modern Catholic Biblical scene is to be found in J. Levie, S.J., *The Bible, Word of God in Words of Men* (New York, P. J. Kenedy & Sons, 1961). It might be well at the outset to clear up possible misconceptions concerning the authority of the Church and the freedom of Catholic Biblical scholars by the following remarks: First, I am not aware of any text in the Old Testament whose meaning has been defined by the Catholic Church. This would include Genesis 3, 15, Isaiah 7, 14, and many others whose interpretation might be regarded as settled by some Catholics. Secondly, the decrees of the Papal Biblical Commission were not designed to cut off scholarly research, even if modern history shows that they succeeded in doing this. I subscribe to the interpretation of their authority which was given by the secretary of this commission in 1955, namely, "the interpreter of Holy Scripture can pursue his scientific research with full liberty" (*Catholic Biblical Quarterly* 18, 1956, pp. 23–29). Two qualifications are given: texts that are connected with truths of faith and morals are excepted; for example, as a Catholic, I am not free to deny that the Old Testament proclaims the Lord as creator. It is in such broad areas that the exception will occur. Also, the authority of the teaching power of the Catholic Church (*salva semper auctoritate magisterii Ecclesiae*), means that my role as an exegete is modified by the fact that I read the Bible in and with the Church; I listen to the voice of the Church when it speaks authoritatively through its teaching power, as in the definition of articles of belief. Thirdly, what is the position of the Catholic Church vis-à-vis dogmatic beliefs and the Holy Scriptures? Catholic dogma represents the manner in

which the Church hears the Word of God down through the ages. No one
dogma is an exhaustive statement or final truth; it is truth, but dogma develops. The Church is able to refine her understanding of God, however much
it falls short of the divine reality.

2 See Robert Gordis, *Judaism for the Modern Age* (New York, Farrar, Straus
& Co., Inc., 1955), pp. 94, 96, 100.

3 *Geschichte der historisch-kritischen Erforschung des Alten Testaments*
(Neukirchen Kreis Moers, Neukirchener Verlag, 1956).

4 *The Old Testament in Modern Research* (Philadelphia, 1956).

5 *Einleitung in das Alte Testament* (Tubingen, Mohr, 1964); an English
translation from B. Blackwell of Oxford has been announced.

6 *Genesis* (New York, Doubleday & Company, Inc., 1964).

7 See Martin Buber, *Moses: The Revelation and the Covenant* (New York,
Harper and Row, Publishers, 1958), *The Prophetic Faith* (New York, Harper
and Row, Publishers, 1960); see also Arthur Cohen, *Martin Buber* (New York,
Hillary House Inc., 1957), and Maurice Friedman, *Martin Buber. The Life
of Dialogue* (Chicago, Chicago University Press, 1955). Heschel's most influential, exegetical work is *The Prophets* (New York: Harper & Row, Publishers, 1963).

8 Yehezkel Kaufmann, *The Religion of Israel,* translated and abridged by
Moshe Greenberg (Chicago, University of Chicago Press, 1960).

9 One of the best expressions of this fact is to be found in J. L. McKenzie,
S.J., "Problems of Hermeneutics in Roman Catholic Exegesis," *Journal of
Biblical Literature* 77, 1958, pp. 197–204, for example, "Indeed, if all scholars
were perfectly objective, entire unanimity should be theoretically possible in
exegesis itself; for the meaning of the Bible has been determined by its
authors, not by its interpreters" (p. 199), ". . . unanimity in textual criticism,
in historical investigation, in exegesis, and even in a theological synthesis of
the Bible is theoretically independent of confessional differences" (p. 204).

10 One may note here the serious and intelligent opposition to this approach
by the late M. D. Cassuto, whose study has been translated from Hebrew
into English, *The Documentary Hypothesis and the Composition of the
Pentateuch* (Jerusalem, Magnes, 1961). However, his point of view has not
rallied much support from Jewish or Christian scholars.

11 For the following examples, see Speiser, *op. cit.,* pp. xxxvii–xliii and also
the commentary at the appropriate places. A long list of studies on this topic
could be given, but a reference to John Bright, *A History of Isreal* (Philadelphia, The Westminster Press, 1959), pp. 69 ff., will suffice, since it contains
numerous references to the pertinent literature.

12 This has, however, been skillfully controverted by Moshe Greenberg,
"Another Look at Rachel's Theft of the Teraphim," *Journal of Biblical
Literature* 81, 1962, pp. 239–248. Another Jewish scholar has interpreted the
Machpela purchase (Genesis 23), out of the background of Hittite law, al-
though this does not seem to be accepted by Speiser; see M. Lehmann,

"Abraham's Purchase of Machpelah and the Hittite Law," *Bulletin of the American Schools of Oriental Research* 129, 1953, pp. 15–18.

[13] This is worked out in detail in his perceptive article, "The Biblical Idea of History in its Common Near Eastern Setting," *Israel Exploration Journal* 7, 1957, pp. 201–216.

[14] See the two articles by G. E. Wright in *The Biblical Archaeologist* 22, 1959, pp. 98–100; 101–108.

[15] Without pretending to be exhaustive, one may single out the commentary of Gordis, *Koheleth—the Man and His World* (New York, Bloch Publishing Co., Inc., 1955), and the commentary of Segal, *Sēper ben Sîrā' ha-šālēm* (Jerusalem, 1958).

[16] The studies of these men have appeared in several journals; readily available would be A. Malamat, "The Kingdom of David & Solomon in its Contact with Egypt and Aram Naharaim," *The Biblical Archaeologist* 21, 1958, pp. 96–102; B. Mazar, "The Campaign of Pharaoh Shishak to Palestine," *Vetus Testamentum* Supplement IV (Leinden, Brill, 1957), pp. 57–66; W. Hallo, "From Qarqar to Carchemish," *The Biblical Archaeologist* 23, 1960, pp. 34–61.

[17] See note 7; Neher has written *Amos. Contribution à l'étude de prophétisme* (Paris, Vrin, 1950).

[18] E. Bickermann, *Der Gott der Makkabäer* (Berlin, Schocken, 1955).

[19] *Ugaritic Manual* (Analecta Orientalia 35, Rome, 1955).

[20] Of the many scholarly contributions of these men may be mentioned Ginsberg's translations in J. Pritchard, *Ancient Near Eastern Texts* (Princeton, Princeton University Press, 1950); Cassuto, *The Goddess Anath* (Jerusalem, Bialik, 1963); Gaster, *Thespis* (New York, Doubleday & Company, Inc., 1961).

[21] A general survey can be derived from M. Dahood, S.J., "Ugaritic Studies and the Bible," *Gregorianum* 43, 1962, pp. 55–79.

[22] There are many studies concerning this edition in C. Rabin, (ed.), *Textus* I-III (Jerusalem, Magnes, 1960–63); see also B. J. Roberts. "The Hebrew Bible Since 1937," *Journal of Theological Studies* 15, 1964, pp. 253–264. The names of M. H. Goshen-Gottstein, E. Kutscher, and S. Talmon are also well-known.

[23] A summary of the state of research in these areas can be found in G. A. Buttrick, (ed.), *The Interpreter's Dictionary of the Bible* (Nashville, Abingdon Press, 1962) IV, pp. 591–592; 273–78. See also D. Barthélemy, *Les devanciers d'Aquila*, Supplements to Vetus Testamentum, 10 (Leiden, Brill, 1963).

[24] S. Yeivin, *A Decade of Archaeology in Israel 1948–1958* (Leiden, 1960). The Israeli are also producing important Biblical studies, such as *Scripta Hierosolymitana*, edited by C. Rabin, Volume 8 (Jerusalem, Magnes, 1961), and a Biblical encyclopedia, now in its fourth volume.

[25] In addition to the four, substantial volumes on the excavation, con-

venient summaries can be found in the reports by Yadin in *The Biblical Archaeologist* 19, 1956, pp. 1–12; 20, 1957, pp. 33–37; 21, 1958, pp. 30–47; 22, 1959, pp. 2–20; in the same journal are the preliminary reports on the activity near Engaddi, 24, 1961, pp. 34–50; 86–95.

26 This is quoted by Moscati in "In Memoriam Father Alfred Pohl, S.J.," *Orientalia* 31, 1962, pp. 1–6.

27 Perhaps the best introduction for a Christian to this body of literature is H. L. Strack, *Introduction to the Talmud and Midrash* (New York, Meridian Books, 1959), or A. Cohen, *Everyman's Talmud* (London, 1932).

28 Perhaps the best introduction for a Jewish reader would be J. Quasten, *Patrology I–III* (Westminster, Md., The Newman Press, 1950–60), and for medieval exegesis, the volumes by H. de Lubac, *Exégèse médiévale* (Paris, Aubier, to 1964).

29 See my article, "The Relationship Between the Testaments," *Catholic Biblical Quarterly* 26, 1964, pp. 349–359, for a discussion of these books, and also for an exposition of current Catholic thought (C. Larcher, P. Grelot).

30 This is the title of an article by J. van der Poeg, O.P., in *Ephemerides Theologicae Lovanienese* 39, 1962, pp. 417–434.

4

�֎ Freedom of Conscience

RABBI ROBERT GORDIS

Freedom of Conscience: A Jewish Perspective

RABBI ROBERT GORDIS, *Professor of Bible at the Jewish Theological Seminary, has also served as Rabbi of Temple Beth-El of Rockaway Park, N.Y., for over three decades. Past President of the Rabbinical Assembly of America and the Synagogue Council of America, he is also a Consultant for the Fund for the Republic's Center for the Study of Democratic Institutions, a member of the Advisory Council of the project, Religious Freedom and Public Affairs of the National Conference of Christians and Jews, and a member of the Board of Directors of the Institute of Church and State of Villanova University and of America's new John LaFarge Institute.*

Rabbi Gordis is author of nine books, including a commentary on the book of Ecclesiastes and, most recently, The Root and the Branch— Judaism and the Free Society *(University of Chicago, 1962).*

I

Religion has made many great contributions to civilization, but freedom of religion is not among them. The ideal of religious liberty is essentially a gift we owe to the secularists. To be sure, there were individual, great-souled believers who had recognized the ideal of freedom of conscience before the modern era. History also knows of a few religiously motivated communities which had established religious freedom before the eighteenth century.

Perhaps the earliest instance of such societies is the Tartar

kingdom of the Chazars in Central Russia, between the Volga
and the Don rivers, which lasted from the sixth to the tenth century. The rulers and upper classes of Chazaria had adopted
Judaism as their faith in the eighth century, and they accorded
full religious liberty to Christians and Moslems as well.[1] The
Dutch kingdom established by William the Silent in the sixteenth
century adopted the principle of toleration, though there were
limitations on the doctrine in practice. Roger Williams, in establishing the colony of Providence Plantations, or Rhode Island,
in the New World, made full freedom of conscience the basis of
the commonwealth. The Catholic Lord Baltimore extended the
right of worship to Protestants. But these were isolated and
exceptional cases.

By and large, the principle of freedom of conscience became
widely held and increasingly operative only with the Age of
Reason. This revolutionary epoch shook both Jews and Judaism
to their foundations through the impact of two related yet distinct forces, the Emancipation and the Enlightenment. In the
wake of the libertarian ideals of the new age, the Emancipation
broke down the walls of the ghetto throughout Western and
Central Europe and admitted the Jews of Europe to full-fledged
citizenship in the lands of their sojourning. In the process, the
structure of the Jewish community and its authority over its
members were all but completely dissolved, the only bonds remaining being purely voluntary on the part of individual Jews.[2]

Even before the Emancipation was complete, the Enlightenment had begun to undermine many of the presuppositions of
traditional religion. Christianity had met major challenges before and was therefore able to fend off these attacks with a fair
measure of success. Judaism, which for centuries had been
isolated from the mainstream of Western culture, found itself
almost helpless before the impact of the Enlightenment, particularly at the outset. The various schools of thought in contemporary Judaism represent different efforts at meeting the
challenge of the modern world.

Yet, however unsettling the ideas of the Enlightenment proved to traditional religion, they had the positive influence of creating a spirit of mutual tolerance among the great faiths. Lessing's famous drama, *Nathan der Weise,* highlighted the new spirit. The drama, which had a Mohammedan Sultan and a Jewish sage as its protagonists, contained the famous parable of "the Three Rings." These rings, which were identical in appearance, had been fashioned by a father for his three sons, because he could not bear to give his priceless, ancestral heirloom to any one of them. The overt message of the parable was clear. The three rings symbolize the three monotheistic religions of Judaism, Christianity, and Islam, all of which represent an expression of God's love for His creatures and of the reverence they owe Him in return. Scarcely beneath the surface was another implication —none of the three faiths can reasonably insist that it alone represents the true revelation of God and should therefore be granted a privileged position in a free society.

While there were individual saints and sages who had found it possible to unite tolerance of diversity with a fervent attachment to their own vision of God, for most men freedom of religion was the fruit of the rise of secularism. With the weakening of religious attachment among large segments of the population came the conviction that "one religion is as good as another." This pronouncement is, in many cases, a euphemistic restatement of the unspoken sentiment that one religion is as bad as another. But whatever its motivations, secularism is to be credited with making freedom of religion not only a working principle but also an ideal goal for modern men. In this sense, if we may adopt a phrase of Horace M. Kallen, secularism may be described as the will of God.[3]

II

While we may be truly grateful for this gift of the spirit, it is evident that the ideal of religious liberty on secular foundations suffers from several grave limitations. Its first obvious weakness is that, given its secular origin, the principle of religious liberty would work best where religious loyalty is weakest or nonexistent. If the soil from which freedom of conscience grows is religious indifference, if all religions are regarded as equal in value or in lack of value, it is obvious that the effectiveness of the principle will be gravely compromised for those who regard religion as of supreme significance in human life and particularly for those who look upon their own religious tradition as possessing a unique measure of truth. Yet the history of mankind has shown that the doctrine of freedom of conscience is most essential in instances where religious loyalty is fervent and the danger of hostility to those outside the group is correspondingly greater. Thus a secularly motivated doctrine of religious freedom can serve least where it is needed most.

Moreover, liberty of conscience in a secular framework can create, at best, only a truce and not a state of peace among the religious groups. This truce is dependent upon the presence of a secular policeman, be it the State or a society in which religious loyalties are weak. On the other hand, if the members of a given social order hold their religious commitments fervently, neither law-enforcement agencies, nor official opinion, nor even a constitution is likely to sustain religious liberty in practice for long. If Supreme Court Justice William O. Douglas is right in his now famous dictum. "We are a religious people whose institutions pre-suppose a Supreme Being," freedom of religion will be in grave jeopardy when Americans take their pretensions to religiosity seriously, if the doctrine remains rooted only in a secular outlook.

Finally, even if religious believers accept the practice of religious liberty, but do not relate it to their religious world view, it will have no binding power upon their consciences. They may extend freedom of religion to those who differ with them, but it will be, at worst, a grudging surrender to *force majeure,* and, at best, a counsel of prudence, limited in scope and temporary in application. Unless a nexus is established between the religious tradition to which the believer gives his allegiance and the doctrine of religious liberty, he will still be in danger, even if he takes no overt act in that direction, of violating the divine commandment, "You shall not hate your brother in your heart" (Leviticus 19, 17). Thus, the integrity of the ethical code by which he lives will be gravely compromised.

In summation, a secular doctrine of religious liberty suffers from all the liabilities to which secular morality is subject.[4] It can deal only with gross malfeassance and not with the subtler offenses of attitude and spirit—what the Talmud calls "matters entrusted to the heart." Nor can it supply the dynamic for an enduring allegiance to the ideal, even when it is within the power of a given group to impose its will on others.

For all these reasons, it is necessary for each religious tradition which takes seriously its obligation to live and function in a pluralistic society to go back to its own resources in order to discover what it can contribute to a religiously oriented theory of religious liberty. This article seeks to explore the bases in Judaism for a doctrine of freedom of conscience.

III

At the outset, we need to recall that the concept of religious liberty possesses three distinct yet related aspects. Like so many ethical values, its roots lie in the instinct of self-preservation. In other words, *the first and oldest aspect of religious liberty is the right which a group claims for itself to practice its faith without interference from others.* The extension of this right to other individuals and groups is a great leap forward both in time and insight, which requires centuries to achieve and has all too often remained unattained to the present day. Indeed, even in our age, instances are not lacking of groups in virtually every denomination who define the right to religious liberty as the right to deny religious liberty to those who differ with them.[5]

In this respect, religious liberty is no different from any basic right, such as freedom of speech or assembly, which is first fought for and achieved by a group in its own behalf. Only later—and often half-heartedly—is *freedom of conscience extended to other groups who differ in belief and practice.* Finally, the third and most difficult stage in religious liberty emerges—and it is far from universal—when *a religious group, dedicated to its belief and tradition, is willing to grant freedom of thought and action to dissidents within its own ranks.*

The Jewish people have played a significant role in the emergence of religious liberty in its first aspect. With regard to the two other aspects, we believe that Judaism and the Jewish historical experience have some significant insights to offer all men. Finally, no other large religious group has as great a stake in the present and future vitality of the doctrine as has the Jewish community.

It is true that virtually every religious group finds itself a minority in one or another corner of the globe and, unfortunately, can point to infractions of its right to worship and propagate its faith. Protestants are exercised over the situation in Spain and parts of Latin America. Catholics are troubled by the status of the Church in communist lands. Christians generally find themselves in difficult positions in parts of Africa and in Moslem autocracies in the Middle East.

Jews have had the sorry distinction of being a minority almost everywhere and always. In the thirty-six hundred years that separate Abraham from David ben Gurion, the Jewish people have been master of their own destiny as an independent nation in Palestine for a small fraction of their life. This status prevailed less than five hundred years during the days of the First Temple, for eighty years during the Second Temple, and during a decade and a half of the existence of the State of Israel in our day. These six hundred years constitute no more than one-sixth of the recorded history of the Jews. Moreover, even during these periods of independence and autonomy, there were large Jewish communities outside Palestine, more populous by far than the Jewish population in the homeland. The survival of these Diaspora communities was directly dependent on the degree of religious liberty they enjoyed. Hence, the curtailment of religious liberty may pose a major problem for all denominations; it is an issue of life and death for the Jewish group.

There is, therefore, historic justice in the fact that the people for whom religious liberty is so fundamental were the first to take up arms in defense of this right. The earliest recorded war for religious liberty is the struggle of the Maccabees against the Syrian Greek King Antiochus Epiphanes, which broke out in 168 B.C.E. The Maccabean struggle was inaugurated not for the sake of political liberty, territorial aggrandizement, national honor, or booty. It represented the armed resistance of a group in Palestinian Jewry who were resolved to protect their religious faith and way of life in a world where a determined effort was being made to impose the uniform pattern of Hellenistic culture and pagan religion on the entire Middle East.

Had the Maccabees not fought, or had they fought and lost, the Hebrew Scriptures would have been destroyed, Judaism would have perished, Christianity would not have been born, and the ideals of the Judeo-Christian heritage, basic to Western civilization, would have perished. There was, therefore, ample justification for the practice of the early Church, both in the East and West, which celebrated a festival on August 1, called "the Birthday of the Maccabees," testifying to the debt which Christianity, as well as Judaism, owes to these early, intrepid defenders of freedom of conscience.[6]

Thus the long struggle was launched for the first and oldest aspect of the concept of religious liberty. From that day to this, there have been communities which have conceived of religious liberty almost exclusively in terms of their right to observe their own beliefs and practices. For such a group, the degree of religious liberty in a given society is measured by the extent to which it, and it alone, is free to propagate its faith. Religious liberty is defined as "freedom for religion" and "religion" is equated with the convictions of the particular group.

This limited conception of religious liberty has a long and respectable history behind it. It is noteworthy that the only instances of forcible conversion to Judaism were carried out by descendants of the very same Maccabees who had fought for religious liberty. The Maccabean Prince, John Hyrcanus (135–104 B.C.), forced the Idumeans, hereditary enemies of the Jews, to accept Judaism. His son, Aristobulus, Judaized part of Galilee in the northern district of Palestine.[7] These steps were dictated less by religious zeal than by practical considerations, a universal characteristic of mass conversions to our own day.

For centuries, the doctrine that "error has no rights," unmitigated either by intellectual subtlety or by practical considerations, continued to hold sway. Heresy, that is to say, dissident views within dominant religious organisms, could be suppressed either individually or collectively, by peaceful persuasion or physical force. For heresy was viewed as illegitimate and sinful and hence worthy of the heaviest penalties. With the rise of Protestantism, which emphasized "private judgment" and the reading of the Bible as the unmediated Word of God, a multiplicity of sects emerged. What was equally significant, their legitimacy was, at least in theory, not open to question by the State. Religious liberty now became a practical necessity for the body politic as well as a burning issue for minority sects. Basically, it is to these minority groups that the world owes a debt for broadening the concept of religious liberty.

Yet, by and large, the ideal to which the various sects gave their loyalty was religious liberty for themselves. When the Puritans left England and later emigrated from Holland to Massachusetts, they were actuated by a passionate desire for freedom of conscience, but in this limited sense only. Protestant dissenters, Catholics, Jews, and nonbelievers could expect scant hospitality in the Bay Colony, and when any appeared within its borders, they were given short shrift. Various disabilities for non-Protestants survived in some New England states as late as the nineteenth century. Only slowly and painfully has religious liberty, which began as a practical policy designed to establish articles of peace between opposing sects, emerged as an ideal to which men have given their loyalty quite distinct from ulterior considerations.

Freedom of religion in an open society must necessarily presuppose two elements which were less obvious in the stratified societies of earlier days. *It must include religious equality,* for there can be no true religious liberty if the formal freedom of worship is coupled with legal, psychological, or financial liabilities. To be sure, the minority group cannot reasonably expect the same level of importance in society as the majority, but it has the right to demand that there be no restrictions or liabilities placed upon it by the State. In other words, full religious liberty means that the State will recognize the equality of all believers and nonbelievers, even though in society the relative strengths of various groups will necessarily impose disadvantages upon the poorer and less numerous sects.

To cite a hypothetical case, a Protestant worshipping in a modest dissenter's chapel or a Jew offering his devotions in a simple prayer room could not reasonably object to the presence of a magnificent Catholic church in the community. But they would have legitimate grounds for objecting to a legal ordinance forbidding the building of a large Methodist church or an elaborate Jewish synagogue in the area, as would a Catholic finding himself restrained from erecting a church, a monastery, or a parochial school.

There is one additional element essential to full religious freedom: *religious liberty is not being truly safeguarded if it is purchased at the cost of religious vitality.* Frequently the position of the Jewish community on questions of Church and State is misunderstood, because it is attributed solely to the desire to avoid religious disabilities for itself and other minority groups, including secularists. It is true that the position of minorities in regard to freedom of religion may parallel that of nonbelievers who also oppose utilizing the power and resources of the State to buttress the claims of religion. But there is another and at least equally deep motivation for the Jewish position: a sincere concern for the preservation of religious vitality. Here majority groups have as direct an interest as the minority.

A striking illustration is at hand in the acute controversy that arose when the U.S. Supreme Court outlawed as unconstitutional the prayer proposed by the Board of Regents of the State of New York for the public schools. Now that some of the smoke has cleared away, though by no means all the fire, it is clear that the Supreme Court was not "banishing God from American life." By the same token, it should be clear that Jews who, with few exceptions, wholeheartedly applauded the position of the Supreme Court (as did many other Americans) were not allying themselves with secularists and nonbelievers. They were defending what, according to their lights, represents the cause of the vitality of religion as well as its liberty.

To be sure, the Regents' prayer was nonsectarian, but as anyone genuinely committed to religion knows, there are some religious practices that are more nonsectarian than others! A good case in point was afforded by the "nondenominational" Decalogue which, thirty-two hundred years after Moses on Sinai, was revealed to the School Board of New Hyde Park, Long Island. From the most praiseworthy of motives, these guardians of the local public school system created a new text for the Ten Commandments which was neither Jewish, nor Catholic, nor Protestant, but one undoubtedly superior to them all. In their version the First Commandment read, "I am the Lord thy God who brought thee forth out of the house of bondage." With one fell swoop, the entire, historic experience of Israel, which lies at the basis of the Judeo-Christian tradition, was eliminated.

The Hyde Park version of the Decalogue is also an impressive demonstration of the ecumenical spirit, an achievement which has not been sufficiently appreciated. As is well-known, there are differences in the enumeration and division of the Ten Commandments by Jews, by Roman Catholics, by Lutherans, and by other Protestants.[8] These divergences were resolved by the Hyde Park School Board by the happy expedient of agreeing with everyone. The only remaining problem, minor as it is, is that the new version of the Decalogue now contains eleven Commandments. It should therefore properly be called the "Hendecalogue," a name to conjure with!

One may seriously doubt that this new version of the Ten Commandments contributed to the vital, religious faith of the children. Similarly, in opposing such practices as nonsectarian prayer and nonsectarian grace at meals, and such intersectarian practices as joint Christmas-Hanukkah and Easter-Passover celebrations in the public schools, Jews are manifesting a deep concern not merely for religious liberty, but for religious vitality.

IV

This concern for the safeguarding of religious equality and religious vitality lies at the base of the Jewish approach to the problem of religion in public education. Elsewhere, we have sought to spell out the implications for such crucial and controversial issues as "the teaching of religion" or "the teaching about religion" in the public school system—elementary, secondary, and collegiate—and the even more emotionally charged issue of governmental aid to religious schools from public funds, on a non-preferential basis.[9] Suffice it to say here that the Jewish community is deeply conscious of the massive, practical problems that confront their Catholic fellow citizens in the maintenance of their great system of parochial education. Moreover, the Jewish community is profoundly concerned by the Jewish religious and cultural illiteracy so widespread among contemporary Jews, even among those who possess a high general culture—indeed especially among them. For such a religious tradition as Judaism, which is centered in a vast literature written in an ancient tongue and oriented to the laity, ignorance is not merely dangerous, but catastrophic.

To meet this threat, the Jewish community in all its groupings has created a far-flung and complex network of schools ranging from the one-day-a-week Sunday School, through the supplementary afternoon Hebrew and Religious School which meets three, four, or five times weekly, to the all-inclusive Day School, in which general and Hebraic studies are taught. Vast energies are mobilized for the enrollment of children, the recruitment of teachers, the elevation of educational standards, the building of adequate school structures, the creation of textbooks, the establishment of adequate supervision, and countless other needs in the field of education. The budget for Jewish religious education runs into tens of millions of dollars in the United States. This represents a tremendous drain on the resources of the Jewish community, even at a time when far too many Jewish children are not reached by Jewish education at all.

Moreover, Jewish education suffers from a grave shortage of competent personnel, both in teaching and in administration. To no slight degree the difficulty involved in recruiting workers for this field stems from the fact that the structure of Jewish religious education is entirely voluntary, so that most schools are completely autonomous and the destiny of teachers is subject to all the fluctuations of popular fancy. Hence Jewish educators feel a lack of status and security in their calling, and this impels many to seek their calling elsewhere.

In spite of all these problems, the Jewish community seeks to shoulder the burden of religious education for its children, unaided by public funds, and, with few exceptions, feels unable to support the demand made in many Catholic circles for governmental aid to religious schools. This attitude does not stem from indifference to religious education or from a lack of sympathy for their Catholic brothers.

Most American Jews, whatever their religious, social, or political orientation, tend to support wholeheartedly the broad interpretation of the First Amendment which forbids even non-preferential aid to religion. They regard the principle of separation of Church and State not as right because it is constitutional, but as constitutional because it is right. As members of a community which has been the object of religious discrimination, intolerance, and persecution for centuries, American Jews are profoundly convinced that the separation of Church and State can best serve the cause both of religious equality and religious vitality. Being members of a minority group, American citizens of the Jewish faith cannot enforce their views at the ballot box. They can hope only to persuade the members of the powerful majority of the validity of their position, because they believe that the majority is moved by a genuine sense of fair play toward the minority and by a deep desire to preserve the inherent values of religion and liberty for all.

V

We have dealt thus far with the first aspect of the ideal of religious liberty: the right which every religious group claims for itself to practice its faith freely, without restriction or interference from others. With regard to the two other aspects of the ideal of religious liberty—more theoretic in character—we believe the specific Jewish historic experience has significance for other religious groups and for the preservation of a free society itself.

As we have noted, there is, theoretically at least, no problem with regard to the doctrine of freedom of conscience for those who maintain that all religions are equally good—or bad. Years ago, when communism was making substantial inroads among American college youth, the writer participated in a symposium on "Communism and Religion." Among the panelists were a Methodist bishop, a Presbyterian minister, two rabbis, and Earl Browder, then a leading spokesman for communism in the United States. As the various speakers for religion sought to develop their positions vis-à-vis communism, Mr. Browder turned to us and declared, to the manifest delight of the youthful audience, "The communists are the only ones who can establish peace and equality among all the religions—because we do not believe in any of them!" The history of twentieth-century totalitarianism has demonstrated that religious intolerance is far from impossible under communism and fascism. Religious bigots can learn many a lesson in practicing their craft from the anti-religious bigots of our age. The crude and brutal persecution of religion by atheistic regimes today makes the classic instances of religious intolerance of the past seem almost idyllic by comparison.

Nonetheless, it is true that the problem of evolving a theory of religious tolerance and practicing it is genuine and complex, particularly for those believers who are convinced that they are the repositories of religious truth and that their fellow men who differ from them are not so blessed. In this connection the attitude of Jewish tradition is particularly interesting. It arose within a religion which believes profoundly that it is the authentic revelation of God and that all other faiths possess, by that token, a greater or less admixture of error. Since such a standpoint is widespread among communicants of most creeds, it should be useful to examine the theory and practice of *religious liberty within Judaism*—the approach of the Jewish tradition toward dissidents within its own community. Even more significant for the world at large is the theory and practice in

Judaism of *religious liberty toward non-Jews*—the attitude of the Jewish tradition toward the rights of non-Jews seeking to maintain their own creeds, and the legitimacy of such faiths from the purview of Judaism.

In order to comprehend the Jewish attitude toward religious differences within the community, it must be kept in mind that Judaism was always marked by a vast variety of religious experience, which is given articulate expression in the pages of the Hebrew Scriptures. The Hebrew Bible contains within its broad and hospitable limits the products of the varied and often contradictory activities of priest and lawgiver, prophet and sage, psalmist and poet. It reflects the temperaments of the mystic and the rationalist, the simple believer and the profound seeker after ultimate truth. The reason inheres in the fact that the Hebrew Bible is not a collection of like-minded tracts, but is, in the words of a great modern exegete, "a national literature upon a religious foundation."[10]

This characteristic of the Bible set its stamp upon all succeeding epochs in the history of Judaism. It is not accidental that the most creative era in its history after the Biblical era, the period of the Second Temple, was the most "sect-ridden." Even our fragmentary sources disclose the existence of the Pharisees, the Sadducees, the Essenes, and the Zealots, to use Josephus' classic tabulation of the "Four Philosophies." We know from the Talmud, which is a massive monument to controversy, that the Pharisees themselves, the dominant group in number and influence, were divided into various groups which held strongly to opposing positions, with hundreds of individual scholars differing from the majority on scores of issues. Although, unfortunately, very little is known about the Sadducees, the same variety of outlook may be assumed among them. With regard to the Essenes, the discovery of the Dead Sea Scrolls has indicated that the term, Essenes, is best used of an entire conspectus of sects who differed among themselves passionately. The Samaritans were also a significant group of dissidents, highly articulate in their divergence from a Jerusalem-centered Judaism. It was in this atmosphere that the early Jewish sect of Christians first appeared, adding to the charged atmosphere of vitality and variety in Palestinian Judaism. There were also countless additional patterns of religious nonconformity in the various Diaspora communities.

To be sure, all these groups of Judaism shared many fundamentals in their outlook, but there were important divergences, both within each sect and among them.[11] The Talmud records that among the Pharisees, the differences between the schools of Hillel and Shammai were deep-seated and broke into physical violence at one point.[12] Nonetheless, the Talmud declares, the Shammaites and the Hillelites did not hesitate to intermarry and "He who observes according to the decision of Beth Hillel, like him who follows the school of Shammai, is regarded as fulfilling the Law," because "both these and the others are the words of the Living God."[13] No such encomiums were pronounced on the Sadducees, who contradicted the fundamentals of normative Judaism. Those holding Saducean views were stigmatized as "having no share in the world to come."[14] In this world, however, it is noteworthy that neither the Sadducees nor any others of these sects were ever officially excommunicated.

In the Middle Ages a variety of factors combined to contract this latitude of religious outlook in the Jewish community. First of all, the constantly worsening conditions of exile and alien status required, it was felt, a greater degree of group-homogeneity. Secondly, most of the earlier dissident viewpoints disappeared. Thus, the standpoint of the super-nationalist Zealots was now totally meaningless, while that of the Sadducees, who centered their religious life in the Temple at Jerusalem, was completely irrelevant to the life of an exiled people. Thirdly, the widespread emphasis on religious conformity imposed by the medieval world on its aberrant sects also proved a model and example. Father Joseph Lecler points out in his massive, two-volume work, *Tolera-*

tion and the Reformation, that St. Thomas Aquinas was "relatively tolerant toward pagans and completely intolerant toward heretics." As Father John B. Sheerin notes, St. Thomas explicitly stated that "to accept the faith is a matter of free will, but to hold it, once it has been accepted, is a matter of necessity."

No such precise and logical theory was ever elaborated in Judaism. The Jewish community lacked the power to compel uniformity of thought, even in the relatively rare instances when the leadership was tempted to embark upon such an enterprise. Nonetheless, some efforts *were* made to restrict religious liberty in the Middle Ages. The history of these undertakings is significant for the intrinsic nature of the Jewish tradition.

Somewhat paradoxically, the attempt to impose a measure of uniformity on religious belief was due to the emergence of medieval Jewish philosophy, which was nurtured in Aristotelianism, and to lesser degree in Platonism. Maimonides, the greatest Jewish thinker of the Middle Ages, confidently proposed a set of *Thirteen Principles,* which he hoped would serve as a creed for Judaism. Though his statement attained wide popularity, and was printed in the traditional prayerbook as an appendix, lesser men did not hesitate to quarrel with both the content and the number of articles of belief in his *Creed,* and it never became an official confession of faith.

An even more striking illustration of the enduring vitality of the right to religious diversity in Judaism may be cited. Uncompromisingly rationalistic as he was, Maimonides declared that to ascribe any physical form to God was tantamount to heresy and deprived one of a share in the world to come. Nowhere is the genius of Judaism better revealed than here. On the same printed page of the Maimonides' *Code* where this statement is encountered, it is challenged by the remark of his critic and commentator, Rabbi Abraham ben David of Posquières who writes: "Better and greater men [than Maimonides] have ascribed a physical form to God, basing themselves on their understanding of Scriptural passages and even more so on some legends and utterances, which give wrong ideas."[15] The critic's standpoint is clear. Rabbi Abraham ben David agrees with Maimonides in denying a physical form to God, but he affirms the right of the individual to maintain backward ideas in Judaism without being read out of the fold on that account. The right to be wrong is the essence of liberty.

Nonetheless, it is clear that the spirit of medieval Judaism was far less hospitable to religious diversity than had been Rabbinic Judaism in the centuries immediately before and after the destruction of the Temple. Thus, while none of the earlier sects had ever been excommunicated, the medieval Karaites, who rejected the authority of the Talmud in favor of the letter of Scripture, were excommunicated by various individual scholars. At the same time, other scholars refused to invoke the ban against them and ultimately a more lenient attitude prevailed.[16]

Excommunication was invoked again against religious diversity in the eighteenth century, this time against Hasidism, a folk movement, pietistic in character, which arose in Eastern Europe. Ultimately, the sect abated its hostility toward Rabbinical Judaism. Today the Hasidim and their rabbinical "opponents," together with a mediating group, are all within the household of Orthodox Judaism.

In the nineteenth century, when the Reform movement first began to appear in Central Europe, some Orthodox rabbis in Central and Eastern Europe sought to stem the tide by invoking the ban against the innovators. It had proved largely ineffective in the field of ideas even in the Middle Ages; now it was completely useless. It served only to drive deeper the wedge between the traditionalists and the nontraditionalists, and was tacitly abandoned.

In summary, religious liberty within the Jewish community exists *de facto*. It is recognized *de jure* by all groups in Reform and conservative Judaism and by substantial elements in Orthodoxy as well.

It need hardly be added that divergences among the groups—and within them—are often sharp, and the antagonisms among some of the advocates of different positions are, all too frequently, even sharper. The upsurge in some quarters of "religiosity," which followed in the wake of the irruption of Nazi savagery and the mass bestiality of World War II, had a powerful impact upon Jews as well as upon Christians.[17] It has strengthened the tendency to withdrawal and insulation against the world among many survivors of the Hitler holocaust and exacerbated their hostility to all those outside their particular group. This spirit is very much in evidence today, but it is a mood of the day, if not of the moment, and it will pass. If history is any guide, these attitudes of isolation and hostility will be softened with time and the impact of gentler experiences. The harrowing events of the last three decades cannot abrogate the tradition of three millennia.

An observation is here in order with regard to the status of religion and the State in Israel. The Israeli Cabinet includes a Minister of Religions (in the plural), who is charged with the supervision and the maintenance of the "holy places" of all the three great religions and with the support of their institutional and educational requirements. It is paradoxical, but true, that at present there is full freedom of religion in Israel for everyone —except for Jews! Catholic and Protestant Christianity, Islam and Bahai, all enjoy the fullest freedom of expression, including the opportunity for missionary activity among Jews, a situation which has aroused not a little antagonism. In addition to the Minister of Religions, Israel has three Chief Rabbis who are of unimpeachable Orthodoxy, except for those Orthodox groups who deny their authority. In accordance with the legacy of Turkish and British law, the Chief Rabbi (like his Christian and Islamic counterparts), has authority in the field of personal status, notably marriage, divorce, and inheritance, and, to a lesser degree, in the maintenance of religious observance in the army and public institutions, and in the supervision of religious education.

At present, there exists a type of religion-and-state union in the State of Israel. To be sure, the effort is made to invest the contemporary situation with the halo of tradition. The historical truth is, however, that the very existence of the office of a Chief Rabbi in Israel represents not a return to Jewish tradition, but an innovation, the value of which is highly debatable. The death of the late Chief Rabbi Isaac Herzog precipitated a controversy as to his successor, and it lasted for several years.

With the Chief Rabbinate as its symbol, Orthodoxy is the only officially recognized religious group in Israel today. Yet here, too, the innate tradition of dissent finds uninhibited expression. Thus, when the new and magnificent headquarters of the Chief Rabbinate was erected in Jerusalem, many of the leading Orthodox scholars announced that it was religiously prohibited to cross the threshold of the building! Side by side with these tensions within Israel Orthodoxy are various other groups, Reform, Conservative, and Reconstructionist, representing a wide spectrum of modernism. In spite of harassment and opposition, they have already established a foothold in the country and ultimately will demand and receive full recognition.

No long-term conclusions may therefore be drawn from the present union of religion and State in Israel. It is partial and subject to increasing strain and stress. Whether the ultimate pattern of religion-state relationships will approximate the American structure is problematic, though the American experience is frequently invoked as an ideal. The disestablishment of religion in any sectarian form is, however, inevitable.

The conclusion is unassailable that the nature of Judaism, buttressed by its historic experience, makes the freedom of religious dissent a recognized reality for virtually all members of the

community *de facto,* even by those who would not recognize it
de jure.

VI

The attitude of Judaism toward religious liberty for those
professing other creeds derives, in large measure, from another
unique characteristic of the Jewish tradition, one which is frequently misunderstood not only by those outside the Jewish
community, but by many who are within it. This trait, deeply
rooted in normative Judaism, is the balance between particular-
ism and universalism.[18] The Jewish conception of freedom of
religion is the resultant of two forces: the retention of the
specific, national, Jewish content in the tradition on the one
hand, and, on the other, an equally genuine concern for the
establishment among all men of the faith in one God and obedience to His religious and ethical imperatives.

It is frequently argued that with the appearance of Judaism
intolerance became a coefficient of religion. It is undoubtedly
true that in a polytheistic world view, tolerance of other gods is
implicit, since there is always room for one more figure in the
pantheon, and the history of religious syncretism bears out this
truth. On the other hand, the emergence of belief in one God
necessarily demands the denial of the reality of all other deities.
The "jealous God" of the Old Testament who forbids "any other
god before Me" therefore frequently became the source of religious intolerance. So runs the theory.[19]

It sometimes happens, however, that a beautiful pattern of
invincible logic is contradicted by the refractory behavior of life
itself. An apposite illustration may be cited. The French Semitic
scholar, Ernest Renan, declared that the monotony of the desert
produced a propensity for monotheism among the ancient Hebrews, whereas the variety in the physical landscape of Greece,
for example, with its mountains and hills, its valleys, rivers and

streams, necessarily suggested a multitude of divinities indwelling in them. This plausible theory enjoyed considerable vogue until it was learned that the pre-Islamic nomadic Arabs, who inhabit the vast stretches of the Arabian Desert, possessed a very luxuriant polytheism, and that all the Semitic peoples, whose original habitat was the same desert, also had very elaborate pantheons. Thus the list of gods in the library of King Ashurbanipal contains more than 2,500 gods, and modern scholars have added substantially to the number.

Now it is true that Judaism was strongly exclusivist in its attitude toward paganism. It insisted upon the uncompromising unity of God and refused to admit even a semblance of reality to other gods. Nonetheless, Biblical Judaism reckoned with the existence of paganism from two points of view. Though logicians might have recoiled in horror from the prospect, the fact is that Hebrew monotheism, the authentic and conscious faith in the existence of one God, did accord a kind of legitimacy to polytheism—for non-Jews. In part, this may have derived from a recognition of the actual existence of flourishing heathen cults. In far larger degree, we believe, it was a consequence of the particularist emphasis in Judaism. Dedicated to preserving the specific group character of the Hebrew faith, the Jewish tradition was led to grant a similar charter of justification to the specific ethos of other nations, which always included their religion.

Whatever the explanation, the fact is clear. No book in the Bible, not even Isaiah or Job, is more explicitly monotheistic than Deuteronomy: "You shall know this day, and consider it in your heart, that the Lord is God in heaven above, and upon the earth beneath; there is no one else" (4:39). Yet the same book, which warns Israel against polytheism, speaks of "the sun, the moon and the stars . . . which the Lord your God has assigned to all the nations under the sky" (4, 19, compare 29, 25). Thus the paradox emerges that the particularist element in Judaism proved the embryo of a theory of religious tolerance.

The second factor that helped to grant a measure of value to non-Jewish religion is one more congenial to sophisticated religious thinkers. A broadminded exponent of monotheism would be capable of recognizing, even in the pagan cults against which Judaism fought, an imperfect, unconscious aspiration toward the one living God. Perhaps the most striking expression of this insight is to be found in the post-Exilic Prophet Malachi: "For from the rising of the sun to its setting, My name is great among the nations; and everywhere incense is burnt and pure oblations are offered to My name, for My name is great among the nations, says the Lord of hosts" (1:11).

This is not the only instance of universalism in our biblical sources. The human sympathy of the author of the Book of Jonah, who exhibits the pagan sailors in a far more favorable light than he does the fugitive Hebrew prophet, the warm compassion of the Book of Ruth, and the breadth of view of the Book of *Job*, which pictures the Patriarch not as a Hebrew observer of the Torah, but as a non-Jew whose noble creed and practice is described in his great *Confession of Innocence* (chap. 31), all testify to the fact that it was possible to maintain the unity and universality of God, while reckoning with the values inherent in the imperfect approximations to be found in the pagan cults.

Thus the two apparently contradictory elements of the Biblical world view—the emphasis upon a particularist ethos and the faith in a universal God—served as the seedbed for the flowering of a highly significant theory of religious tolerance in post-Biblical Judaism. To this concept, known as the Noachide Laws, we shall return.

Nonetheless, it was self-evident that a universal God who was Father of all men deserved the allegiance and loyalty of all His children. A steady and unremitting effort was therefore made to counteract the blandishments of paganism and to win all men for Jewish monotheism through the use of persuasion. The Biblical *Deutero-Isaiah*, the Apocryphal *Sybilline Oracles*, the life-long activity of Philo of Alexandria—indeed the entire apologetic literature of Hellenistic Judaism were designed to win the allegiance of men for the one living God of Israel.

Holding fast to their conviction that Judaism alone represents the true faith in the one God, the Prophets had looked forward to its ultimate acceptance by all men: "For then will I turn to the people a pure language, that they may all call on the name of the Lord, to serve him with one accord" (Zephaniah 3:9). "And the Lord will be king over all the earth; on that day shall the Lord be one, and His name be one" (Zechariah 14:9).

This faith for the future did not cause Judaism to overlook the realities of the present. It did not deny the values to be found in the religious professions and even more in the ethical practices of many of their pagan fellow men. From these facts there emerged one of the most distinctive concepts of monotheistic religion, a unique contribution of Judaism to the theory of religious liberty, the doctrine of the Noachide Laws, which actually antedates the Talmud. The Apocryphal *Book of Jubilees,* written before the beginning of the Christian Era, could not conceive of untold generations of men before Moses living without a divine Revelation. It therefore attributes to Noah, who was not a Hebrew, a code of conduct binding upon all men:

In the twenty-eighth jubilee, Noah began to enjoin upon his son's sons the ordinances and commandments and all the judgments that he knew and he exhorted his sons to observe righteousness and to cover the shame of their flesh and to bless their Creator and honor father and mother and love their neighbor and guard their souls from fornication and uncleanness and all iniquity. (7, 22)

This injunction is elaborated in the rabbinic tradition under the rubric of the Laws of the Sons of Noah.[20] According to this rabbinic view, all human beings, by virtue of their humanity, are commanded to observe at least seven fundamental religious and moral principles. These commandments include the prohibition of idolatry, sexual immorality, murder and theft; the avoidance of blasphemy and of cruelty to animals by eating the limb of a living creature; and the establishment of a government based on law and order. When these principles, upon which all civilized society depends, are observed, Judaism regards the non-Jew as worthy of salvation, no less than the Jew who observed the entire rubric of Jewish law. Hence, there is no imperative need for the non-Jew to accept the Jewish faith in order to be "saved."

These Laws of the Sons of Noah, it may be noted, seem to be referred to in the New Testament as well: "But that we write unto them, that they abstain from pollutions of idols and from fornication, and from things strangled, and from blood . . . That ye abstain from meats offered to idols, and from blood and from things strangled and from fornication: from which if ye keep yourselves, ye shall do well. Fare ye well" (Acts 15, 20, 29).

This doctrine of the Noachide Laws is extremely interesting from several points of view. It represents in essence a theory of universal religion which is binding upon all men. Characteristically Jewish is its emphasis upon good actions rather than upon right belief as the mark of the good life. Ethical living rather than creedal adherence is the decisive criterion for salvation. Its spirit is epitomized in the great rabbinic utterance: "I call Heaven and earth to witness, that whether one be Gentile or Jew, man or woman, slave or free man, the divine spirit rests on each in accordance with his deeds."[21] In its all-encompassing sweep, this passage recalls the famous words of Paul: "There is neither Jew nor Greek, neither bond nor free, there is neither male nor female, for ye are all one in Christ Jesus."[22] Significantly, the equal worth of all men in the rabbinic formulation does not derive from common doctrinal belief, nor does it depend upon it; it requires only loyalty to a code of ethical conduct.

Many contemporary religious thinkers are now seeking a theory which will combine complete loyalty to a specific tradition while accepting wholeheartedly the postulates of a democratic society which is committed to pluralism as a reality and to religious liberty as a good. The issue is one which profoundly agitates Americans in our day because of its practical importance in government and politics.

There is more than academic interest, therefore, in this rabbinic adumbration of a theory of religious tolerance resting upon a concept of "natural law." This doctrine of the Noachide Laws, be it noted, was not the product of religious indifference. It arose among devotees of a traditional religion who not only loved their faith, but believed that it alone was the product of authentic revelation. Yet they found room for faiths other than their own, as of right and not merely on sufferance.

VII

The principle of the Noachide Laws had originated in a pagan world. It obviously proved even more valuable when two mono-theistic religions, Christianity and Islam, replaced paganism. Both "daughter faiths" sought energetically to displace the mother and deny her authenticity. The mother faith sought to repulse these onslaughts as effectively as possible by calling attention to what she regarded as their errors. But she did not, on that account, ignore the elements of truth which her more aggressive offspring possessed.

The attitude of Judaism in the Middle Ages toward these two religions necessarily differed with the personality of each partic-ular authority, his environment and his own personal experience. The proximity of the Christian and the Jewish communities in Europe, and the consequent economic and social relationships upon which Jewish survival depended, compelled the medieval rabbinic authorities to reckon with reality. In the Talmud con-siderable limitations had been placed upon Jewish contacts with pagans, particularly at heathen festivals and with regard to objects of worship. In the Middle Ages the rabbis could not maintain the position that Christians were pagans and that all the Talmudic restrictions upon intercourse with idolaters applied to them. By and large, these modifications of Talmudic law were originally *ad hoc* improvisations and limited to specific practices upon which the livelihood of Jews depended.[23] But what began as a practical necessity led to the rise of an appropriate theory.

Among the most painful features of medieval Jewish-Christian relations were the public religious disputations forced upon Jews, often at the instigation of Jewish converts to Christianity.[24] Nonetheless, these debates led to one positive result. They gave the Jews the impetus to re-evaluate the general principles governing their attitude toward non-Jews and to recognize that there were significant differences between the pagans of antiquity, to whom the Talmud refers as "idolaters," and the Christians who were their contemporaries in the Middle Ages.[25]

Thus the tragic disputation, convened in Paris in 1240, involving the convert Nicholas Donin and four Jewish representatives, led to the public burning of twenty-four cartloads of Hebrew books. The chief Jewish spokesman was Jehiel ben Joseph of Paris, and he was assisted by Moses of Coucy. It is a tribute to the greatness of Moses' spirit that, in spite of this grim exhibition of fanaticism, he developed a new insight into the character of the dominant faith, an insight undoubtedly stimulated by his participation in the debate. Time and again he called upon his brethren to maintain scrupulous ethical standards in dealings with Christians, basing himself on broad religious and moral considerations.[26] Not expediency, but regard for the honor of Israel and the avoidance of *Hillul Hashem,* "the desecration of the Holy Name," became the fundamental motivations.[27]

The practical need of a *modus vivendi* between Jews and Christians could not be denied, since they lived in closest proximity with one another throughout Europe. Simultaneously, the outlines of a theory of religious tolerance were being laid by Jewish thinkers living in Mohammedan as well as in Christian countries. The teaching of the second-century Talmud Sage, Rabbi Joshua, "There are righteous among the Gentiles who have a share in the world to come,"[28] was slightly but significantly broadened by Maimonides into the generalization, "The righteous among the Gentiles have a share in the world to come."[29] Thus the principle that salvation was open even to those outside the Jewish fold remained normative and served as the basic principle underlying the Noachide Laws. The medieval poet and philosopher, Judah Halevi, wrote, "These peoples [i.e., Christianity and Islam] represent a preparation and preface to the Messiah for whom we wait, who is the fruit of the tree which they will ultimately recognize as the roots which they now despise."[30]

Rabbi Menahem Meiri, who lived in thirteenth-century France when several expulsions of Jews from that country took place, wrote, "Those among the heathen of the ancient days who observe the seven Noachide precepts, i.e., refrain from idol worship, desecration of God's name, robbery, incest, cruelty to animals, and have courts of justice, enjoy the same rights as Jews; how much the more so in our days, when the nations are distinguished by their religion and respect for law! We must, however, treat equally even those who have no systems of law, in order to sanctify the Name of God."[31] He distinctly declares that "in our days idolatry has ceased in most places," and describes both Muslims and Christians as "nations disciplined by the ways of their religions."[32]

Moreover, even the trinitarian concept of Christianity, which Judaism emphatically repudiated as impugning the unity of God, was not generally regarded as sufficient to deny to Christianity the character of a monotheistic faith. The twelfth-century Talmudic commentator, Rabbi Isaac the Tosafist, set forth a legal basis for the view that belief in the Trinity was legitimate for Christians in his statement: "The children of Noah are not prohibited from *shittuf*, i.e., associating the belief in God with that in other beings".[33] This utterance achieved such wide scope and authority that it was frequently attributed by later scholars to the Talmud itself.

Maimonides, with his penchant for systematic canons of thought, was strongly critical both of Christianity and of Islam. Living all his life in Islamic countries, with few direct contacts with Christians, Maimonides tended to react negatively to the trinitarianism of Christianity and to its Messianic claims for Jesus as the Savior. On the other hand, the uncompromising emphasis upon the unity of God in Mohammedanism, with which he was in constant contact, gave him a greater degree of tolerance for Islam, although he castigated the sensuality of the Prophet Mohammed. Even the adoration of the Ka'abah, the black stone of Mecca, was regarded by Maimonides as a vestige of polytheism which had been reinterpreted in Islam—a remarkable anticipation of modern research.

In a passage in his great code, *Mishneh Torah* (which appears mutilated in the printed texts because of the censor) Maimonides rejects the claim that Jesus was the Messiah, on the ground that Jesus failed to fulfill the Messianic function as envisioned in Scripture and tradition. Maimonides then proceeds:

The thought of the Creator of the world is beyond the power of man to grasp, for their ways are not His ways and their thoughts are not His thoughts. All the words of Jesus the Nazarene and of Mohammed, who arose after him, came into being only in order to make straight the road for the King Messiah, who would perfect the world to serve God together, as it is said, "Then I shall turn all the peoples into a clear speech, that they may all call upon the Lord and serve Him shoulder to shoulder."

How is that to be? The world has already been filled with the words of the Messiah, and the words of the Torah and the commandments. And these words have spread to the furthermost islands among many people uncircumcised of heart or of flesh, who now discuss the Commandments of the Torah. Some declare that these commandments were true, but are now no longer obligatory and have fallen into decline, while others declare that there are secret meanings within them, not according to their obvious intent, and that the Messiah had come and disclosed their secret connotations.

But when the true King Messiah will arise, he will succeed and be raised to glory and then they will all return and recognize they had inherited falsehood, and that their Prophets and ancestors had misled them.[34]

Maimonides elsewhere declares that Christians are idolaters because of their trinitarian beliefs.[35] In this regard, he goes further than the warrant of his rabbinic sources. Nor was his attitude shared by most of his contemporaries. Thus, his great predecessor, Saadia (882-942), the first great figure in medieval Jewish philosophy and who also lived under Islam, declared that the Christians' belief in the Trinity is not an expression of idolatry, but the personification of their faith in life, power and knowledge.[36] In his negative view, Maimonides not only ignored the Talmudic passage quoted above, but was in sharpest variance with most Jewish scholars, such as Rashi and Meiri, who lived in Christian countries, knew Christians at first hand, and recognized their deeply-rooted belief in the One God.

Later such rabbinic authorities as Moses Rivkes, Hayyim Yair Bacharach (1638-1702), and Rabbi Jacob Emden (1697-1776) explicitly recognized a common tradition linking Judaism and Christianity when they pointed out that Christians believed in God, the Exodus, Revelation, the truth of the Bible, and *creatio ex nihilo*.[37]

In the eighteenth century, Moses Mendelssohn wrote a famous reply to the Protestant minister, Johann Casper Lavater. Therein he expounded the traditional Jewish doctrine, speaking in the accents of eighteenth-century Enlightenment:

Moses has commanded us the Law; it is an inheritance of the congregation of Jacob. All other nations we believe to be enjoined to keep the law of nature. Those conducting their lives in accordance with this religion of nature and of reason are called "virtuous men from among other nations," and these are entitled to eternal bliss (*sind Kinder der ewigen Seligkeit*).

There was an obvious apologetic intent and a consequent exaggeration in his next statement:

The religion of my fathers, therefore, does not desire to be spread. We are not to send missions to Greenland or to the Indies in order to preach our faith to these distant nations. The latter nation, in particular, observing as it is the law of nature better than we do here, according to reports received, is in the view of our religious doctrines an enviable nation.

It is true that an active missionary campaign has not been carried on in Judaism ever since the pre-Christian centuries when Hellenistic Judaism won untold pagans for "reverence for God" and thus helped lay the foundation for the rapid spread of Christianity. In the Middle Ages the external facts of history united with the inner nature of Judaism to preclude large-scale efforts to win non-Jews to Judaism.

Today, some voices are being raised in the Jewish community in favor of a more active effort to bring the message of Judaism to religiously uncommitted non-Jews, though without employing conventional missionary techniques.[38] A warm discussion on the question is now going on among Jewish religious leaders and laity. But both those who favor and those who oppose such an active effort are at one in recognizing the legitimacy of non-Jewish faiths, the availability of salvation to all who observe the basic spiritual and ethical principles embodied in the Noachide Laws, and the right of all men to the fullest liberty of religious practice and belief.

VIII

The attitude of Judaism toward religious liberty may now be summarized as follows:

1. Judaism insists on total freedom of religious belief and practice for itself, which will include full equality before the law and no attenuation of vital religious commitment freely given.

2. Judaism accepts the existence of differences within the Jewish community and accords to dissidents the right to their own viewpoint and practice, at least *de facto*.

3. Judaism recognizes the existence of other religions among men and their inherent right to be observed *de jure*.

There inheres a measure of naivete, as there is of the overly simplified, in Albert Einstein's utterance, "I thank God that I belong to a people which has been too weak to do much harm in the world." But more than mere incapacity inheres in the Jewish attitude toward religious liberty. The balance between the universal aspirations of Judaism and its strong attachment to the preservation of its group-character have impelled it to create a theory that makes room in God's plan—and in the world—for men of other convictions and practices.

Moreover, the deeply ingrained individualism of the Jewish character, its penchant for questioning, and its insistence upon rational conviction have made dissent a universal feature of the Jewish spiritual physiognomy. As a result, all groups within the Jewish community have achieved freedom of expression and practice. Efforts to limit or suppress this liberty of conscience have not been totally lacking and undoubtedly will re-occur in the future. But such attempts are invariably accompanied by a bad conscience on the part of the apostles of intolerance, who thus reveal their weak roots in the tradition that they are ostensibly defending and betray their predistined failure to achieve their ends.

Finally, the millennial experience of Jewish disability and exile in the ancient and the medieval worlds has strengthened this attachment to freedom of conscience among Jews. In addition, the modern world has demonstrated that the material and intellectual position and progress of Jews, individually and collectively, is most effectively advanced in an atmosphere of religious liberty.

Thus all three elements, tradition, temperament and history, have united to make religious freedom, both for the Jewish community and the larger family of mankind, an enduring ideal and not merely a temporarily prudential arrangement. Undoubtedly Jews have fallen short of the lofty standards of their tradition in this as in other respects. Yet it remains true that, by and large, they have maintained their loyalty to the ideal of freedom of conscience for themselves and for all men.

NOTES

[1] On the Chazar kingdom, see A. B. Pollok, *Khazaria* (Hebrew), Tel Aviv, 1951; D. M. Dunlop, *The History of the Jewish Khazars* (Princeton, 1964). For a brief account see M. L. Margolis and A. Marx, *A History of the Jewish People* (Philadelphia, 1927), pp. 525 f.

[2] On the medieval community, see Salo W. Baron, *The Jewish Community, Its History and Structure to the American Revolution*, III (Philadelphia, 1942). The impact of the Enlightenment and the Emancipation is treated in all works dealing with modern Judaism. The reader may be referred to R. Gordis, *Judaism for the Modern Age* (New York, 1955), for a brief discussion of the revolutionary changes that followed in their wake.

[3] Cf. his provocative book bearing the same title, *Secularism as the Will of God* (New York, 1954).

[4] We have developed the theme of the relationship of ethics to religious faith in *A Faith for Moderns* (New York, 1960).

[5] Instances are to be found, even today, in every religious group. Thus, several months ago, a furore was created in the State of Israel when members of the ultra-Orthodox community of Me'ah She'arim in Jerusalem sought to prevent vehicular traffic on the Sabbath by stopping and even burning the cars coming through the Mandelbaum Gate. When the police arrested the leaders of the group, their sympathizers in New York demonstrated in front of the Israeli consulate carrying banners in the name of the "Committee for Religious Freedom in Israel."

The *New York Times* (Dec. 18, 1964) reported that the Most Rev. Louis Alonso Munoyerro, titular Archbishop of Sion and Catholic Vicar-General for Spain's armed forces, gave an interview to the newspaper *ABC* in Madrid, in which he denounced full religious liberty for Protestants in Spain as part of an international conspiracy that was seeking "to make Catholic unity disappear from our fatherland."

The archbishop urged Spaniards to learn from history to be "circumspect" and not to "join the chorus of those champions of liberty who judge the success of the Vatican Council by whether it produced the enslavement of the conscience of Catholic peoples, and among them the Spanish people."

Fortunately, these attitudes are not representative of Catholicism or Judaism as a whole. Nor is religious intolerance rare among atheists. It is, of course, well known that the Soviet Constitution guarantees "freedom of religion and the right of anti-religious propaganda." This right to "freedom of religion" is felt to be entirely compatible with the heavy disabilities visited upon virtually all religious institutions and leaders, the prohibition of religious education, and all but complete suppression of Judaism.

6 Cf. the judicious comments on the subject of the role of the Maccabees in Christian thought in T. K. Cheyne, *The Origin and Religious Content of the Psalter* (New York, 1895), p. 29.

7 Cf. Josephus, *Antiquities* XII, 9, 1; 11, 3.

8 In Exodus, chapter 20, Jews reckon verse 2 as the First Commandment, verses 3–6 as the Second, and verse 17 as the Tenth. Roman Catholics and Lutherans consider verses 3–6 as the First Commandment, and verse 17 as containing the Ninth and Tenth. Most Protestants count verse 3 as the First, verses 4–6 as the Second, and verse 17 as the Tenth.

9 Cf. our paper, "Educating For a Nation of Nations" in *Religion and the Public Schools* (Santa Barbara, Cal., Center for the Study of Democratic Institutions, 1961) and *The Root and the Branch: Judaism and the Free Society*, (Chicago, 1962), pp. 94–114.

10 Cf. A. B. Ehrlich, *Die Psalmen* (Berlin, 1905), p. vi.

11 The literature on the religious movements in the Judaism of the two centuries B.C.E. is enormous. For a brief presentation of some of the differences among the sects, see *The Root and the Branch: Judaism and the Free Society*, pp. 34 f.

12 Cf. *B. Sanhedrin* 88b, *Shabbat* 17a.

13 Cf. *Mishnah Eduyot* 4, 8.

14 Cf. *Mishnah Sanhedrin* 10, 1.

15 Cf. Maimonides, *Mishneh Torah, Hilkhoth Teshubhah* 3, 7.

16 On the uses of the ban in medieval Judaism, and the famous though atypical excommunications of Uriel Acosta and Benedict Spinoza, cf. *Judaism for the Modern Age*, pp. 292–306.

17 The tendency to extreme pietism reappears after major catastrophes with sufficient regularity, we believe, to be called a "law." The validity of this contention deserves to be examined by a study and analysis of the historical evidence.

18 On this fundamental aspect of Judaism, cf. *The Root and the Branch: Judaism and the Free Society*, pp. 23–27.

19 This contention has been a staple in the thinking of Arnold Toynbee. The same view is set forth by Leo Feffer, who cites the same commandment

(cf. his paper "Church and State: A Jewish Approach" in Jacob Freid, ed. *Jews in the Modern World* [New York, 1962] I, p. 210). This is particularly astonishing, since, aside from Feffer's general insight into Judaism, he himself cites Roger Williams who utilized the Decalogue (which includes this commandment), as the foundation for his theory of religious tolerance. Cf. Feffer, *ibid.*, pp. 219 f.

20 Cf. *B. Sanhedrin* 56a–602; *Tosefta, Abhodah Zarah* 8, 4–8.

21 Cf. *Yakqut Shimeoni* on Judges, sec. 42.

22 Cf. Galatians 3, 38.

23 On the history of Gentile-Jewish relationships in Christian Europe, see the excellent study of S. Katz, *Exclusiveness and Tolerance* (Oxford, 1961). On religious tolerance in Judaism, see A. Altmann, *Tolerance and the Jewish Tradition* (London, 1957), and *The Root and the Branch: Judaism and the Free Society*, chap. 3, esp. pp. 47–52.

24 The texts of many of these disputations are assembled in J. D. Eisenstein, *Otzar Vikkukhim* (New York, 1928), albeit in uncritical form. Cf. also Katz, *op. cit.*, pp. 106 ff. and the bibliography there cited. The most recent study of the subject is that of O. S. Rankin, *Jewish Religious Polemic of Early and Late Centuries* (Edinburgh, 1956).

25 The modifications of the Talmudic laws by great legal authorities in the early Middle Ages are analyzed by S. Katz, *op. cit.*, pp. 12–36.

26 Cf. Katz, *ibid.*, pp. 102 ff.

27 Cf. the moving passage in his *Sefer Mitzvot Hagadol* (Venice ed., 1547), pp. 152 c–d, cited by Katz, *op. cit.*, p. 104.

28 Cf. *Tosefta, Sanhedrin* 13:2.

29 Maimonides, *Hilkhoth Melakhim*, 8, 11; *Hilkhoth Teshuvah*, 3, 5; *Milkhoth Eduth* 11, 10; the *Commentary on the Mishnah, Sanhedrin*, 10, 12; *Teshuvoth Ha-Rambam ve-' Iggerothav* (Leipzig, 1859), part 2, p. 23b.

30 Cf. his *Kuzari*, 4, 23.

31 Cited in Bezalel Ashkenazi, *Shittah Mequbbetzet*, 1761 ed., pp. 78a.

32 His descriptive phrase, *'ummoth hageduroth bedarkhei hadathot*, means literally, "nations restricted by the ways of religion." Cf. Katz, *op. cit.*, pp. 114–115, for a careful and well-balanced treatment of Meiri's views.

33 Cf. *Tosafot* on *B. Sanhedrin* 63b.

34 Cf. *Mishneh Torah, Hilkhoth Melakhim* 1, 4.

35 Cf. *Mishneh Torah, Abodah Zarah* 9, 3; *Commentary on the Mishnah, Abodah Zarah* 1, 3.

36 Cf. *Emunot Vedeot*, 2, 5.

37 Cf. Moses Rivkes, *Be'er Hagolah* on *Shulhan Arukh, Hoshen Mishpat* 525, 5.

38 On the history of proselytism in Judaism and the issues involved, cf. *Judaism for the Modern Age*, chap. 16.

MOST REVEREND JOHN J. WRIGHT

Conscience and Authority: Catholic Reflections

THE MOST REVEREND JOHN J. WRIGHT *has been Bishop of Pittsburgh since 1959. He was educated at the Boston Latin School, at Boston College, at St. John's Seminary in Brighton, Mass., and at the North American College in Rome. Following his ordination to the priesthood in Rome, our contributor served in the Archdiocese of Boston as Professor at the Seminary and, later, as Secretary to the Archbishop of Boston. Consecrated as Auxiliary Bishop of Boston on June 30, 1947, Bishop Wright was installed as the First Bishop of the newly created Diocese of Worcester on March 7, 1950. Nine years later, on March 18, 1959, he was installed as eighth Bishop of Pittsburgh.*

Bishop Wright is the Episcopal Advisor to the Lay Retreat Movement in the United States and to the Mariological Society of America. He has served as President General of the National Catholic Education Association and as a member of the Theological Commission of the Second Vatican Council. Author of books on Catholic social teaching as well as of many magazine articles and books, Bishop Wright holds honorary degrees from numerous American and Canadian colleges and universities and is a member of the American Academy of Arts and Sciences.

Bishop Wright's reflections on "Conscience and Authority" are the substance of a lecture originally given, under this title, to the Thomas More Associates in Chicago and printed in The Critic.

By coincidence both Dr. Robert Gordis and I were prevented by illness from actually participating in the Latrobe colloquy.

However, he had kindly provided the text of his contribution to the discussion on conscience in which we were to take part. And so, thanks to Dr. Gordis, I had some opportunity to consider preliminary reactions to his paper.

Quite apart from the fact that we had no opportunity for such mutual exchange of criticism as the round table might have occasioned, our papers turn out to be parallel presentations of our respective Jewish and Christian concepts of conscience, rather than confrontations which either conflict or mesh.

I would note, however, two reservations which I intended to express at the symposium. Dr. Gordis appears to link, both conceptually and historically, the notions of *freedom of conscience* and of *freedom of religion* more intimately than I think to be well-founded logically or factual historically. Throughout his paper Dr. Gordis seems to equate the two as co-extensive concepts. I would agree that they usually overlap in one or another degree, that they often turn out to be bound up with one another in cases of attack on either, and that not less often the one is in the condition of the other. But I suggest that notionally and historically they are not quite the same thing, nor are they as interchangeable as Dr. Gordis' paper might lead one to conclude.

If I read correctly certain historic positions of the Jewish community toward those of its own members who, presumably following conscience, have changed their religion, it would seem that some, at least, of the Jewish understandings of freedom of conscience are neither philosophically nor historically consistent with Dr. Gordis' reading on this point. A sharper distinction between the two rights at issue, sharper than that which he makes, appears to have been traditional among other Jews; their social controls and reactions would seem to be closer to those followed in other orthodox religious patterns, sometimes being even more stern in their expressions, at least in the realms of changes in religion and inter-religious marriages. On this point, the sympathetic Catholic critic will find Dr. Gordis' argument a trifle sanguine.

Moreover, I cannot help considering Dr. Gordis to have been generous beyond warrant to secular and political authorities in his estimation of their role in the development of the right of conscience. Here reveals itself, I suspect, the inadequacy of his distinction, at least historically, between freedom of conscience and freedom of religion. That both freedoms have been nourished by whatever has strengthened either is undisputed, but the concern of the secular State has been different with respect to each. The heavily pragmatic problems of what we now call "the pluralistic society" have occasioned a practical policy with respect to *religious* freedom much more developed and widespread than any philosophical or practical concepts of even modern States with respect to the right of *conscience*. "Conscientious objectors" under many post-Age of Reason regimes might bear witness on this point, but so could greater numbers of citizens who, while enjoying fairly full freedom of religion, invoke with only limited success the right of conscience in connection with educational problems, social questions, and the like.

The concept of freedom of religion, one might conclude, has gained greatly from the modern secular approach to the problems of peaceful co-existence of large religious groups in a pluralistic society; the concept of freedom of conscience, however, owes its greatest strength, in my opinion, to a specifically religious witness in its behalf which is as old as the preaching of the Hebrew prophets and the resistance of the Hebrew people to the tyranny of their captors. It is a concept enormously enriched, directly and *ex professo*, by the New Testament and the Christian dogmatic and moral tradition. It is to this, with the reservations I shall try to indicate, that my own paper is addressed within the special theme of a Christian understanding of the relation between conscience and authority.

Conscience and authority are always at work and often in conflict in the general society, in the family, in professional life, in the university world—wherever there are persons in societies of whatever kind or origin. The most bitter arena of conflict between conscience and authority in our century is probably in the area between conscience and the modern State which, in all its forms, tends to be characterized by a certain absolutism creating grave problems for even the natural conscience. This absolutism of the modern State causes tormenting antagonisms for the consciences of those who believe in a supernatural or divine order transcending and subordinating the claims of secular authority.

I refer here, however, to the concepts of conscience and of authority within the Church. I do so because when these concepts and their mutual relations within the Church are clear, when a Christian conscience is soundly formed, a model is proposed for other societies, and Christians are the better prepared personally to face up to parallel tensions elsewhere and socially to contribute to the easing of these in their other forms and areas of conflict.

In thus limiting my discussion to the Church, I note that Pope Pius XII distinguished sharply between the spirit of authority in the Church and the spirit of "authoritarianism." I recall his careful distinction between the structure of authority in the Church and that in totalitarian regimes, insisting that these latter "can claim no point of resemblance to hierarchical constitutions of the Church," precisely because of the respective attitudes of these and of the Church toward "the clear and incontrovertible dictates of conscience," "the laws of individual and social living written in the hearts of men" and "the freedom and improvement of the human person . . ."

And yet, even among Christians there is much seemingly tentative and even hesitant talk about the relations between conscience and authority. In fact, however, the present debate on the conflict between conscience and authority is relatively modern in time and not even now universal in its geography, the contemporary statement of the problem of conscience being linked to relatively recent and almost regional claims with respect to the sovereign independence of the individual person. Jacques Leclercq (*Liberté d'Opinion et Catholiques*) contends that citizens of the Western world suffer from a certain optical illusion when they adjudge the sovereign independence of the individual person to be one of the major themes of human literature, political, moral and other. On the contrary, this theme—above all, its statement in terms of personal conscience—is even now almost confined to Western Europe, North America, Great Britain, plus some contiguous and scattered zones influenced by ideas transplanted from these.

In the Western world, however, the theme of the supremacy of conscience, in a valid sense but also with some exaggerations, has been compared to a steadily expanding river, flooding in all directions; it has become an *idée fixe*, a master theme, perhaps the master theme of Western civilization. People have become accustomed to link, in a somewhat overly simplified way, its origins to controversies arising out of sixteenth-century religious disputes. The controversy passed from the religious to the political arena in the seventeenth century, reaching its first high political plateau with the French concepts of the rights of man in the eighteenth century and pressing forward thereafter in politico-social movements inspired by the idea of liberty—above all, personal liberty—and thus becoming associated with movements and points of view that came to be called "liberal."

There is, of course, a long history of the concept of conscience prior to modern times. And yet, conscience is one of those words which everyone uses readily enough as not only basic but also very simple, even though an invitation to define it usually reveals confusion and embarrassment. People can feel very strongly about conscience and be quite fierce in asserting its claims, while being little prepared to say what it is, even though, as they might point out, "everyone knows what it is." It is something like a spiral; we all know what a spiral is, but when pressed for a definition, we most helplessly wiggle our fingers in the air.

In seeking to define conscience, some do so in inspirational terms, such as those which little George Washington used when he wrote in his copy book, "Labor to keep alive in your breast that little spark of celestial fire—conscience." Still others speak in the more negative terms of the so-called "accusing conscience," that stern, tormenting voice that only speaks to you when you have done something wrong and which many suppose to be the only true sense of conscience. This, I think, is what people usually mean when they use such a phrase as "a New England conscience," which, under study, often means the guilty recognition that you have spent too much money, or that you are likely to be found out in some indiscretion and find your name in the paper, or, what is worse, to have forfeited your credit in the local bank.

Some, particularly at the moment, seem to suppose that it is conscience which makes things sinful or innocent. This, of course, is false in any warranted sense of the word. Conscience may declare individuals innocent or guilty, but it does so on the subjective level of conscious innocence or conscious guilt, not on the level of what is and what is not objectively sinful. *Conscience is not a legislator; it is a judge. Conscience does not make actions objectively right or wrong; it declares one guilty here and now or innocent, here and now.* In this here and now moral judgment, conscience may be right or wrong, but in any case it does not legislate the objective rightness or wrongness of actions; at most, it indicts, dispenses or exculpates subjectively the person who acts from honest conviction.

A working description of conscience is that by Sir William Hamilton, the nineteenth-century Scottish philosopher (not to be confused with the husband of Lord Nelson's mistress, they having the same name, overlapping dates, but somewhat different preoccupations): "Man, as conscious of his liberty to act, and of the law by which his actions ought to be regulated, recognizes his personal accountability, and calls himself before the internal tribunal which we denominate *conscience*. Here he is either acquitted or condemned. The acquittal is connected with a peculiar feeling of pleasurable exultation, as the *condemnation* with a peculiar feeling of painful humiliation—remorse."

But such definitions or descriptions leave us with several unsolved problems. The first is the problem of the relationship of the dictates of internal conscience to the demands of external authority, the heart of our present reflections. Another is that of how and whence conscience derives its knowledge of the law by which its actions are to be regulated; in a word, how is conscience formed or illumined? What norms, other than its own *ipse dixit,* does conscience have?

Protestant Christian theories include explanations often bound up with illuminatism or even direct, divine inspiration, if not revelation; others, more often in the eighteenth and nineteenth centuries, relate (as did Sir William Hamilton and the even greater Sir William Blackstone) the concept and function of conscience to the concept of natural law, a source of knowledge of God's will which a solid Protestant tradition once exalted much higher than does any Catholic doctrine of natural law, since the interpretation of the demands and sanctions of Natural Law for Catholics has always been within the context of the mind, or understanding, of the Church where revelation serves to illumine, to purify, and to warm areas of natural law which are otherwise obscure, harsh or unduly rigorous.

The development of the Catholic Christian understanding of the concept and range of conscience includes divers theories regarding the nature of conscience, while agreeing on its claims and its power. The theories of Albert the Great and Thomas Aquinas are intellectualistic, those of Alexander of Hales and Bonaventure are voluntaristic. Both general schools are consistent with Father Haring's own contention, typically Catholic as distinct from "direct voice of God" concepts of conscience, that God is indeed at work in the depths of conscience, at work as a person "who calls and invites, a judge, living, absolute, the source of the summons and the law," but that we ourselves contribute, out of

our natures, something which must be trained to play its part in
the decisions of conscience. "It is the voice of God, but in the
sense that we must contribute something of our own in the
formation of the decision of a conscience which is right in God's
sight. Error is possible in our decision, but we are able to trace
it to its source." That source, and it operates commonly, is in
ourselves, not God, and it is, of course, the presence and perils of
it which so complicate the discussion of conscience itself and its
relations with authority.

This is particularly true when there is talk of the freedom of
conscience as that further concept is debated in our day. The fact
is that, contrary to a general but loose impression, conscience
binds far more than it loosens. Conscience is not something by
which I am set free from obligations so much as it is something by
which I am bound, controlled, and on occasions sternly rebuked.
It is necessary to get this unpleasant fact (if it is unpleasant) in
clear focus at the outset of any discussion of conscience. This is,
of course, what befogged much discussion, outside the Ecumenical
Council, of the progress of the debate on Religious Liberty as an
aspect of freedom of conscience: it also made extremely delicate
the debate on freedom of conscience in the Council itself.

Bishop Emil De Smedt of Bruges, Belgium, whose magnificent
address introducing the draft on Religious Liberty was universally
applauded at the Council, was painfully aware of the widespread
confusion on his point not only among possible critics of his
position, but also among some who have no idea about what he
is talking and who might, in fact, reject it if they did, but claim
him as their champion.

Hence, De Smedt cannot safely, as an honest Christian, or
prudently, as a competent debater, leave his case on the apodictic
assertion of Pope John (*Pacem in Terris*): "Every human being
has the right to honor God according to the dictates of an upright
conscience, and therefore the right to worship God privately and
publicly . . ." He is obliged to shoot at enemies from half a dozen

directions, those who wish to scuttle his ship and who clamber over its prow in the honest effort to sink it, and those who are scampering aboard in the aftersection and all around the sides in an effort to sail under his banner into harbors for which De Smedt is not destined and of which he wants no part.

And so, De Smedt is obliged to devote whole sections of his Council speech to explaining what he is *not* talking about, since what he *is* talking about is highly mysterious to a generation which talks passionately of conscience, but often to the confusion of the cause.

Accordingly, my chapter on conscience will quote at length from Bishop De Smedt's speech to the Council, beginning with the section in which he says:

> When religious liberty is defended, it is not asserted that it is proper for man to consider the religious problem according to his own whim without any moral obligation and decide for himself according to his own will whether or not to embrace religion (religious indifferentism).
>
> Nor is it affirmed that the human conscience is free in the sense that it is, as it were, outside the law, absolved from any obligation toward it (laicism).
>
> Nor is it said that falsehood is to be considered on an equal footing with truth, as though there were no objective norm of truth (doctrinal relativism).
>
> Nor is it admitted that man in any way has a quasi-right to maintain a peaceful complacency in the midst of uncertainty (dilettantistic pessimism).

Such positive claims of conscience as these are set forth in St. Thomas Aquinas and in a very brief, but very forceful phrase of the Fourth Lateran. The Lateran Council said that anyone who acts against conscience acts so to his damnation. St. Thomas specifically relates the possibility of damnation to the relations between the dictates of conscience and those of authority when there may be conflict between the two. He does so in many passages, one of

which will suffice: "Therefore conscience is more to be obeyed
than authority imposed from outside. For conscience obliges in
virtue of divine command, whether written down in a code or in-
stilled by natural law. To weigh conscience in the scales against
obedience to legal authority is to compare the weight of divine
and of human decrees. The first obliges more than the second, and
sometimes against the second" (*De Veritate,* 17, 5).

Wherefore, our next concern is obviously the concept of
authority. The concept and fact of authority are not merely
widely discussed at the moment; they are also universally
threatened. Within the family, within political society, in the
world of teaching and philosophy, in the realm of morals and
religion, authority is of all concepts the least popular.

However, authority is not just a word; it is a profoundly
ethical, religious, political and social reality, a *fact* whose manifestations everybody accepts or endures. In every society, political
and religious, public and private, necessary and voluntary, authority is essential as a cause of united action even in the smallest
and most compact community; it is necessary also for the very
volition, let alone the attainment of the common good. Considered in its essential functions, therefore, authority is neither
a necessary evil, nor a lesser good, nor lesser evil, nor the consequence of any evil or deficiency. It is, like nature and society,
unqualifiedly good. Even Bertrand Russell, without theological
premises or preoccupations of any kind, develops the pragmatic
but significant contention that a healthy society requires both
central control and individual initiative: without control there
is anarchy; without initiative there is stagnation. I suggest that
without certain metaphysical and even theological realities
beyond these correlative forces, neither the individual initiatives
nor the central controls are likely to stand up very long. For
authority, as the word itself demonstrates, is bound up with
the origins, divine and human, of our being; wherefore, contempt
of the authority of parents, as of any other human sources of what

we are, grows fatally in proportion as our recognition of the mystery of creation and the fact of God grows more and more agnostic, however sentimental, and finally atheistic. It is this theological fact which makes instinctive the mutual interplay of conscience and authority, as a result of which conscience instinctively seeks the guidance of authority and presupposes its existence, even as genuine authority by its very nature postulates the existence and freedom of conscience; authority cannot exist, function or accomplish its divinely appointed purposes save in a moral universe where conscience is alive and at work.

Both authority and obedience, then, presuppose conscience and both are related to the most intimate and profound notion of being itself, the ultimate root and meaning of authority being found in the reality conveyed by the word "author."

This is the same point, philosophical and semantic, that Romano Guardini makes. It involves the mystery of creation and the meaning which that mystery gives to the authority of God; it suggests the limited but analogous nature of human authority, limited because all human authority is devoid of that character of absolute authorship which belongs to God alone; analogous, however, because men can be the "authors" who increase or develop (*augere*) the growth of that to which God has given existence.

Creation does not mean for many of our contemporaries what it does for Christians; neither, therefore, does authority. But for the believer, the concept of authority, on whatever level, will be shaped and hallowed by the mystery of creation, directly and fully in what pertains to God, analogously and proportionately in what pertains to anyone less than God. Christian doctrine suggests that human authority is at once a phenomenon and a service whose origin is in God's creative act. Everyone who exercises authority is invested therewith by God and will have to answer to God for the use he makes of it.

For this reason, it is established Christian doctrine that one who holds authority stands to his subjects in the place of God. But this must be understood in its most positive and fruitful sense; it must not be limited to meaning that the superior, natural or religious, only represents the authority of God in any merely negative or inhibiting sense. Understood as God, who works through the constitution of nature and the dispensations of grace and who must intend it for the building of His Kingdom, authority, communicated to others by God, must mean that he who holds it represents divine love not less than divine authority, divine mercy not less than divine justice and, in sum, the *life-giving* power of God, as Father Corbishley states it.

This means that authority is not only established to regulate, to control, to order and, on occasion, to forbid, all in analogy to God; it means also what is usually much more important and urgent, namely, that authority is given to inspire and to encourage the initiatives of others, as does God by His grace; to coordinate the purposeful lives, strivings, aspirations, undertakings, and energies of others, to press forward, leading, directing and challenging others, as God, by His grace and through the voice of conscience, is constantly calling to new levels of excellence those subject to His sway and responsible to His authority, even as He sometimes, by a grace or a rebuke of conscience, dissuades, prohibits or overrules them.

This all presupposes, of course, a sense and the reality of community within the influence of which the role of authority is refined and checked, even as conscience is formed and given direction. When Christians are most consistent with and faithful to the spirit that unites them, they are in essence, always and everywhere, a community; at first they even lived as a community, wrote to each other as members of a community, were martyred as representatives of a community, prayed as a community. The very fact of being constantly subjected to possible outbreaks of persecution reinforced this sense of the community; it still should. Even the failures of Christians in the moral problems of life were principally failures to maintain the "concord and harmony" of the community; they should still be so seen. In such a community the conscience of the Christian early acquired a formation which preserved it from individualism and moral solipsism.

On the side of authority, also, the situation was (and essentially is) such that Father Yves Congar, in *Problems of Authority,* can write:

In the early Church authority was that of men who were like princes in a community which was wholly sanctified, *plebs sancta,* and overshadowed by the Spirit of God. The Church leaders were all the more conscious of their authority in that they saw it as the vehicle of the mystery of salvation which God wishes to accomplish in his Church. They wanted to be, and knew that they were, moved by the Spirit, but they also knew that the Spirit inhabits the Christian community and in the exercise of their authority they remained closely linked to this community.

But consciences, too, were moved by the same spirit; the formation of conscience was accomplished by a single spirit through the shared teachings of the single Mother Church, and this with the result that, although conscience was warmly personal as the Christian conscience must be, it was never sharply individualistic, as later influences have made the human conscience and most things else, once the sense of community grew weaker and weaker in the Middle Ages, so that finally the whole accent of expression between, roughly, the eleventh and sixteenth century, falls increasingly on the first person singular when we ordinary people are speaking, and on the third person plural when people invested with authority are speaking—a very significant shift, indeed, from earlier usages. All this prepares us for the later tendency to emancipate conscience itself more and more from the formative influence of anything but one's own insights, separate graces, and private judgments.

This fuller expression of the individual, as distinct from the communal side of the human person, has been, of course, not without good effects in the development of human culture and even of those divine purposes by reason of which all things turn out for good for those who love God. But the passing evil out of which came the permanent good was sometimes evil indeed; it was particularly hurtful to profound devotion, to the authentic image of the Church and to Christian concepts of conscience and authority. Medieval and Renaissance developments gave impetus to new branches of dogmatic, moral and mystical theology and inaugurated discoveries in psychology which uncovered intimate facets of the human person as an individual; this period in our history made contributions both sound and lasting. But it was unfortunate insofar as it concentrated excessively on the individual, stressing too much the importance of purely individual experiences and emotions and leading to an individual sensitiveness, with complications unsettling to the delicate balance of society as well as that of the person.

All this threatened to dissolve the sense of the human community; it has already weakened the very sense of membership in the Church, tending as it did to turn religion into a wholly private affair. It made the ordinary man chafe under the guidance of authority and it tempted him to excessive confidence in his own spiritual strength apart from the Communion of Saints in the company of the Church. In terms of conscience, it accounts for the total difference between the Catholic position of St. Joan, even as late as the fifteenth century, and the completely Protestant position of Luther only a century later.

What happened in later history explains the dismay of a present-day Anglican scholar over what has happened to the New Testament concept of conscience not only in modern society, but in the Church as he knows it. In his book, *Conscience in the New Testament,* the Kaye Prize Essay for 1955, Professor C. A. Pierce contends that it is one thing to teach that conscience

is inviolable and that no authority would be justified in over-
ruling it when it speaks out against an action or command which
alerts it to protest, but that it is something quite different to
suppose that conscience is infallible. He protests that should the
Church offer men no better guidance than only "act according
to conscience," she would abdicate the office to which she is appointed and be apostate to the first article of her Creed, namely,
that Jesus is Lord. He contends that the word conscience has
been so torn out of its Christian context that in any conflict between conscience and Christ Himself, the modern opinion would
make Christ come out second best!

As a result, not all the rhetoric which has extolled the sovereignty of the modern individual conscience can cover the
pathetic moral state in which it has so often left individuals.
This rhetoric has, however, blinded us to the ugly fact that
exaggerated sense of the autonomy of individual conscience can
give those whose individual consciences become not only the
norm of their own moral lives, but also their putative title to
dominate the lives of others.

Individual conscience is not always on the side of freedom,
nor of life, nor of God, nor of love, nor of man: "modern conscience" can mean moral solipsism, the arrogance and arbitrari-
ness of which can be more horrendous, because more inaccessi-
ble to protest, than almost any despotism and certainly than
any duly constituted authority which must function under
written law—civil or canon. Consider, for example, what appears
to be the moral philosophy of the followers of Ayn Rand.

And so it becomes important to reflect on the role played by
society and social institutions on the formation of conscience;
obviously I must invite you to consider the role of the Church
in such formation. The need to do so is made the greater by
recent developments in Protestant moral theology which have
not been without side effects in the thinking of some Catholics.
It reveals itself, of course, in connection with moral judgments

generally, including those on social justice; but, given the pre-occupations of our generation, it has become publicized chiefly in connection with moral assessments of contraception, abortion, divorce and euthanasia.

As we have seen, the traditional Protestant concepts of personal conscience were linked to the objective word of Scripture, how-ever sometimes privately interpreted, or to norms of natural law, seen as God's law almost as Scripture is God's Word and, therefore, as a control on and guide to conscience. But in the particular case of contraception Father de Lestapis sees a revolu-tionary change in the Protestant understanding of the nature of conscience: "The believer, as he faces his God, is the only judge in conscience, not only of the intentions which lead him to desire to limit birth, but also of the validity of the means he employs for the purpose."

The moral philosophers who put forth this "law of liberty" wish to defend some binding force for moral laws; but, as Father Gerald Kelly points out, in principle they cannot admit an ab-solute binding force covering every concrete case because they think this would conflict with the liberty of God and also with the liberty of the Christian as the child of God. Hence, while admitting that the moral laws are good general guides to what is right, some influential Protestant theologians defend as the ultimate standard of moral conduct what they call the "law of liberty" or the "law of love" in the New Testament. This law of love is superior to all other laws and may contradict them. The individual knows this law as it applies to him in the con-crete situations of everyday life, not through any verbal formula, but rather through a sort of divine inspiration received within his own soul. In other words, in the depths of the soul there is an immediate contact with God—an intuition of love, as they call it—and this is the ultimate guide for individuals in their moral choices. This direct word of "permissive love" from God Himself is what the voice of conscience appears to have become in this recent school of some (by no means all) Protestant moral philosophy; it has had traces of effect or perhaps parallel in the thinking of certain Catholics. One notes, for example, the possibly cynical but certainly inexact use by Dr. John Rock (in a Notre Dame lecture recently) of Cardinal Newman's quip about toasts to conscience and to the Pope.

It was on this "law of liberty" concept of conscience that Pope Pius XII commented in a searching and significant radio broadcast made on "Family Day," March 24, 1952, when he talked on "Conscience and Education." Although delivered directly to the people of Italy, the talk was a commentary on the most urgent aspect of the general problem of conscience in the present revolutionary transition from an age of individualism to an age of new, potentially good, potentially unfortunate, communal emphasis. It is the problem of the formation of the just and objectively justified conscience.

For Pope Pius XII conscience is "that which is deepest and most intrinsic in man"; it is "the innermost and most secret nucleus in man. It is there that he takes refuge with his spiritual faculties in absolute solitude: alone with himself, or, rather, alone with God—whose voice sounds in conscience—and with himself. There it is that he decides for good or evil; there it is that he chooses between the way of victory and that of defeat . . . Hence conscience, to express it with an image as old as it is fitting, is a sanctuary on the threshold of which all must halt, even, in the case of a child, his father and mother. . . ."

How, then, can one talk of the formation or education of conscience? We cannot do otherwise, of course, in the light of the Incarnation and claims of the Word of God in Christ and the consequent Christian obligation in matters of faith and morals to accept the will and the commandments of Christ and to conform one's life to them, i.e., each single act, inner or exterior, which the free human will chooses and decides upon. But what is the spiritual faculty, if not conscience, that, in each particular

case, gives guidance to the will so that it may determine its actions in conformity with the divine will? Conscience, the Pope
argued, must be clear reflection of human action's divine pattern. "Therefore, expressions such as 'the judgment of the Christian conscience,' or 'to judge according to the Christian
conscience' mean this: that the pattern of the ultimate and
personal decision for a moral action must be taken from the
word and will of Christ. In fact, He is the way, the truth, and
the life, not only for all men collectively, but for each single
one; the mature man, the child, and the youth."

And so, the formation of the Christian conscience consists,
above all, in illuminating the mind with respect to Christ's will,
law, and way; guiding it, also, so far as this can be done from
outside, freely and constantly to execute the divine will. This
is the highest present task of moral education, and moral education pre-supposes authority; it is the first contact between conscience and authority, that of the parent, of the teacher, above
all, of those who teach divine law—and of all these within the
Church. Nor is anything more consistent with the traditional
Christian concept of conscience. For conscience, as Father Bernard
Haring reminds us, since it is not an oracle which draws truth
from its own obscure depths, by its very nature seeks illumination
and guidance.

God, the ultimate norm, the truth to which every conscience must
conform, . . . always instructs conscience in accordance with its nature:
the natural conscience through the order of nature, the conscience endowed with the supernatural grace of faith through supernatural revelation. Just as it is not alien to natural conscience to draw from the
natural revelation expressed in creation and to learn from the natural
communities which correspond to it, so it is also "according to nature"
for the believing conscience elevated by grace and steeped in humility
to harken to the word of revelation communicated to us in the
Church . . . .

. . . . and only one with a totally perverted concept of the real nature and function of conscience would repudiate the infallible *magisterium* of the Church in the name of conscience. Only a conscience which itself enjoys creative plenitude of infallibility in its own native right could *a priori* reject as contradictory every intervention of objective authority.

Nor are Catholics alone in their sense of urgency concerning the role that authority, and especially the teaching Church, must play in the formation of the enlightened conscience. The Anglican scholar whom we have already cited, Professor Pierce, quoting a traditional Protestant source, argues appositely:

Dreadful consequences are derivable to society . . . (from the use of) . . . a plausible word wrested from its proper sense. It has been imagined that, provided men follow directions of their own "consciences," they are justified in whatever mode of conduct they may adopt, which (as the term "conscience" is now too generally understood) is . . . in other words to say that, because men are persuaded a thing is right, therefore it cannot be wrong . . .

When men therefore talk of "liberty of conscience," they would do well to consider whether it is not, as the phrase is now understood, rather a liberty of their own making than any portion of that liberty with which Christ has made them free.

For this reason, Pierce sees the Church as having five main duties, plus the resources for performing them, in connection with that training of personal "choice and conscience" which Pius XII found the urgent need of our civilization. He sees the Church as bound to make herself "the best possible environment" for the formation of conscience, a role of the Church that is no longer served when the concept of the Church evaporates from the notion of Christian community to that of an ecclesiastical center visited from time to time for ritualistic observances, conceived as strictly private duties. He speaks of the spiritual manner in which the Church must influence the secular environment in which her members have to live, since this, too, shapes conscience; he describes the teaching responsibility on specific moral questions which the Church has, beyond her general witness to the truth, and how she must set before her members, and anyone else who will listen, the relevant facts on these specific issues, beginning with the great truths of revelation and the doctrines necessary to salvation, but including also the wisdom of her own experience, which is the sum of that of her countless members plus the corporate insight that comes from her immemorial dialogue with the cultural, political and religious systems of all humanity. Above all—and here the Anglican echoes Pope Pius—she must proclaim not only the teachings of Christ, but His life-giving Person as the pattern to be emulated, making the influence of everything which Christ said, and did, and was penetrate the deepest depths of human intellectual, appetitive, instinctive and emotional life where conscience stirs. Mindful that conscience can, while still claiming the name of conscience, be lulled, anesthetized, even deadened, the Church has the duty to seek the development in all her children of a moral sensitivity so acute that conscience would not merely react negatively to deviation from Christian perfection, but impel positively toward personal perfection, social reform, and the building of the kingdom of God.

Greater appreciation of this latter office of the Church in the formation of conscience would offset the temptation to pretend that the claims of authority to obedience have so stifled the initiative and freedom of devout consciences as to diminish the effectiveness of the Gospel and the Church. But Father Daniélou proclaims the authentically heroic understanding of true obedience when he writes: "Christianity would have had greater influence on social institutions if we had always had the courage to show that obedience to God, as an absolute duty, effects man's whole temporal, political, professional, and family life. If Christians have not been more revolutionary, it is not because they lacked freedom, but because they have not been sufficiently obedient . . . This is problem number one and it involves fully relating conscience to authority, above all, the authority of God. How?"

The answer to Father Daniélou's "How?" is found largely in the study and experience behind Cardinal Newman's final judgment on the part of the Church in the formation of a Christian conscience. Newman was excruciatingly aware of the need for objective criteria for evaluating the dictates of conscience and no small part of his life was a search for such criteria in what pertained to the basic moral act—the act of faith. He could not find such criteria in unaided nature alone, particularly given the fallen state of man which was, of all dogmas, the one most clear to Newman. He could consider Scripture in itself neither an adequate objective means to the formation of conscience nor norm for judging its dictates; in Luther's protestation that his conscience was "captive to the Word of God," Newman would find the cry of a sorry captive, indeed, as long as the Word of God meant merely the *letter* of Scripture alone; but Newman could find no adequate guide or objective norm for conscience in Tradition or the teachings of the Fathers, and it is the point of his life that he could not find the rule of conscience in a National Church. The Universal Church, he decided, endowed with infallibility and teaching through divinely-appointed channels, must be the spiritual country in which authority brings supernatural doctrine to the direction of that conscience which is the herald of the natural law; such a Church alone provides adequate objective criteria for the evaluation of those dictates of the sincere conscience which the upright man is bound to follow.

The English Cardinal scholar, although the eager and unmistakable champion of conscience, was no partisan of "modern conscience" or of moral liberalism. Like C. A. Pierce among recent Protestants and Bishop De Smedt in the Catholic Ecumenical Council, Newman must include in his defense of the rights of conscience a repudiation of its caricatures and counterfeits. He exposes the scientific and literary efforts to be rid of conscience entirely, the "resolute warfare . . . against that spiritual, invisible influence which is too subtle for science and too profound for literature":

As in Roman times, and in the middle ages, its supremacy was assailed by the arm of physical force, so now the intellect is put in operation to sap the foundations of a power which the sword could not destroy. We are told that conscience is but a twist in primitive and untutored man: that its dictate is an imagination: that the very notion of guiltiness, which that dictate enforces, is simply irrational, for how can there possibly be freedom of will, how can there be consequent responsibility, in that infinite eternal network of cause and effect in which we helplessly lie? And what retribution have we to fear when we have had no real choice to do good or evil?

Then Newman sketches the present "notion of conscience in the popular mind." The sketch remains lifelike after a century:

There, no more than in the intellectual world, does "conscience" retain the old, true, Catholic meaning of the word. There too the idea, the presence, of a moral governor is far away from the use of it, frequent and emphatic as that use of it is. When men advocate the rights of conscience, they in no sense mean the rights of the Creator, nor the duty to Him, in thought and deed, of the creature; but the right of thinking, speaking, writing and acting according to their judgment or their humor, without any thought of God at all. They do not even pretend to go by any moral rule, but they demand what they think is an Englishman's prerogative, for each to be his own master in all things, and to profess what he pleases, asking no one's leave, and accounting priest or preacher, speaker or writer, unutterably impertinent, who dares to say a word against his going to perdition, if he likes it, in his own way. Conscience has rights because it has duties; but in this age, with a large portion of the public, it is the very right and freedom of conscience to dispense with conscience, to ignore a Lawgiver and Judge, to be independent of unseen obligations. It becomes a license to take up any or no religion, to take up this or that and let it go again, to go to Church, to go to Chapel, to boast of being above all religions and to be an impartial critic of each of them. Conscience is a stern monitor, but in this century it has been superseded by a counterfeit which the eighteen centuries prior to it never heard of, and could not have mistaken for it if they had. It is the right of self-will.

But for Newman himself, beginning in his earliest Anglican days, conscience was a cognitive and affective act of profoundly theological overtones, God-centered, God-sanctioned, sensitive and responsible to God above all else. It involved the faculties by which man discovers God and by which he pleases God.

Again, then, conscience and authority not merely admit of reconciliation, they demand one another. Newman wrote: "The general sense of right and wrong, which is the first element in religion, is so delicate, so fitful, so easily puzzled, obscured, perverted, so subtle in its argumentative methods, so impressed by education, so biased by pride and passion, so unsteady in its flight . . . this sense is at once the highest of all teachers, yet the least luminous; and the Church, the pope, the hierarchy are in the divine purpose the supply of an urgent demand" (*Difficulties of Anglicans*).

But however "obscured" and "unsteady" conscience may be, it is still, says Newman, "a messenger from Him Who, both in nature and in grace, speaks to us behind a veil, and teaches and rules us by His representatives. [It] is the aboriginal Vicar of Christ . . ." Hence authority depends on conscience not only for the holy exercise of its claims; it depends on conscience for the very acceptance of these. The authority, that of the Pope included, which would be unmindful of conscience or hold it in contempt would be suicidal, destructive of itself; but the conscience, even otherwise enlightened, which would not recognize its need of authority—above all, the teaching authority in the Church—would be similarly destructive of its own purposes. Both are within a community; both are social; both are conditioned, bound up with social, never merely individual purposes, and these purposes are bound up with those of God and of His providence. Every sensitive person, every conscientious wielder of authority, dimly, at least, discerns this. The saint perceives it clearly and therefore becomes the witness unto death of the things we have been considering—conscience, authority, and both within the spiritual community that is the Church. Take, for example, the case of St. Joan of Arc (whose memory for reasons historical, theological, and perhaps sentimental I must cherish precisely because I am a bishop), one bound by conscience, charged with authority, and tied by great love to the Church.

Jean Guitton, the first of the lay auditors admitted to Vatican Council II, has promised a book precisely on these aspects of the haunting case of St. Joan. No case in twenty centuries presents so dramatically nor in such brutal completeness the most extreme anguish of the conflict between conscience and authority. No others ever caught in this conflict, certainly not Galileo and most certainly not any usually cited as "modern Galileos," hold a candlelight of moral splendor to the solar brilliance with which St. Joan illumines the Catholic concept of martyrdom for conscience' sake.

St. Joan has so much to teach us about the claims of conscience, the pitfalls of authority, and why the Church, one with Christ, is supremely to be loved, no matter what. Joan reminds us that neither conscience nor authority amount to anything, in final terms, except as means to an end greater than either or both, and that end is neither the freedom that conscience claims nor the order that authority imposes, but it is the sanctity to which conscience must bind us and authority must serve. Joan reminds us that the Church is on the side of conscience and canonizes those who follow it; the Church is on the side of authority and commands those who exercise it; but the

Church is, above all, the kingdom of *sanctity*, and to sanctify everything, conscience and authority and all else, is utterly subordinate.

Joan has other things to teach us and these, too, Jean Guitton promises to develop in his book. He suggests that Joan is not only the saint of conscience, but she is specifically the saint of conscience impelling one to vocation, a vocation within the Church, even though often involving tension with the institutional side of the Church and, therefore perhaps, with authority.

This makes ours "the age of Joan" in yet another dimension, since in our age the very sense of *vocation* has grown tenuous and vague, almost in proportion as conscience, for all the talk about its freedom and its sovereignty, has become more and more divorced from the voice of God. A whole literature is growing up around this subject, thank God, and its emphasis is happily on the relationship of vocation to personal liberty and of both to enlightened conscience.

Bernard Shaw links St. Joan to all this in one of the most perceptive sections of the preface to his provocative play on Joan. For Shaw, Joan exemplifies the conflict between genius and discipline, by which he means the conflict between vocation and institution as one aspect of the conflict between conscience and authority. For the pursuit of vocation, whether clerical or lay, always pre-supposes dictates of conscience and sooner or later brings one into collision with one or another form of authority. Sometimes it is the authority of God, impelling one to the vocation of a needed but unattractive work. Sometimes it is the authority of parents, resisting a son's vocation to priesthood, to marriage, or to one of those harebrained ventures which so frequently turn out to the good name of the family and the glory of God. Increasingly in our day it is the authority of the State, seeking to regulate our vocations, sometimes through work authoritatively imposed (as in compulsory military service) and sometimes through the impersonal requirements of the Planned Society, rightist, leftist or secular democratic. This may easily prove the great source of collision in an age of technocracy.

See how pertinent, therefore, to the concept of vocation, which is, in turn, so pertinent to the vitality of human culture as well as of the Church, is this question of conscience and authority. See how important it is that conscience and authority be harmoniously related, but that neither be annihilated.

In fact, not only must each be strong, but the synchronizing of both must still leave a tension between them. In the dynamic society—and the Church must always be such—there is a tension as well as a harmony between the liberty that, unchecked, could degenerate into chaos and the control that, unchecked, could freeze into despotism. Hence in the Church, where the basic relations are in order and both forces are strong, we shall not regret the occasional painful stresses and perhaps embarrassing strains which reveal that the tension between individual conscience and collective authority is at work. Quite the contrary: we shall rejoice in the evidence this gives of organic vitality, recognizing not only that the tension remains even after the two forces are harmoniously reconciled, but that the tension is essential to the harmony itself.

This truth has its parallel everywhere. It is symbolized in the "basic dualism" that Curt Sachs finds at work in the world of art where the to and fro of shaping trends of perfections depends on two ideals alternately acting as magnetic poles. Sometimes this polarity and tension in art is set forth in metaphor from physics; then it is termed "static-dynamic." Sometimes the antinomies are described, as the Greeks expressed them, in terms of *ethos* and *pathos*. There is a tension underlying the harmonies of music, where the order of rules is imposed on the spontaneity of sound. Biology reveals the "balance of nature"; a certain tension is everywhere in art and life or there is no harmony and no health.

So for moral health, whether in the person or in society, a certain tension is as inevitable and necessary as we saw authority itself and the impulse of conscience to be. It is in fostering and forming both, in the guidance it gives to conscience and the controls it imposes on authority, with the tensions arising from their mutual interplay, that Holy Church gives glory to God, makes its greatest contribution to civilization, and helps reveal our vocations, temporal and eternal, to her children.

5

✪ Religion and the Public Order

RABBI MARC H. TANENBAUM

The Role of the Church and Synagogue in Social Action

RABBI MARC H. TANENBAUM, *National Director of the Inter-Religious Affairs Department of the American Jewish Committee, was ordained at the Jewish Theological Seminary in New York. A member of the Rabbinical Assembly and a former Executive Director of the Synagogue Council of America, he was the only Rabbi in Vatican City at the time of the introduction of the Jewish Decree at the Ecumenical Council.*

Rabbi Tanenbaum has served as a Vice-Chairman of the White House Conference on Children and Youth, the White House Conference on Aging, the Religious Advisory Committee of the President's Committee on Equal Employment Opportunity, as a Consultant to the Children's Bureau, and with the White House Conference of Religious Leaders on Race, in addition to numerous other positions with the United States Government and United Nations Advisory Committees. Our author was Program Chairman of the historic National Conference on Religion and Race and is regarded as an authority on Christian-Jewish relations. He is the Jewish consultant to the Pius XII Religious Education Resource Center and the Sister Formation Conference.

A few years ago, a Hebrew book, published by American Jews in Israel, but written in Soviet Russia, was called to my attention. This book was an exchange of correspondence between two rabbis in Soviet Russia—one the Rabbi of Bobruisk, the other the Rabbi of Pavlograd in the south of Russia.

The topic they had been discussing for a number of years in their correspondence was "Whither Soviet Jewry?" What is the future of Russian Jews?

In one of his first letters to the older rabbi, the Rabbi of Pavlograd asked whether or not he should remain in the rabbinate. Why this question? He says, "We have a Synagogue—it's empty. We have no *Talmud Torah* [Jewish religious school]. We have no *heder* [elementary school]. We have nothing. But somehow a couple hundred of Jews living in Pavlograd are afraid of remaining without a Rabbi. But I have nothing to do. Wouldn't it be more desirable to resign and become a factory worker in Russia and at the same time remain a pious, traditional Jew as I am?"

The other rabbi advised him not to resign. The line of the argument he used and the criterion he applied to what a rabbi is or should be is very interesting. A rabbi should be in his world an almost functionless person. His only function is to study and to pray, and his house should be open to other people; that is the only function of a rabbi.

I tell you this story about the book not because I want you to adopt on the American scene that criterion for the rabbi—or, by inference, for the priest or minister—but because the Rabbi of Bobruisk referred to something else.

In his semi-rabbinical language, the rabbi referred to an idea about cycles in history. There are various cycles in human history, the rabbi writes in one of his letters. Fundamentally, there are only two—the naturalistic cycle and the metaphysical cycle. Now we are in the midst of a new naturalistic cycle, as the rabbi said, a materialistic, secularistic, and naturalistic cycle in highly industrialized countries, in countries with a technological civilization or in countries aspiring to create a technological civilization. And our duty "is to be patient and wait. This new naturalistic cycle is going to commit suicide."

"I see already the germs of death in this cycle, in this new naturalism," wrote the Rabbi of Bobruisk. "And then a new wave of the metaphysical outlook will seize Soviet Russia; not only Russia, the world as a whole; and the Jew will again find his place in the world and his language will be more understood than it is today. But in order to welcome the emergence of the new metaphysical cycle we must have you in Pavlograd and you must have me in Bobruisk, and there must be hundreds of others like us in other places. That is your task."

This Dostoievskian *midrash* might well be viewed as a parable on the situation of the Church and Synagogue in the twentieth century. Without subscribing to the conclusions of the Rabbi of Bobruisk, nor to his overly simplified and apocalyptic views on "the cycles of history," I cite this episode because it is suggestive, symbolically and metaphorically, of these three larger themes with which I should like to deal in this paper:

1) The existential situation of the Church and Synagogue at this moment in history, and some implications of the present condition for social action.

2) Some of the theological and historical factors that have formed the relations of the Church and Synagogue with the social order.

3) The challenges, the dilemma, and the possibilities in social action for the religious communities.

The Existential Situation

Any informed observer of the social-action arena in the United States and abroad, but especially in the United States, over the past two decades may confidently assert that a virtual revolution has taken place within the religious communities—within them as well as between them. The impressive record that Father John S. Cronin[1] documents of the accomplishments in such social-action areas as race relations, anti-poverty campaign, civil liberties, and the pursuit of peace (with some qualifications) is a decisive testimony to this growth of collective social consciousness and witness on the part of denominations, singly and cooperatively. More than one Congressman and civil-rights leader has publicly testified that the collective action of the Catholic, Protestant, Orthodox, and Jewish leadership was a crucial factor in passage of the 1964 Civil Rights Act.

Nevertheless, the term "revolution" should not be used unqualifiedly. In the face of the glaring moral corruptions and social injustices that pockmark our society; in the wake of the even more overwhelming problems of potential nuclear holocaust and of poverty, disease, and illiteracy that afflict most of that two-thirds of the human family so callously called "underdeveloped"; in confronting the fantastic challenges of the "triple revolution" of cybernation, weaponry, and human rights, it is evident that the Kingdom of God is far from being realized and that a posture of (*cf.* "The Church, The Synagogue, and the World," Father Cronin's contribution to this Colloquy) denominational or interreligious triumphalism is unwarranted, and, worse yet, dangerous because it creates an illusion of achievement which is the greatest enemy of growth and development, the fruits of realism.

In point of fact, the social action enterprises of the churches and synagogues cannot be adequately comprehended apart from a recognition of the transcendant reality of this time; that is, the contradictory existential situation in which the West, and in particular, the Western religious communities find themselves.

The ultimate contradiction, quite obviously, is that posed for the entire human family by the nuclear age itself. The science and technology which hold out the possibility for the first time in man's recorded history of banishing the scourges of poverty, disease and ignorance, are at the same time a Pandora's box of apocalyptic terror that enables modern man to "overkill" himself at least 125 times!

In the middle of the eleventh century the Catholic Church was in a position to enforce a "Truce of God" which greatly restricted the time when it was permissible to carry on warfare. By means of the Truce of God, the Church prohibited warfare between contending parties from Wednesday evening to Monday morning of each week, and during the period of Church festivals. Thus, there were at least theoretically only eighty days for fighting in each year, never extending over more than three consecutive days. The difference between the unitary, feudal society of the Middle Ages in which the Church held effective political power and the relative impotence today of all the churches combined to affect, for example, the decisions for the prevention of the proliferation of nuclear bombs is too obvious to require comment. Nevertheless, this paramount "social action" question must be confronted with a new seriousness as to whether the prophetic, moral, and spiritual resources of the world's major religions cannot be asserted at this critical hour to help achieve a twentieth-century "Truce of God" before the world destroys itself in a nuclear-missile holocaust, and, almost tragi-comically, either through mechanical error or human miscalculation.

There are other decisive factors which have undergirded the renewal and reform of religious communities, and foremost among them has been the recognition on the parts of Pope John of blessed memory, Pope Paul, and other Catholic, Protestant, Orthodox, and Jewish leaders of the radically altered new realities which confront all Western religions, and the West itself. (There is substantial evidence that certain forms of *aggiornamento* are taking place among the major Oriental religions—Islam, Buddhism, Hinduism—but this paper is confined primarily to a survey of the Church and Synagogue of the Occident.)

For the first time since the emergence of Christianity in the fourth century as an established, organized religious community, Christians—and allied with them Jews and all others who count themselves as citizens of the West—find themselves at one and the same time as a minority and a majority. Out of the 3.3 billion people who inhabit our planet today, less than one billion are

Christians and Jews. Every year 22 million non-whites, non-Christians, non-Jews are born into the world as contrasted with eight million who are born Christian or Jewish. The annual population growth rate in Asia, for example, is 2.6 per cent, as compared with 1.6 per cent in the United States, and 0.7 per cent in northern and western Europe. Roman Catholics today number some 18 per cent of the total world population, and population projections indicate that by the year 2,000, the world Catholic community will number 11 to 12 per cent of the 6 billion inhabitants of the earth. In light of such statistics, Father Karl Rahner's insistence on the "Diaspora" situation of Christians takes on concrete human meaning and is not just a charming Biblical metaphor to be taken abstractly (it takes on meaning for Jews, too, but apparently Jews are veterans of the Exile and suffer less trauma, having come to grips with the condition some time ago at Babylon).

The "diaspora" situation of Christianity (and Judaism) is profoundly shaped by other forces as well. The emergence of communism as a global, pseudo-Messianic religion with an effective missionary enterprise and a determined anti-theistic ideological program represents the most powerful and unprecedented opponent in the 1,900-year human experience of Christianity. Since the end of World War II, fourteen formerly "Catholic" countries have become Communist satellites and more than 100 million Christians are now behind the Iron Curtain. The largest Communist parties in the world, outside of the Iron Curtain, are found in predominantly "Catholic" countries, namely, France and Italy. The Communist inroads in Cuba and the considerable hold of communism in other parts of Central and Latin America are sources of profound anxiety to the West. None of the dominant nations in the world today are "Catholic" as contrasted with the pre-World War II situation when Catholicism was a major political force in France, Italy, and the Balkans, and in Europe generally—and Europe was the major force in the world.[2]

Another dimension of these "new realities" is the rise of nationalisms in Africa and Asia. In many of these countries, Christianity is regarded as the "white man's religion," the handmaiden of Western imperialism and colonialism. (In many ways Jews are involved in Asia and Africa through the activities of the State of Israel which has been carrying on significant programs in technical assistance. To some extent, the Israelis have also been looked upon as agents of the "Western-imperialist-colonialist" world). The tragic massacres of missionaries in the Congo and Angola reveal the depths of the hostility of the African toward peoples of the West, even if the European was at one time considered a Christian benefactor. The harassment and banishment of Christian missionaries in the Sudan is only one of the more recent of a long series of acts in many parts of Asia and Africa that have reduced Christians to tolerated minorities.

According to the Methodist publication, the *Christian Advocate,* the establishment of Islam as the official religion of Malaysia resulted in a ban on religious teaching by missionaries and on the use of the radio for evangelical purposes. In Nepal, Methodist missionaries were allowed to open a hospital on the promise that they would not evangelize and that the government could take over the equipment in five years if it so desired. In Ceylon, the government has nationalized 2,500 Catholic and Protestant schools which served 140,000 students. In the United Arab Republic, a Christian school is permitted to stay open on the condition that a Moslem teacher be allowed to come into the classroom and explain the Koran.

Accompanying the rise of nationalism is the resurgence of the Oriental religions, once regarded as moribund. Of the 242 million Africans, for example, there are 35 million Christians (Roman Catholics number 23 million; 7 million are Protestants; 5 million are Eastern Orthodox; of the remaining Africans, 160 million are classified as animists, and 89 million are Moslems). Islam, which numbers some 430 million adherents in the world, has the most aggressive missionary outreach in Black Africa. Islam converts seven Africans for every one African converted either to Catholicism or Protestantism. Every embassy of the United Arab Republic in Africa has an "attaché" for Islamic affairs—a euphemism for a Moslem missionary. Similarly, Buddhism (153 million adherents), Hinduism (335 million), and Confucianism (300 million) have been undergoing a renaissance, are rapidly developing a political sophistication which reflects itself in effective social organization (the new Buddhist quasi-political structures in Viet-Nam are a powerful example), and have become increasingly competitive with Western Christianity.

A statement on "the Pope's Plan for Latin America" which appeared in *The Catholic World,* contained a report by CELAM, the Episcopal Conference of Latin America, which discusses frankly the situation of some 200 million souls there.[3] This report says that it is not unusual to find cases where 60 or 70 per cent of the couples are without religious marriages. Some, said to be Catholics, have not even been baptized. There is one priest for every 5,000 people compared to one for every 700-800 in the United States. In a recent survey in Chile, 60 per cent of the men favored abortion. The Latin American population is increasing faster than that of any other continent in the world. There is not a single government in Latin America that is not threatened by economic upheaval and political instability—fertile grounds for the marauding of the Castroites and Communists, on the left, and for the Peronists and fascists (such as the Tacuara movement in Argentina, in alliance with the thick nest of Nazi emigrés and the Arab League), on the right.

The "contradictory" aspect of the existential situation, to which I earlier referred, grows out of the fact that at the moment when Christians and Jews are becoming collectively a "minority" living in the "diaspora," they are at the same time experiencing an unprecedented growth and strength as a "majority" in the United States. The churches and synagogues in America, and their auxiliary bodies, today have the highest rate of growth, the highest levels of per-capita contributions, the most extensive building programs, the highest rate of attendance at religious services and of enrollment of children in religious schools, the most carefully developed social welfare programs for youth and the aged—the highest in comparison to their growth in the past and in contrast to churches and synagogues anywhere else in the world. This growth has taken place—not incidentally—in a free, voluntary, pluralistic society, and not in a confessional Church-State arrangement. But this very growth and this very strength have given many Christians and Jews—and other Americans—a "buffered" vision of the world at large. The description of the American state of mind by Bishop Fulton J. Sheen is tragically accurate: "Americans live in a sumptuous palace in the midst of a vast slum."

The problems of religious liberty, freedom of conscience, the question of proselytization or witnessing, freedom of movement, the relationship of Church to State, racial and religious discrimination—once regarded as the preoccupation of Westerners and Christians in the internal relationships between Catholics and Protestants, on the one hand, and Christians and Jews on the other—have now been catapulted onto the world scene. In an age in which there is instantaneous global communication, rapid transportation and mobility, it is no longer possible either to "keep under wraps" for long or to withhold from the judgment of a restive and interdependent human family any acts or attitudes which reflect contempt for the human person or which deny him his "natural rights."

An attack on a Negro in Birmingham today will tomorrow be condemned editorially in a Ghana newspaper. The harrassment of Christian missionaries in Jerusalem will be protested at once on the front pages of Christian newspapers and the general press in various parts of the world (I write here in defense of the rights of responsible missionaries, not the "rice missionaries" who deceive children and exploit the desperate poverty and confusion of newly-arrived Jewish immigrants from Arab countries). The denial of the religious rights of a Protestant or Jew in Spain or in Colombia will become the subject of a consultation within hours in New York or Geneva. The banishment of priests and nuns from Indonesia results in immediate protests from far-flung parts of the world.

From the foregoing I would here summarize three conclusions:

1. A world, teetering on the brink of nuclear destruction, can little afford the perpetuation of an atmosphere of hatred, division, and suspicion.

2. The human society, both East and West, threatened by moral decay and materialism, needs every human and spiritual resource to meet the overwhelming needs and challenges of our age. Repressive, mutually antagonistic religious, racial, and ethnic group conflicts will paralyze mankind in its effort to meet the challenges of survival. The monopolies and hegemonies of the past must give way to a global pluralism in which, in the words of Pope John's *Pacem in Terris,* "the universal common good, that is, the common good of the entire human family" is promoted.

3.Religion itself will be irrelevant if it continues to perpetuate the glaring contradiction between preaching high moral principles of love, sympathy and charity, and allowing the undisciplined practice of the opposite in the forms of race prejudice, anti-Semitism, anti-Catholicism, anti-Protestantism, and other ethnocentric blasphemies.

Theological and Historical Factors

"Are the churches (and synagogues) exerting even as much as 10 per cent of the influence which they could—or should—be exerting in the fields of peace and social justice? Are they tooled for such a task by intention, declaration, organization, program, finance, staff?"

E. Raymond Wilson of the Friends Committee on National Legislation posed this question in his article, "Are We Serious about Social Action?" (*Christian Century*, Feb. 10, 1965). On the basis of a sampling of Protestant denominational social action, Wilson comes to several striking and chastening conclusions (which, I would argue, are virtually applicable without much qualification to that of the Catholic and Jewish communities as well):

First, "Through the past two decades there has been considerable growth in church social action programs at national, state, and local levels, but that growth has been slight in comparison with the many opportunities available for effective action." For example, Mr. Wilson writes, "What is needed now is enlightened and continued support, backed by testimony that is competent, relevant and effectively presented, of such objectives as wider development of United Nations operations; more far-reaching steps toward disarmament: enlarged but more discriminating mutual aid and technical assistance projects to overcome world hunger, ignorance, disease and poverty; and expansion of programs for population control. Such issues get no appreciable supporting mail from churchmen, in contrast to the stream of letters inspired by the isolationists, the 'fright peddlers' and others who would have our national concern limited to the part of the human race labeled 'American' . . ." He adds that in the area of negotiations dealing with the ending of the spiraling arms race, "it is disheartening that, so far as I know, no religious organization has a full-time staff person dealing with disarmament problems."

Secondly, "There is with all of us a temptation to confuse resolutions and pronouncements with social action. Such statements do serve to register a certain degree of concensus, but they are not self-executing."

Thirdly, an appraisal committee of the National Council of Churches' Division of Christian Life and Work has reported that "of the council's 31 constituent communions only ten have agencies with one or more full-time staff members engaged in social education and action, while six others have voluntary commissions or committees to work in the field. In other words, only one-third of the member churches have assigned full-time staff members to the specific task of supplying local congregations with pertinent information and helping them engage in social action endeavors."

Mr. Wilson adds that "a survey of the denominations (other than the historic peace churches) which are particularly active in social action indicates that the proportion of their central funds devoted to support of their departments in that field varies from ½ to 4 per cent, and that average expenditures per member vary from four to 15 cents. [Here he indicates that these figures do not take into account the funds expended on health, welfare, and home-missions work at home or on relief and service to refugees abroad.] How can we hope to achieve such goals as disarmament, world peace, or racial justice when the average church member's annual sacrifice to keep his denomination at work in those areas on the national level is no greater than his expenditure for one candy bar, one soft drink?"

How does one explain such relatively limited action on social issues? Mr. Wilson seeks to offer several reasons. One is financial: "yet throughout the nation expensive new buildings are being constructed by congregations whose social budgets are starved for funds or are nonexistent". Another is the fact that "conservative boards and ecclesiastical hierarchies" are frequently unwilling to approve new endeavors that compete for funds and attention with entrenched programs." A third reason which Mr. Wilson offers is the "theological," and he explains it in these words: "For far too many, Christian religion is merely a personal matter having no relation to the unsolved problems of national and international life. If a wider horizon exists, it is likely to be confined to the foreign mission enterprise; if ethical concerns intrude, they are often limited to the effect on the public of smoking, gambling and drinking." Related to that, he adds, is the view that "the church shouldn't 'get into politics.' Lobbying is something nice people don't do . . . The church should stay out of controversy."

Schleiermacher has written that "underlying every philosophy is a conviction." I would submit that the reverse is also true: "underlying every conviction is a philosophy." At the very heart of the question of the relation of the Church and Synagogue to social action is the theological and philosophical issue of the orientation of the religious traditions to the world. A good deal of the behavior of the religious communities in response to contemporary social challenges can be understood primarily in light of theological positions whose origins stem back to the foundations of the faith communities.

In his perceptive study, *Christ and Culture* (1952), H. Richard Niebuhr set forth the five main ways in which Christians have understood the relationship between the Church and the world: Christ against culture (e.g., Tertullian); Christ of culture (e.g., Locke, Ritschl, Barton); Christ above culture (e.g., Thomas Aquinas); Christ and culture in paradox (e.g., Luther); and Christ the transformer of culture (e.g., the "conversionism" of F. D. Maurice).

Thus, four of these historic formulae involve a separation of religion from the public domain—if not a separation, then certainly a primary emphasis on personal salvation or otherworldly concerns. The views of St. Augustine are most frequently cited as the proof texts of the classic Christian view that the ideal world is always above and not at the end of human history.

"Two loves," says St. Augustine in *De Civitate Dei*, "have made two cities, love of self unto contempt of God, the Earthly City; love of God unto contempt of self, the Heavenly City," the City of God. The *Civitas Dei* is a "mystical society" of all the elect, past, present and future. The *Civitas Terrena*, the Earthly City, is identical neither with the earthly State, nor with any particular earthly State such as the Roman Empire, nor with any merely human society; it too is a "mystical society," that of the impious, the damned.

In an essay on "Aspects of Medieval Thought on Church and State," Gerhart B. Ladner (*The Image of Man*) writes: "St. Augustine's concept of the City of God is a specifically Christian ideal of community life . . . It is only natural that notions of such perfection as that of the City of God or of the Church itself which in one of its aspects is 'the only human society engaged in building the City of God' tended to depreciate the state as conceived by pre-Christian antiquity. St. Augustine is indifferent towards the state as community and territory." Ladner adds that Augustine's views were "rather generally held in the patristic period and was an important factor in the development of early medieval political theory."

An eminent Protestant church historian, A. C. McGiffert, in his introduction to *Protestant Thought Before Kant*, traces mainstream Christian ideas about human nature and temporal society back to the teachings of St. Paul.

The theological system of the Middle Ages was in its controlling principles as old as the Apostle Paul. He was led by his own experience to draw a sharp distinction between the fleshly man, who is essentially corrupt, and the spiritual man, who is essentially holy. The one is natural, the other supernatural. The one is doomed to destruction; the other is an heir of eternal life. The spiritual man does not come from the natural by a process of development and growth, but is a new creature born directly from above. Wherever Paul may have got the suggestion which led him to interpret his experience in this way, his low estimate of man and his contrast between flesh and spirit revealed the ultimate influence of oriental dualism which was profoundly affecting the Hellenistic world of the day. A sense of moral evil, a conviction of human corruption and helplessness, and a recognition of the worthlessness of the present world were becoming more and more common, and men everywhere were looking for aid and comfort to supernatural powers of one kind or another. The later Platonism, from which the theological thinking of the great fathers chiefly drew its sustenance, was completely under the sway of this spirit.

With the traditional view of human nature was correlated the notion of the present world as evil, sharing in the curse of man and doomed to destruction as he is. To escape from it was the one great aim of the serious-minded man. Salvation meant not the salvation of the world itself, its transformation into something better and holier, but release from it in order to enjoy the blessedness of another world altogether. The dominant spirit was that of other-worldliness. To be a Christian meant to belong to another sphere than this, to have one's interest set on higher things, to live in the future, and to eschew the pleasures and enjoyments of the present. Asceticism was the Christian ideal of life.

The practical implication of this theological world view, according to McGiffert, was that "social service on a large scale was postponed to modern times." It was not a mere accident that this was so, he explains; "rather, it was because of an altogether different ideal, and an altogether different estimate of the present world."

The emergence of Protestantism, particularly in a certain tradition of Martin Luther's teaching, it would seem, represented a radical break with this line of Pauline and Catholic teaching. Luther's conception of salvation as being wholly a matter of divine forgiveness (man is saved by faith and not by works, as developed in *The Liberty of the Christian Man*) led to the belief that the Christian is free from the necessity of earning his salvation by engaging in particular religious practices and performing works of special merit; this, in turn, also meant the sacredness of all callings, even the most secular and the most humble, and the possibility of serving God in worldly profession, business and trade as truly as in monastery and priesthood.

It looks like a great thing when a monk renounces everything and goes into a cloister, carries on a life of asceticism, fasts, watches, prays, etc. . . . On the other hand, it looks like a small thing when a maid cooks and cleans and does other housework. But because God's command is there, even such a small work must be praised as a service of God far surpassing the holiness and asceticism of all monks and nuns. For here there is no command of God. But there God's command is fulfilled, that one should honor father and mother and help in the care of the home (*Luther's Primary Works*, V, p. 100, as quoted by McGiffert).

But Luther, a complicated man, often contradicted himself, and his views on the relation of salvation to moral and ethical responsibility were no exception. The Protestant historian, McGiffert, quotes Luther's contradiction as it appeared in his essay, *Against Latomus*: "As wrath is a greater evil than the corruption of sin, so grace is a greater good than the perfect righteousness which we have said comes from faith. For there is no one who would not prefer (if this could be) to be without perfect righteousness than without the grace of God."

McGiffert observes:

It was a religious and not an ethical motive which controlled him; not to attain moral purity, but to be on good terms with God was the supreme need of his being. To claim that the Protestant Reformation was due primarily to ethical considerations, and was the result of dissatisfaction with the moral state of the world, and of the desire to raise the moral tone of society, is nothing less than a travesty upon the facts.[4]

John Calvin, the great formulator of the Reformed theology whose *Institutes of the Christian Religion* (1536) became "the theological textbook of all Western Protestantism," was even more rigorous than Luther in conceiving of man in terms of his "corruption and depravity" as a correlative of his doctrine of unconditional predestination and God's omnipotent will. As Calvin says in his *Institutes* (Book III. chap. ix.), "With whatever kind of tribulation we may be afflicted, we should always keep this end in view, to habituate ourselves to a contempt of the present life that we may thereby be excited to meditation on that which is to come" (§1). "There is no medium between these two extremes, either the earth must become vile in our estimation, or it must retain our immoderate love. Wherefore if we have any concern about eternity, we must use our most diligent efforts to extricate ourselves from these fetters" (§2).

Protestant scholasticism as expressed in the *Formula of Concord* (1580), which was widely adopted as the official doctrinal standard of the Lutheran churches, served to stereotype this view of human nature and the negative relation of religion to life. As in all scholasticism, according to McGiffert, the importance of a particular doctrine came to depend upon its place in the closed system rather than upon its practical relation to life.

In response to the rigidities of scholasticism, the emphasis upon formal orthodoxy, the absorption of leading churchmen in theological controversies, and also in reaction to the depressed religious and moral life that ensued on the heels of the Thirty Years' War (1618–48), there emerged in Germany under the advocacy of Philip Jacob Spener (1633–1705) the Pietist movement that became a dominant force in German religious life down to the eighteenth century, even influencing the reconstruction of theology at the beginning of the nineteenth century. Both in his organization of Bible-reading groups, commonly known as *collegia pietatis,* and in his introduction to the mystical work, *Pia Desideria,* Spener emphasized the practical nature of Christianity, which consists not in the knowledge, but in the conduct, and particularly in the exercise of mutual love and service. Spener, an orthodox Lutheran, insisted that personal piety, the bent of the heart and life, the feelings and will at the expense of the intellect, personal faith, and growth in Christian perfection were more important than doctrinal soundness.

Spener interpreted Christian conduct in other-worldly terms. His ideal was not, as with Luther, victory over the world, but es-

cape from it. Piety was to show itself in devotion to spiritual and
supernal things, and in the transfer of affection and interest from
this world to another. As McGiffert profiles the movement:

> The pietism of Spener and his followers was essentially medieval in
> its estimate of man and the world. Distrust of human nature and de-
> spair of the salvability of society were both characteristic of it. Salva-
> tion meant escape from an evil world for a few elect souls who banded
> together for spiritual communion and mutual edification, and these
> elect souls were not the Christian Church but a small circle within the
> larger body . . .
> The vitalizing of Christian piety, the breaking of scholasticism's con-
> trol, the recognition of religious experience as the chief basis of
> theology, the emphasis of the will instead of the intellect in religion,
> the prominence given to the emotions, above all the individualism given
> to the whole movement and its hostility to ecclesiasticism, sacramen-
> tarianism, and sacerdotalism, meant much for days to come. Pietism
> was one of the forces which brought the modern age in the religious
> life of Germany.

Without succumbing to the temptation of employing history as
the "imperialism of the present," one can understand the warrant
which justified Franklin Littell, in his examination of the moral
collapse of the Lutheran churches under Nazism, to conclude that
"a sentimental and degenerate personal piety pervaded the established churches of Europe, secure in the stagnant swamp of
culture-religion."

German pietism, in turn, influenced English Evangelicalism
through the impact of the Moravians on John Wesley (1738),
founder of British Methodism. Calvinist and Arminian evangelicalism, through Wesley communions and the preaching of
Wesley's associate, George Whitefield, influenced the New England theology of America, especially through the revivalist
activity of Jonathan Edwards. Like the German pietists, the
Evangelicals were ascetic in their tendency. Their ideal was to

live with heart set constantly upon the future, and natural human
interest in the present world was condemned as irreligious.
"Friendship with the world," Wesley said, "is spiritual adultery."
But, as church historian McGiffert points out (p. 168):

The Evangelicals were not as consistent and thoroughgoing as their
medieval prototypes; they did not advocate retirement from the world
and seclusion in a monastery. But they denounced many of the ordinary pursuits and pleasures of society, commonly looked upon as indifferent matters, and insisted that they ought to be eschewed by the
Christian. Card-playing, dancing, gaming, horse-racing, theatre-going,
elaborate dressing, and frivolity of all kinds came in for most vigorous
condemnation. To be a Christian very commonly meant above all to
turn one's back upon such employments. Thus there grew up an
externality of religion and an artificiality of practice even more complete than anything witnessed in medieval Catholicism.[5]

Both in England and in the United States (in the former under
the impact of the industrial revolution and in the latter under the
force of pressures exerted by a frontier society) evangelicals and
revivalists did not overlook responsibility for the welfare of one's
fellows. Love and service were an important part of Christian
virtue, and the evangelicals gave themselves to humanitarian and
social labor on a large scale and with great effectiveness. It meant
much for the future that not rationalists, and deists, and unbelievers alone were fired with a growing enthusiasm for humanity,
but that the great representatives of a revived Christianity shared
the same spirit.[6]

This survey of some of the theological factors which have
helped shape the contemporary stance of religious communities
toward the social order has concentrated mainly thus far on the
Hellenic, that is, Platonic, dualistic element in Christian tradition.
But there has been another formative influence at work, namely,
the Hebraic, which requires comment.

In an essay entitled, "The Present Heritage of the Long Encounter between Christian Faith and Western Civilization,"[7] Reinhold Niebuhr asserts that "the civilization of Europe has been created by a culture in which the Christian faith has been a chief component." Among the "distinctive qualities" which he regards as "possible ultimate causes of unique aspects of European culture," Prof. Niebuhr cites three which have their origins in Jewish religious thought and tradition:

1) The hazardous affirmation that history is meaningful and the temporal process is not merely a corruption of the eternal.

2) The emphasis on the value and dignity of the life of the individual and the equally important affirmation that the unique freedom of the individual is the source of evil as well as of virtue. [Niebuhr cites Pascal's phrase of "the grandeur and misery of man" as affirming Augustinian realism as reflected in the emphasis that "the freedom of the self is the root of both the creative and the destructive possibilities of human action."]

3) The attitude toward the whole temporal process, which is not regarded as divine (as in systems of cosmic pantheism), or as evil or illusory because it is not divine (as in systems of acosmic pantheism). The Hebraic component of Western culture contributed this sober attitude toward the temporal and the natural, making it possible for Western man to regard nature, in Santayana's phrase, as "man's stamping ground and system of opportunities."

In *Moral Man and Immoral Society* Niebuhr elaborates his view:

It was the peculiar genius of Jewish religious thought that it conceived the millenium in this-worldly terms . . . Whenever religion concerns itself with the problems of society, it always give birth to some kind of millennial hope, from the perspective of which present social realities are convicted of inadequacy, and courage is maintained to continue in the effort to redeem society of injustice. The courage is needed, for the task of building a just society seems always to be a hopeless one when only realities and immediate possibilities are envisaged.

In his Harvard essay, Niebuhr observes that the Jewish idea of the Messiah, "the hope in a future fulfillment of history in which, under a Messianic king, power and virtue would be perfectly coordinated, was the most potent . . . of the various solutions to the problems of historical meaninglessness." He adds, however, that "the radical transformation by New Testament faith of Old Testament messianism was one of the two greatest revisions of the Hebraic faith (the other being the emphasis on grace, rather than law, as a saving power). The revision was expressed in viewing the Messianic fulfillment in the crucified Christ, rather than in the triumphant Messiah," and this view assumed "a perennial variance, even contradiction, between historical achievements and the divine."

But this radical revision, Niebuhr observes, did not completely suppress the original messianic or eschatological vision. The early church was dominated by the imminent Parousia of the promised triumphant Messiah, at the price, says Niebuhr, of the lack of a responsible attitude toward all the proximate solutions of the communal problems of a sinful world. He continues: "An historical religion must have the tension supplied by an eschatological vision. But the vision must not be so pure or so determined as to destroy responsibility for proximate goals—a fact which Karl Barth evidently does not understand."

From the point of view of Jewish concerns about the social order, this tendency of Christian thought toward a "neutralism" or irresponsibility for historic tasks in this world has been one of the fundamental departures from the prophetic view, and has stood in radical contrast to a mainline emphasis in Judaism. In the judgment of Rabbi Abraham Joshua Heschel, there has been a tendency on the part of Christian theologians to affirm mystery at the expense of history, but Christianity is both proclamation and event.

It may be worthwhile to recall that the characteristic Jewish experience of God is the awareness of His presence in human events. Every aspect of the Jewish tradition is pervaded by the memory of His redemptive act in the exodus from Egypt. Almost the whole of the religious calendar is an act of recalling the past experience of the Jewish people as a record of God's relationship to it. The emphasis of Jewish faith is therefore neither on metaphysical speculation nor on dogma, but on human action. Life is the arena of moral choice, and man can choose the good. He can make himself worse than the beast or he can ascend to but little lower than the angels. Every man plays his role, for good or ill, in the redemptive history of mankind, for man is God's partner in the work of creation. In *imitatio Dei*, the Jew is obligated to seek justice and pursue it, to care for the widow and orphan, and the stranger at the gate.

This is not to say that rabbinic Judaism denies dualism altogether. The concept of the *yetzer hara* (the evil inclination) in constant tension with the *yetzer tov* (the good inclination in man's nature), of Kodesh (holiness) and of *chol* (this-worldliness) are intimations of a recognition of the *homo duplex*. But it is characteristic of rabbinic thought that these are *experienced* as "value-concepts" by the individual alone or in community, rather than "congealed in a static, hierarchical system of thought."[8]

The growth of involvement in social action on the part of the Christian community has, indeed, been a radical response to external forces of the twentieth century, such as those elaborated earlier in this chapter: population explosion, anxieties of the nuclear space age, communism, emerging new nations, resurgent Oriental religions, secularism, and pluralism. But it owes whatever deeper meaning it possesses to interior forces at work in the life of Christianity and Christendom, namely, the Biblical, liturgical and theological renewals. In its concerted effort to recover the Hebrew mode of thought by restoring the Scriptures to a more central place in study and worship (see Father Roland Murphy's chapter in this volume), the Church has moved decisively to overcome the bifurcating and "abstractifying" of life that was one of the by-products of Scholasticism.

The emphasis in Vatican Council II's schema on *"De Ecclesia"* (On the Nature of the Church) which speaks of the Catholic Church ("while on earth it journeys in a foreign land away from the Lord . . . like an exile") and its conception of itself as "the people of God" related providentially to "Israel according to the flesh" finds resonance in the non-Catholic ear.

Especially compelling have been the declarations of several Council Fathers at the Ecumenical Council during the third session as they discussed Schema 13, "The Church and the Modern World." Bishop Remi Joseph De Roo of Victoria, British Columbia, said, "Christians achieve their total vocation when they engage themselves in the structures of the world, share in its struggles and commune with the inner dynamism of humanity. A Christian must immerse himself in the world. He dare not consider himself as foreign to or above the world, belonging to a church which condescendingly imparts gifts reserved to her by God alone."

The late Cardinal Meyer of blessed memory, whom I was privileged to know both in connection with my work as program chairman of the National Conference on Religion and Race as well as in Rome during the third Council session in September, 1964, in commenting on Schema 13, said that he missed in the draft "a sound theological basis for joyful acceptance of the world and a correction of the false dualism which would separate soul and body, the Church from the world, spirit from matter." In essence, said Cardinal Meyer, all creation goes together. Men must realize that their daily work is a part of the plan of salvation. The Redemption was total. It was not a snatching of man's blithe spirit from the weight of his body, nor did it imply a hopeless break between the world of the spirit and world of flesh, matter and physical energy. In the divine economy, redemption meant much more than the salvation of souls; it meant also the resurrection of bodies and indeed the resurrection of the universe itself.

That this reorientation of the Church toward the world and its values is profound, more than a matter of perfunctory or isolated ecclesiastical statements, is reflected in a survey of current Catholic and Protestant theological thought contained in an article by Thomas E. Clark, S.J. (*America,* May 29, 1965), whose subtitle significantly is: "Christian secularity finds positive values outside the institutional Church." Father Clark identified the two movements of modern Christian thought, *immanence* and *secularity,* as today "coming into vital confrontation in our effort to adopt a new Christian posture before the world and its values."

Citing the contributions of such Catholic thinkers as Maurice Blondel, de Lubac, Von Balthasar, Karl Rahner, Jacques Maritain, Père Chenu, E. Schillebeeckx, and John Courtney Murray, as well as of such Protestant thinkers as Dietrich Bonhoffer, John Robinson, Paul Van Buren, and Harvey Cox, Father Clark stresses that "for over a half century now . . . the insistence has been on the *unity* rather than on the distinction of natural and supernatural orders, the immanence of the Christian in the human (rather than on its transcendence of the human)." In a revelatory exploration of the meaning of "secularity" for modern Christianity, Father Clark makes many assertions that will startle conventional ears, but what he affirms has a greater ring of relevance than has been heard for a very, very long time from religious quarters:

Christian secularity excludes instrumentalization. The goodness of the creature (and not merely its non-evilness), of the world, of time and temporal institutions, is a central conviction of Christian secularity. Any *purely* instrumental approach to the world—that is any attitude that would see in it merely a tool for Christian evangelization, that would neglect its innate values, its own immanent dynamisms and finalities—is incompatible with Christian secularity. The world is to be taken seriously. As Father Robert Johann has put it: "Whatever ultimate meaning life may have . . . life is a call to share in the world's making."

Why do I, and probably a great many other Jews, welcome this profound reorientation in Christianity and Christians?

First—and I must ask you to indulge me here if this smacks of Jewish triumphalism, but you will grant that two millenia of "grandeur and misery" in the diaspora is a long time to wait—the very Jewishness of Christendom's posture today seems to confirm the mission of the Jews to serve as "a light unto the nations." Perhaps all our witnessing across the millenia to the Covenant and to the mandates of the Prophets is getting through after all. More seriously, it helps make sense and give reality to the teachings of Maimonides and other Jewish sages who regarded Christians (and Moslems) as the missionary outreach of Judaism, charged by Providence to bring the idea of God and of obedience to His word to the heathen of the world.

Secondly, in light of their history, Jews have a special stake in a peaceful social order, in concretizing justice and freedom. The Catholic Church, and many Protestant bodies, have become major agencies of social reform. As citizens of the Western world, Jews see themselves increasingly as allies with their Catholic (and Protestant) neighbors in social reconstruction.

Thirdly, involvement in social action is providing Jews and Judaism with new opportunities of service beyond their own group. This is a test of our Prophetic universalism. Heretofore, Jews have been preoccupied with helping to defeat the Nazis and Fascists, rescuing refugees, building and securing the State of Israel, combatting anti-Semitism (which still preoccupies our community for we are deeply concerned about anti-Semitic discrimination in Soviet Russia and in parts of Latin America). As these problems have diminished, Jews have become increasingly free to make contributions to the resolution of problems that are not specifically Jewish—problems such as are related to race relations, the war against poverty, and international affairs. In this sense, Rabbi Louis Finkelstein has formulated this challenge: "Our ancient teachers were right in their admonition that there is a great contribution to be made only by those without power, who are few in number, always a minority, uncertain of their ability to meet alone the challenges of the world . . . We are a pledge to remind the world of its true goal."

Religion and Society; Dilemma and Possibilities

The context in which the present shape of social action is being forged is that of a voluntaristic society within which the Federal Government is assuming ever-increasing initiatives and responsibilities in the achievement of social-welfare purposes. Prescinding from the debate over whether this is good or bad for America, it is one of the overarching facts of the life in our nation that the Government, in building the "Great Society," is calling upon voluntary agencies (conceived as large blocs of influence over substantial constituencies) in order to help advance the goals of health, education, welfare, civil and human rights. Religion, along with labor, business, farm, and education, is unblinkingly conceived of as another of the major blocs. This development has obvious advantages for "religion," for it means that religious institutions are taken into serious account in the affairs of our nation. At the same time, this development brings the Church and Synagogue face to face with acute predicaments.

The first dilemma centers on bureaucracy.[9] In an age of bureaucracies, can a group of "amateurs," joined in small units, still be heard? If the answer is no, the trend toward bureaucratization of the Church and Synagogue would seem to be justified. But when these institutions become just one more bureaucracy, will they say anything worth hearing? Bureaucracy can threaten religion with impersonalism, and when the Church and Synagogue fall victims to impersonalism, the vitality of society and one of the chief sources of a nation's moral strength is affected.

The second dilemma involves the use of power by religious groups. The individual is guided by the higher ethics of selflessness in personal relations; but social cooperation requires coercion. Social organization is structured power, for, as Reinhold Niebuhr has pointed out, "only a romanticist of purest water could maintain that the national group ever arrives at a 'common mind' or 'general will' without the use of force or the threat of force." However, "power is poison," as Henry Adams has said—a poison which blinds the eyes of moral insight and lames the will of moral purposes. The Church and Synagogue can foreswear all use of power in order to remain true to a Biblical and prophetic imperative. But this would render their efforts ineffectual in the social order and may contribute to anarchy or to a moral order based on naked power. (Most forms of social order are better than anarchy, and an order only partly imbued with morality is better than one of no morality at all.) Or the Church and Synagogue can seek power for the sake of the prophetic imperative which demands realization; however, they must recognize the real possibility of becoming compromised in the use of that power. Religious motivation is no protection against such compromise. Experience shows, in fact, that power, wielded in the name of God, is subject to special perversions, one of the most destructive of which is the fanaticism "occasioned by attributing ultimate validity to historically relative norms, purposes, and ends." The only palliative for either religious fanaticism or the secular fanaticism of political religions, as Niebuhr points out in his Harvard essay, "is an open society, as it has developed in the last three centuries, which grants no immunity from criticism or review to any authority proclaiming the truth, whether in the political, the religious, or the scientific realm."

This discussion raises a number of basic questions for which there are no easy answers and which have not yet been adequately examined by Church and Synagogue leaders. For example, what are the theological justifications for the involvement of the *corporate* Church and Synagogue in influencing the public order? And, as indicated above, in what ways are Church and Synagogue to exercise their power? Are the limitations that we would put on Church involvement a result of theological conviction or, rather, of prudential judgment based on certain convictions concerning the nature of the democratic process?

To be specific, if Church and Synagogue leaders can lobby vigorously—literally buttonhole Congressmen—as they did with such effective strategy for the enactment of the Civil Rights bill, why should they not lobby also for a measure that would curb pornography? If Synagogue and other Jewish leaders can threaten congressmen with the loss of votes on an issue that affects the economic welfare of a Jewish Sabbath-observer or that impinges on the welfare of the State of Israel, is it wrong for a bishop to exercise the same threat on such issues as bus transportation for parochial school children or the revision of the divorce law?

What are the rightful areas and responsibilities of the State and Church, together and separately, in their effort to achieve and maintain standards of private and public morality? What is the particular role of the corporate Church and Synagogue— as against that of the individual clergyman and in contrast to that of the layman—as they seek to make religion a significant force in life? How can the Church and Synagogue wield their power and yet maintain respect for those of other faiths who differ? How, too, can they wield their power while maintaining respect for those within the faith community who differ with the Church or Synagogue on those political issues which contain spiritual or religious significance? Where do the political and moral meet? Where do they separate?

As one attempts to respond to what, to this writer, is the most crucial of these questions, namely, the exercise of corporate power by Church and Synagogue, I would submit that, on the one hand, those committed to the prophetic tradition cannot escape the responsibility of moralizing power; on the other hand, they must resist all temptations to make a bid for *direct* power. The religious groups, as I view it, should seek to make effective use of *indirect* methods of pressure, namely, exhortation and persuasion. Of all the steady contributions which religion makes to American life, its creating of a moral atmosphere and consciousness, within which social and political decisions are made, is more significant than that of supplying the basis for these decisions. It is more a policy of the Church and Synagogue indirectly shaping a whole pattern of national thinking than of supplying precise doctrines.

Religious institutions made their most significant contributions by remaining true to their vocations as judges of society, as centers of independent criticism insisting that the nation live up to its own ideals and general standards of morality. Churches and Synagogues that fail to rebuke people when they worship themselves or fall down before nationalistic idols are, by their own standards, guilty of betrayal. By following the example of those saints and sages who cried out against injustice, complacency, and spiritual torpor, religious spokesmen exercise liberty for the benefit of all. By keeping alive before the nation a sense of the Absolute as man's highest ethical aspiration (which eliminates partial perspectives) and a sense of the Divine as Benevolent Will by condemning selfish actions and desires, so that no position of power in the community remains unchecked, the Church and Synagogue contribute to justice and to rendering responsible the exercise of every kind of political power.

Toward working out such generalized positions as these in a concrete situation, Dr. Gibson Winter (*Christianity and Crisis,* May 31, 1965) gives a valuable illustration in his article, "The Churches and Community Organization." In a perceptive analysis of "the political character of community organization" whose purpose is to help the dehumanized and impoverished masses of the ghettos to "regain dignity and independence through self-determination," Dr. Winter raises the question of what "is the method of participation appropriate to the situation and to the nature of the Church." One of the conclusions suggested by Dr. Winter is that "the churches have a servant role to fulfill—not leading but encouraging community organization where possible. They also have a prophetic role to play—not letting community organizations settle for token reprisals but pushing on to a new political and cultural vision for metropolis."

At the same time, the nation has a right to expect religious groups, whatever their theological claims, not to impose their special truths on others by special coercion, by use of economic pressures, political threats, boycotts, or blacklists. A religious absolutist position that attempts to translate beliefs into laws or public practices binding on all represents a genuine threat to freedom.

A third problem of critical seriousness is the lack of communication between religious and secular culture. As William Clancy has written in *Religion and American Society*, "The forces of religion and the forces of liberal culture seem increasingly to be addressing and describing different worlds." Liberal deafness toward theology deprives them of a wealth of humane wisdom; on the other hand, religious leaders often speak in formulas that no longer have meaning for those to whom they are addressed. The absence of communication between religious and liberal culture should be taken as one of the most serious problems of our time. Contrary to the eschatological vision of our Rabbi of Bobruisk (which many religionists share either consciously or unconsciously), the secularistic cycle is not on its way to suicide and will likely be with us for the duration of our civilization.

We are in a new era in man's history, the age of urban secularization, which Harvey Cox describes with shocking power in his book on "technopolis," called *The Secular City*. The secular city (which supersedes not only early tribal society, but also the town culture that has shaped the world since the time of the Greek *polis*) requires not only a renewed message from the Church and Synagogue, but also a renewed language. "We must not define our 'spiritual' resources too narrowly in traditional religious terms," Reinhold Niebuhr asserted in the UNESCO pamphlet, "Our Moral and Spiritual Resources for the International Order." We cannot forget, he adds, that the very creation of our free society was the joint achievement of religious and secular forces. The American consensus has been kept alive over centuries through combined efforts of the Church, law, university, press, and the learned professions.

The secular disciplines, frequently so defective in their ultimate frames of reference, nevertheless provide the discriminating judgments which made it possible for modern man to analyze complex problems of social, economic, and political justice and to puncture the pretensions of religious people who sought to make religious faith an instrument of political power and self-aggrandizement.

In summary, the Church and Synagogue can make effective contributions to America not by putting themselves at the disposal of the nation, or by blessing whatever our society does or hopes to do, but

1. by providing a source of values;
2. by enlightening and inspiring the individual citizen to have courage and patience;
3. by helping the individual and society to become sensitive to the injustices and petty tyrannies that exist in our midst;
4. by providing the individual with motivation for responsible life in our society and with stable standards of moral judgment;
5. by calling men to self-knowledge and personal humility and bidding them to be aware of the unfathomable depths of human personality, keeping the sense of transcendence alive.

NOTES

1 *Triple Revolution,* Information Service, Department of Research, National Council of Churches, New York, May 22, 1965.
2 Cf. *The Challenge to Change,* by Abbé François Houtart (New York, Sheed

& Ward, Inc., 1964, for an excellent summary of global change from a socio-logical and religious perspective; also my articles, "The New Realities" in *Worldview* magazine, published by the Council on Religion and International Affairs, 170 East 64 St., New York 21, N.Y.; and "Confronting the New Realities of the Nuclear-Space Age," published in the *Sister Formation Bulletin*, X, No. 2, Winter 1963–64.

3 Cf. *CIF Reports*, studies of developmental programs in Latin America published by the Center for Intercultural Formation, Guernevaca, Mexico, under the direction of Msgr. Ivan Illich. Also, *Profile of Latin America*, a Protestant analysis by Dr. Stanley Rycroft, research specialist on Latin America for the National Council of Churches, New York, N.Y.

4 *Protestant Thought Before Kant* (New York, Harper and Row, Publishers, 1963), p. 24.

5 *Op. cit.*, p. 168.

6 For an insightful analysis of revivalism and its relation to nativism and American political pietism in the form of radical-right movements, see Franklin Littell's *From State Church to Pluralism*.

7 *Harvard Divinity Bulletin* (October, 1961).

8 For a fuller development of the basic ideas, values, and religious life of Jews and Judaism, see *Judaism* by Rabbi Arthur Hertzberg (George Braziller, Publishers), *The Rabbinic Mind* by Rabbi Max Kadushin (Jewish Theological Seminary Press), and *The Prophets* by Rabbi Abraham J. Heschel (Harper & Row, Publishers). A fuller bibliography is available by writing to me at the American Jewish Committee, 165 E. 56 St., New York, N.Y.

9 Cf. *Religion and American Society* issued by the Center for the Study of Democratic Institutions. This section of the paper is much indebted to this and related Center publications.

REVEREND JOHN F. CRONIN, S.S.

The Church, the Synagogue, and the World

REV. JOHN F. CRONIN, S.S., *Assistant Director of the Social Action Department of the National Catholic Welfare Conference, was ordained a priest of the Society of Saint Sulpice and the diocese of Albany in 1932. He received an S.I.B. in 1932 and Ph.D. in 1935 from the Catholic University of America. Awarded the Benemerenti Medal from Pope Pius XII in 1957, he was three years later presented with the Pro Ecclesia et Pontifice Medal from Pope John XXIII.*

Father Cronin lectures extensively throughout the country on social questions and conducts courses on this field. He founded the Institute of Catholic Social Action for Priests and Seminarians at The Catholic University and completed a series of nationwide broadcasts on "The Catholic Hour," discussing current social problems. Author of many books and articles on economic problems including Catholic Social Action, Problems and Opportunities in a Democracy, *and* Catholic Social Principles, *he was awarded the Pabst Post-War Employment Award for his proposal for the best post-war use of our resources in men and materials. Father Cronin served the U.S. Government as Economic Consultant to the American Administration in Germany in 1951, and was professor of philosophy and economics at St. Mary's Seminary, Baltimore, Maryland, before assuming his present position.*

In thinking about the topic of this chapter, there came to mind an incident which sharply illustrates similarities and differences

197

in the Jewish and Catholic communities as they confront the
problem of social reform in the modern world. About two years
ago, I happened to meet socially a wealthy Jewish clothing manu-
facturer from Baltimore. In mentioning happy memories connected with that city, I told of my close associations with Rabbi
Edward Israel. I mentioned that I was privileged, some twenty
years earlier, to give a radio eulogy on this distinguished social-
action leader.

As I told this story, the face of my new acquaintance lighted
up and he told me of his own recollections of Rabbi Israel. Two
decades had not dimmed his warm memories of a leader whose
fame was widespread throughout the United States. It mattered
little that the Rabbi Israel was a close friend of organized labor
and a supporter of the reform measures of the New Deal. Presumably, representatives of the business community were not
completely happy with the positions he took on these issues, yet
this businessman was ecstatic in his appraisal of the good rabbi.

About the time that Rabbi Israel was exercising leadership in
Baltimore and throughout the nation, Pope Pius XI was writing
his great social encyclicals. In his 1937 encyclical "On Atheistic
Communism," the Pope noted with sorrow that many Catholics
of wealth refused to heed his warnings. Indeed, in one country,
unnamed by the Pope, business leaders suppressed the publication of the courageous message he gave in 1931, "On Recon-
structing the Social Order."

If these were isolated instances, one would hardly trouble to
recount them. Yet they seemed to be fairly typical of experiences
encountered at least in the United States. In Washington, D.C.,
there is a Jewish social-action center, national in scope, established through the generosity of a Jewish business leader from
New England. This same leader is currently active in promoting
racially integrated housing. I know of no comparable donations,
either of time or funds, from Catholics of means and community
stature.

When one compares official pronouncements of religious leaders, Catholic and Jewish, on the critical social issues of our times, there is an astonishing similarity in position, indeed a high degree of unanimity. We all favor racial justice and harmony, the rights of labor, the abolition of poverty, the promotion of international peace, civil and religious liberties, and civic morality in our communities. Each body has active social-action organizations. We have testified, jointly or separately, before legislative bodies in favor of social legislation.

Our doctrinal bases for social reform are quite similar. Those who seek strong, even thunderous, pronouncements on justice toward one's fellow man are more likely to quote the prophets of Israel than the writers of the New Testament. Those who know and love the Psalms realize how pervasive was the concept of the fatherhood of God, and its correlative, the brotherhood of man. In the Books of the Law, we read of remission of debts and the freeing of slaves.

Catholics may quote the social encyclicals of recent popes or the theological writings of St. Thomas Aquinas. Jewish scholars in turn may cite the great rabbis, such as Moses Ben Maimon. Yet St. Thomas often quoted Maimonides as a master whom he revered, and Jewish writers today follow closely the work of Vatican Council II, hoping that its august authority may break down the barriers of prejudice and misunderstanding that have so saddened mankind throughout the centuries.

Nevertheless, here in the United States there are differences between the Catholic and Jewish communities as they confront problems of social reform. Jewish congregations and community-action organizations have, on the whole, a long and distinguished record of seeking social reform. In the Catholic community, one has the feeling that only now are we reaping the benefits of the teachings of socially oriented popes, from Leo XIII to Paul VI, and of such great clerical leaders as Monsignor John A. Ryan and Father John La Farge.

These variations in approach and reaction are not cited for historical reasons, but as a preface to our understanding of current problems. We are discussing reactions of religious communities toward the problems of the modern world rather than merely the official statements of leaders or congregational bodies. Attitudes, actions, and postures must be considered as well as doctrinal pronouncements. We know that in each community there are prophetic souls whose intuitive understanding and courage offer leadership and today give us, as daring proposals, what may be the standard programs of tomorrow. In each community there are also the apostles of the *status quo,* timid souls whose fears inhibit action. Some try to follow the highest ideals; others seem devoid of moral aspiration.

Given these general observations, we now proceed to examine some concrete problems of unusual pertinence, to see how, from a Catholic viewpoint, Church and Synagogue should proceed in the years to come.

Race Relations

In the area of race relations, both communities start from a concept of the dignity of man and the sacredness of the human person. This norm precludes the downgrading of our fellow man through prejudice and discrimination; positively, it impels us toward the ideal of equality, fully realized in the entirety of life —economic, social, political, and cultural. When our brother is hurt, we feel the pain. When he is unjustly imprisoned, our freedom is diminished. When he is despised, our own dignity has been outraged.

Both communities, Catholic and Jewish, have developed programs for securing racial justice. Within each group these programs have grown at different rates, some maturing more rapidly than others. Nevertheless, when the opportunity for a radical breakthrough presented itself in the early 1960's, each was ready to do its share. Even better, each was eager to work with the other (and with powerful Protestant organizations) for a definitive solution of the racial problem in the United States.

From a Catholic viewpoint, the distinctive feature of race relations in the 1960's was the fact that the focus of action shifted sharply. Prior to this time Catholic race-relations activity tended to be mildly parochial, consisting mostly of the work of Catholic interracial councils which labored mainly within the Catholic community, although individual leaders had broad, ecumenical outlooks. Moreover, these interracial councils constituted a fringe, specialized activity in our midst, much like the liturgical movement during these same years. But in recent years two major changes took place. Race relations became the concern of the power centers within the Church and approach to it became heavily interreligious.

For these happy developments, much credit must be given to the conceivers and planners of the 1963 National Conference on Religion and Race, among whom was Rabbi Marc Tanenbaum. Here, for the first time in American history, leaders of the major faiths gathered to develop a common program for meeting a great national problem. The bonds of unity forged in the preparation of that conference, and during the days when nearly 800 national religious leaders met together, were strong and durable. We began to achieve a degree of common action that would have been inconceivable even a few years before.

The fruits of this unity were soon evident. In 1963, representatives of our foremost religious groups achieved other "firsts" of the highest importance. We testified jointly before Congress on civil-rights legislation. Three of us appeared together before congressional committees, using the same written testimony and reinforcing one another's answers to questions. Joining with labor and civil-rights groups, we mounted a massive campaign for the enactment of this legislation.

In 1964, seminarians from the three faiths kept vigil at the

Lincoln Memorial in Washington, D.C., not breaking this vigil until the Civil Rights Act was passed. On April 28, 1964, top national religious leaders presided over a massive rally in Washington, petitioning Congress for the passage of this legislation. Then, after passage of the Civil Rights Act, we gathered in the shadow of the Capitol for a service of thanksgiving. Finally, in November of the same year, we regrouped in a three-day conference of religious race-relations experts, along with more than fifty Government officials concerned with this problem, to plan the future.

This case history is an ideal example of Church-Synagogue relations in facing a major moral problem in the political order. Our agreement in this area was practically total. We accepted the same principles, the same objectives, the same strategy. Yet the task is not finished; indeed our work has only begun. Hopefully we face only mopping-up actions in our fight for equal rights. But the problem of equal opportunity remains, and it may involve a prolonged effort by the entire community. Then there remains the work of healing, especially of those who have been degraded and brutalized by decades of slum conditions and discrimination.

Equal opportunity means, first of all, the ability of Negro youths and adults to get well-paying jobs. Here our problem is not primarily discrimination (although this does exist), but education and incentive. Our slum schools are inferior because, as a rule, they do not have the best teachers or even adequate facilities. Children in these schools return to homes that give them little chance for study and few incentives to try. Yet there are cities in which this problem has been met by intensive teaching programs, by assigning the best teachers to this work, and often by keeping the schools open before and after regular class hours to give opportunities for study and wholesome recreation.

School work may be supplemented by volunteer tutoring, with these same programs being made available to adults, many of whom have scarcely achieved literacy. All this had been done by local initiative, prior to the plans developed under the Economic Opportunity Act of 1964. We, in turn, can now do much to make universally available sound educational programs, both on the basis of principles thus far developed as well as within the framework of the Economic Opportunity Act, with its camps for the jobless and job-training programs for those who remain at home. We can work for scholarships for talented children from our minority groups. Much of this is primarily a civic activity, but religious groups can jointly give inspiration and leadership in these vital areas.

There also is the problem which too often is unmentioned today, as if we were ashamed of what we have done. I refer here to families without fathers—often a third generation on relief—in which children grow up under conditions that almost guarantee delinquency, crime, and vice. All too often society has seemed deliberately to be promoting such conditions, especially by shortsighted and poorly planned relief programs. When these evils are mentioned, we have a tendency to say that the victims should be left to the experts, such as psychiatrists and social workers, overlooking the fact that professional help may not supply the one primary ingredient for building a sense of human dignity and hope in those who have been given little of either. What is needed here is a feeling of belonging, a conviction that someone really cares, and this is not easily given by professional workers, especially when they are surrounded by regulations that discourage personal interest. Religiously minded persons here face a challenge to work out an apostolate for those who have little hope. We can, for example, appeal for help from married persons whose children have grown up, and contacts with these people may be made by young persons who are looking for an outlet for their idealism. Basically, this is the same spirit that motivates our Peace Corps and Vista volunteers, with the direction given by religious rather than governmental agencies.

Equally as important as training for job opportunities is the affording of good housing to those who too often are condemned to slum ghettos. Some Negroes today can afford good housing, but they face a wall of discrimination. The techniques for meeting this situation have been worked out in detail and have proved successful in many parts of our land. Religious groups, especially when they work together, can be an important factor in breaking down ignorance and prejudice in regard to housing.

Here we might mention a program that is modest in scope, but of some value in achieving better racial attitudes. Many religious groups have promoted home-visitation days, in which members of both races meet socially in a pre-arranged fashion. Artificial as this may seem to some, the program has worked wonders in exposing false stereotypes and in promoting racial harmony.

In the more strictly social-action field, there are proposals for using investments in integrated housing. It is suggested that religiously minded persons set aside one-tenth of their investment income for such purposes. In addition, for those who cannot afford private housing, we continue to need public housing. Here religious leaders can help not only in promoting such projects, but also in examining carefully the type of operation involved. We know that many persons are having second thoughts today regarding large, isolated public-housing settlements, and are urging that we use funds instead to renovate neighborhoods that can be salvaged. Thus we do not lose the real values of a neighborhood, values which often are most important in even the poorest of areas.

Our dedicated work for employment and housing cannot be the high-pressure, crash type of operation such as was the crusade for the Civil Rights Act. Rather it will be a long-term project, calling for sustained concern rather than passing enthusiasm— a real challenge for prolonged Church-Synagogue co-operation.

Poverty

Related to the problem of race-relations is that of poverty. While most of our poor are white people, a disproportionate number of minority members belong to the class of the unemployed and the poor. The causes of poverty are more extensive than the factors we noted in connection with racial ghettos. Lack of education, poor home environment, and discrimination are only a few of the factors relevant to deprivation and destitution in our midst. Because the problem is so far-reaching in its implications, our response to it must be equally extensive and complex.

First there are factors which only indirectly engage our competence as religious leaders. These are the strictly economic causes of poverty, such as inadequate growth in our economy or the existence of areas of declining industry and opportunity. Because of our interest in the human problems involved, we are concerned with programs for economic growth, for tax reform, for retraining workers in the coal regions, and for enlarging opportunity in Appalachia. As religious leaders, however, we do not have technical competence in these areas. Here we encourage and motivate those who are expert in economics and political science to remove the scandal of unemployment and consequent poverty in the richest nation in the world.

Sometimes our poor cannot be helped by such economic measures. Certainly this is true of the aged poor in the United States. We may say this also of widowed or separated mothers of young children—it would seem more desirable that they be able to take care of their children rather than be forced to work full-time for a living. We think also of those who are presently considered unemployable: alcoholics, compulsive gambling addicts, the mentally retarded, the physically handicapped, and those burdened with serious personality disorders.

It is unrealistic, most of the time, to seek jobs for those men-

tioned above. Our concern should be to help them with dignity
to live a human type of life in spite of their economic impotence.
Some can be aided in preparing for useful work, and this, too,
should be done with dignity and sensitivity. Often we can prevent
the occurrence of such situations in the future. Proposals such as
Medicare and education for the early detection and cure of
alcoholism and mental disorders can do much to lessen the future
incidence of these problems.

Many of the poverty programs are identical with the education
projects mentioned in connection with equal opportunities for
minority-group members. Our aim should be to secure proper
education and training for all capable of receiving such help. If,
as a result of automation and the electronic age, private industry
finds it more and more difficult to absorb the unemployed, we
should then enlarge our vision of public service, so that those who
fall within our concern should have the opportunity for truly useful employment. Certainly the minimum we can offer those who,
through no fault of their own, are unable to earn sufficient income, is a guarantee of the wherewithal for decent living.

We might mention here a potential source of division between
Catholics and Jews, as we confront poverty both at home and
abroad. Many experts have strong convictions that family planning and population control are needed elements of any realistic
program, either for fighting poverty in the United States or for
economic aid to developing nations. In the past the introduction
of such proposals would have been clearly and extensively divisive. Today, many Catholic scholars are deeply concerned over
both family planning and population control. Some of these, in
fact, call for a broadening of our attitudes toward certain hor-
monal techniques for achieving a decline in fertility. This is still
an open question for many Catholic scholars, and it is known
that Pope Paul VI has appointed a distinguished international
commission to look into the entire question.

Without trying to anticipate any decisions by the Holy See,

it is fairly safe to say that the birth-control problem will continue to be a divisive factor in interreligious relationships, at least in the near future. There is no present prospect of development in Catholic attitudes toward techniques of family limitation to the point that there would be no differences in our major religious communities. There may even be continuing clashes on objectives, since many Catholics find it somewhat puzzling that the richest nation in the world must promote family limitation as a technique for combating poverty in our midst.

It is well to face these difficulties and tensions realistically, since they are bound to recur in a pluralistic society. In the present context, while we may not achieve full agreement on family planning at this time, we may move toward a narrowing of controversies. For example, if we Catholics argue that there should be no elements of compulsion—either for clients, doctors, or social workers—in any community program for family planning, it must be remembered that we are here arguing on a basis much broader than Church doctrine. We are urging a point that could involve the personal dignity and even the civil liberties of poor families.

On the other hand, when advocates of population-planning contend that publicly financed contraceptive services should be made available to those who desire to limit their families, most Catholics would not oppose this position. They would feel that any opposition would amount to an imposition of Catholic doctrinal positions on those who do not share these stands. Already in many cities of the United States there have been compromise programs involving civic aid for family planning. What is particularly encouraging is the fact that a pattern of harmony, achieved in the struggle for racial justice, made adjustments and compromise much easier when more religiously divisive issues arose.

Civil Liberties and Church-State Relations

In the areas of civil liberties and Church-State relationships, we are likewise confronted with problems that could be divisive. There is no question that the historical factors that often condition policy positions led to quite different attitudes in the Catholic and Jewish communities. For many centuries in Europe, the Catholic Church has enjoyed, and often sought, close relationships with the civil State. Its traditional teaching on Church-State contacts—granted that there have been strong dissenters in the past and at present—has favored such close collaboration between the city of God and the city of man. In addition, the formerly dominant Catholic attitude toward religious liberty, also under strong attack today and reversed in Vatican Council II, has been a factor in promoting the religious clashes that constitute a sad factor in European history.

While Catholics in the United States are strong advocates of religious freedom, they have not generally been in the forefront of the struggle for civil liberties. Their preoccupation with the problems of world communism and internal subversion led many to attitudes which other Americans consider dangerous in terms of civil liberties. Moreover, we have been identified with advocacy of censorship in the area of obscenity. In such struggles as those involving Sunday-closing laws and the birth-control laws of Connecticut and Massachusetts, American Catholics have tended to favor retention of the laws, even though they were passed by forces other than our own.

By contrast, as a number of contributors to this volume have pointed out, members of the Jewish community are historically conditioned to fear the union of Church and State since they have all too often been victims of such relationships. They are deeply concerned with civil liberties, for they know too well what can happen to a minority group that is considered unpopular in a given time and place. Their whole history teaches them to fear the power of the censor and the inquisitor.

In presenting these divergences as historically conditioned, I am not ignoring doctrinal positions. Yet doctrine can be incomplete and conflicting, as Pope Pius XII noted in his celebrated 1953 address to Italian Jurists on religious liberty in a multinational union. There the Pope called attention to factors that had been overlooked in the traditional Catholic teaching on religious liberty, noting that the common good not only permits, but may well command a pluralistic State to practice neutrality in regard to religions within its borders. Vatican Council II has already shown in many ways how a narrow concentration on one doctrinal position may lead to policies which conflict with other and more vital doctrines. Thus our previous focusing only upon what divides us from other religious faiths has been superseded by the broad directives of the Schema on Ecumenism.

This trend suggests strongly the need for intensive dialogue among Americans of different faiths with regard to divisive issues in the area of both Church-State relations and civil liberties. Out of such discussions can come a much broader area of agreement than has existed in the recent past. A good beginning would be to classify our broad aims and objectives in one list, and, in another list, the techniques to be used in seeking these goals. We may well find important areas of agreement when objectives are considered. Both communities want the maximum of religious freedom without any domination by the civil State. Both oppose communism; both are concerned with family welfare and public morality; both believe in religious education of children by Church or Synagogue and in the family.

We differ, perhaps less than before, in some of the means used for achieving these results. There are conflicts about religious observances in public schools; about the use of public funds for private, religious schools; about the area of public regulation of morals; about Sunday-closing laws; and, possibly, about techniques to be used in countering domestic subversion.

What is really important is that today we are much better conditioned for calm and unemotional discussion of these potentially divisive issues. In carrying on these discussions, we must be patient and try carefully to distinguish between positions held as a matter of principle and those involving cultural lags and possibly misunderstandings. We can hardly expect full agreement at first—those who have been following Vatican Council II realize how difficult it has been within the same religious community to achieve virtual unanimity on highly controversial issues. What is important is that we move forward calmly and persistently until we have achieved the greatest possible meeting of minds.

Other Social Issues

There are other social issues of high importance which Church and Synagogue must confront, hopefully together. Our experts in labor relations have worked closely together for many years, and we have few differences of any importance in this area. We favor the rights of labor, especially such as the unfortunate migratory and farm workers. We have worked for social legislation, again with very few differences of opinion. In this area, perhaps all that need be said is that we should continue to do in the future what we have done so well together in the past.

Nor are there basic differences among us when we confront issues of world peace and the prosperity of nations. Some of the strongest expressions of approval of Pope John's encyclical, "Peace on Earth," came from Jewish religious and secular leaders. Rabbi Eisendrath has been zealous in promoting joint discussions on this topic, and we all look forward to the time when we may have a national conference on religion and peace comparable to the historic National Conference on Religion and Race.

It would be helpful if both of our communities could consult more closely in such matters as welfare and community-action programs. We may find areas in which joint or parallel action would greatly strengthen the effectiveness of our work. In such discussions we would do well to be aware of two extreme positions that may cause difficulties. At one extreme is the desire to seek artificial interreligious programs, devised mainly to give us an opportunity to work together. Obviously such ill-conceived ventures cannot be fruitful. At the other extreme is the desire to have separate, religiously connected programs in areas where we would do much better work if we did it together.

One field that can stand careful study is that involving civic morality and community standards. We want our neighborhoods to be morally wholesome as well as physically attractive. We want our youths to be safe from purveyors of filth, narcotics, or anything else that might demoralize them. More positively, we wish to give them real challenges in life, constructive programs that will serve as alternatives to the destructive urges that break through as outbursts of delinquency. All of us can gain much from free and extensive discussions of the problems that confront the modern family. Our homes will be better if we can jointly promote a community atmosphere that is inspiring and strengthening to youth.

These, then, are some of the major social and political issues that today confront Church and Synagogue. We are far better equipped than ever before in history to face these problems with a high degree of mutual understanding and common action. Moreover, the process of consulting and working together can be cumulative. As we meet on these issues, we can gradually chip away at age-old antagonisms and misunderstandings. We can increase our respect, one for the other. Worshipping, as we do, the one true God, we can truly then become brothers under this eternal Father.

6

�֍ Israel as Idea and Reality

REVEREND GERARD S. SLOYAN

The Meaning of Israel as Idea and Reality

REV. GERARD S. SLOYAN *has been Head of the Department of Religious Education at the Catholic University of America since 1957 and has served in various offices there since 1950. Ordained a priest in June, 1944 at Trenton, N.J., he received his Ph.D. in 1948 at the Catholic University. He is the author of many books including* Shaping the Christian Message *(Macmillan, 1958),* The Gospel of St. Mark, Christ the Lord, Modern Catechetics *(Macmillan, 1963),* Liturgy in Focus, *and* The Three Persons in One God *(Prentice-Hall, 1964), one of a twelve-book series on the Foundations of Catholic Theology. In 1962–64, Father Sloyan served as President of the National Liturgical Conference. He is currently on the Board of Directors of the Institute of Judaeo-Christian Studies, Seton Hall University, South Orange, N.J.*

I hope to try to tell you the Christian meaning of Israel, both as idea and reality, as I understand it. I am quite aware that it does not have this same meaning for my Jewish brothers, and I do not put it forth in any antithetical spirit whatever. I simply articulate the faith that is in me, so that, in company with Rabbi Agus I may help provide the beginnings of discussion. My attempt shall be that of a man of faith, not a scholar, for, although I make certain pretensions to being a scholar, I am not sure if considerations based on scholarly inquiry are what are needed in a discussion as basic as this.

There is a passage at the close of Shakespeare's *The Taming of the Shrew* in which Kate speaks in praise of woman's master, her spouse.

> Thy husband is thy lord, thy life, thy keeper,
> Thy head, thy sovereign, one that cares for thee,
> And for thy maintenance commits his body
> To painful labour both by sea and land . . .

In return for this service, he,

> craves no other tribute at thy hands
> But love, fair looks and true obedience.

Such was the love affair between the Lord, the great God of the heavens and the earth, and tiny Israel. Indeed, the Bible is filled with little else. Those sacred books tell us nothing, really, except the story of that high romance. Yahweh, God of Israel, is the suitor, the strong lover who will do almost anything to keep the affection of His errant bride. Too often Israel is, in Shakespeare's language, but a "foul, contending rebel and graceless traitor to her loving Lord." She first serves Him, then betrays Him, then repents, only to serve and fall again. Like any husband wronged, Yahweh, grows furious: "Therefore, O harlot, hear the word of the Lord. Thus says the Lord God: Because . . . your shame has been discovered through your adulteries with your lovers . . . behold I will gather together all your lovers with whom you have taken pleasure and all whom you have loved, with all whom you have hated, and I will gather them together against you on every side, and will uncover your shame in their sight, and they shall see all your nakedness. And I will judge you as adulteresses and they that shed blood are judged, and bring upon you the blood of wrath and jealousy" (Ez. 16, 35–38).

Yahweh, of course, God of love and mercy, did no such thing. Instead, He hadn't the heart to do it. Being a God of love and mercy, He promised her reconciliation, a thing unheard of, since it was strictly forbidden by the Law of Moses to take back one's wife after divorce. Yet, through the prophet Jeremiah the Lord says, "Return, O virgin Israel, return to these your cities. How long will you continue to stray, O rebellious daughter? For the Lord has created a new thing upon the earth: the woman returns to her husband [or: must encompass the man]." (Jer. 31, 22)

I begin my presentation—there is no other place to begin— from the holy books which give testimony to the life of a people. These books are not themselves that history, that life, but they testify to it. And their testimony is true.

The two cities where the sacred writings of ancient Israel are held in honor are Judaism and Christianity. The two peoples agree thus far on this, that there should not be two cities of God in the midst of men, but one. The Jew says it is God's will that all the nations of the earth shall drink at the spring of holy wisdom which lies at the heart of his city. The Christian says that in company with Israel the nations have already been let drink of waters purer than mortal man can dream, not as suppliants or petitioners, but as equals and brothers, as dwellers in the city with full rights of citizenship, though not born there. Both Jew and Christian say what they say in faith. They would not dare to speak otherwise.

Meanwhile, the sacred books are the meeting ground where Jew and Christian can consort briefly as one, not two; briefly, because duality always lurks close by. The sacred writings lead to this great matter, somehow if not fully realized, says the Christian. The writings point to that same matter, unfulfilled the Jew must say. And we are two again. But briefly we were one, perhaps to be inseparably one again and forever through these holy books whose author is that God who is the Lord. The Jewish Scriptures in any case represent a hope, and, specifically, a hope for the religious unity of men.

More than all else, the sacred books are the bridge between

brothers who are separated, for their words express the aspirations and the ideals of sons of a common Father. The Spirit of the Lord speaks to our spirit in these writings. Let pass what may, they will remain. They cannot change or lose what force they ever had. They can only be fulfilled in greater divine event, yielding meanings they always possessed, but meanings which men will come to know only slowly and painfully as the years unfold.

Many books, written in our time, seek to remind us of *the* Book. Some are written by Christians who assume that the Israelite experience is true, that the Christian experience is true, and that these experiences are not two, but one. On this assumption, they are one, not as the two sides of a single coin are one, nor as a child is something of its mother and in that sense one with her, but as nothing else in all nature is one, though two.

I can write here neither as a learner from Divine Wisdom who has become more learned nor as an adolescent grown adult without immediately offending Jew and Christian alike, because I should be untrue to the facts. How shall I express in human language the reality I seek to express, when there is mystery—divine mystery—surrounding the people of Israel? With respect to this mystery, perhaps the least apprehended truth is the basic Jewishness of Christianity, the latent Christianity of Judaism, and the near impossibility of speaking of the two in terms of a relation. When there is a condition of identity, the word "relation" has no place; when one regards two things in relation, he thereby assumes them to be distinct, disparate. How useless is our ordinary vocabulary in speaking of this mystery! The very fact that the situation is in some sense inexpressible leads us to realize that we are in the presence of authentic, divine mystery.

The Hebrew Scriptures, we remarked at the outset, tell the story of a great love. One thinks of how exasperating it must be for the Jew to hear that God sent love into the world with His Son, Jesus, and that before Jesus' time there was only covenant, divine justice, and law. And what of the basically unchristian ring to the phrase, "Christian charity," as if Christians were saying that Jesus is "the man who invented *hesed*"? Only if there has first been faith in a divine dispensation through Moses that is all *hesed we emeth*—"love and fidelity, grace and truth"—is it possible to speak of the Word become man as the fullness of grace and truth.

For the Christian, the Scriptures of Israel are a book of instruction and formation, priceless in value—priceless for the Christian, we may say, in their "independent value" (if that phrase does not cut God off from His own work). They are a compendium of prayer; they are the inexhaustible food of contemplation. These holy books are the well of Jacob to which parched and sinful humanity comes to draw water. The God of Jacob is there, waiting to speak to that sinner, to proffer the waters of eternal life.

For the ancient Jew, the world's history was all but synonymous with Israel's history. If there was a significant difference between the two, the ancient Jew never knew it. Adam's sin meant the beginning of sin for all mankind. The relationship between God and man, consequent on that sin, became the accepted condition of men on the earth, as friendship with God had characterized man's primitive state. "The earth was corrupt in the sight of God, and it was filled with violence" (Genesis 6, 11).

But there was Noah, who was blameless. He rode out the storm in trust, and afterwards he knew how to offer holocausts which pleaded with their sweet odor. "When the bow is in the clouds I will look upon it . . . and remember the perpetual covenant between God and every living creature of flesh" (9, 14 f). Nor was God's fidelity fruitless, for a spared humanity meant heirs to the promise: Abram, the son of Thare, received the call

in the metropolitan capital of Ur. "I will make a great nation of
you. I will bless you and make your name great" (12, 2).

Thus does the great alliance, the solemn covenant of friendship, tentatively begin. Later Abraham was to say to the Lord,
"I am but dust and ashes" (18, 27). But he said it bravely and even
ventured to ask, "What if ten [just] be found there?" "I will not
destroy it [the city] for the sake of ten," said the Lord (18, 32).
And God promised him—the God who is faithful to His promise,
"In your descendants all the nations of the earth shall be blessed,
because you have obeyed me" (22, 18).

Since God is true to His word, the happiness of all men is to be
found through this people made up of the descendants of
Abraham according to the flesh. The nations will praise and love
Him because of this people and its relation to Him. And if the
promise means anything, it means that this relationship is eternal.
In the people Israel, in Abraham's seed, "The earth shall be filled
with the knowledge of the glory of the Lord, As the waters cover
the depths of the sea" (Hebrews 2, 14). The heathen make song
and saga, but the prophets of Israel's God speak the truth. They
report His activity in their midst. They record the history of
God with men. Through His promises to Isaac, and Jacob, and
their descendants, His name is made holy. A torrent of grace is
poured out from age to age, and the sacred books record the
flow.

But there must be some means to communicate. In a matter
so important there cannot be guesswork. If God is a living God
and man a living soul, then surely there will be some way to
converse. For His purpose, God uses the words of His prophets.
When there is doubt that the words are really His, they are to
be believed if there is a sign. Truly He is a hidden God (cf.
Isaia 45, 15) who must always act behind some veil of sense.
Were it otherwise, He would not be God, but a man. God spoke
His word on Sinai and upheld it with a sign. "The glory of the
Lord settled upon Mount Sinai. The cloud covered it for six

days, and on the seventh day he called Moses from the midst of the cloud. To the Israelites the glory of the Lord was seen as a consuming fire on the mountaintop" (Exodus 24, 16 f).

This was the way of God with His people: always to communicate through holy ones and in circumstances that reminded His people that He alone is the Holy. "Indeed the Lord God does nothing without revealing his plan to his servants, the prophets" (Amos 3, 7). He is not the God of the philosophers and the sages, available to the subtle inquiries of their minds. No, God is the worker of marvelous works whose deeds and words are unmistakable. After them there can only come faith or unbelief. " 'Learn then that I, I alone, am God, and there is no god besides me' " (Deuteronomy 32, 39). All other worship is idolatry. " 'Now, therefore, put away the strange gods that are among you and turn your hearts to the Lord, the God of Israel' " (Josue 24, 23).

From Adam's day all Israel knew the lie that said, "Your eyes will be opened and you will be like God" (Genesis 3, 5). It was a base lie because no creature is like Him. Only for Him is it worth leaving country, kinsfolk, and a father's house. "To whom can you liken me as an equal? says the Holy one" (Isaia 40, 25), for "I am the first, and I am the last; there is no God but me. Who is like me? Let him stand up and speak, make it evident, and confront me with it" (44, 6).

This jealous God does not see Israel give His glory to another with equanimity, but with wrath. If there is rumor of a town or place in conquered lands that will not have Him for its only God, the inhabitants must be tracked down and put to the sword. All His works are right, and all His ways are just, and He is able to humble those who walk in pride.

God's name is Holy; He is the Lord. "This is my name forever; this is my title for all generations" (Exodus 3, 15). From on high He looks down on the sons of men and, knowing their sinfulness, demands of them the sacrifice—the gift—of an obedient will. He commands that honor be given to father and mother. He requires truthfulness, justice, brotherly love. Most of all, He commands fidelity to Himself. A loving Father, He would have offspring who are one seed. He is the shepherd of Israel, and this people is but one flock. "Have we not all one Father? Has not the one God created us? Why then do we break faith with each other, violating the covenant of our fathers? . . . For Judah has profaned the temple which the Lord loves, and has married an idolatrous woman" (Malachia 2, 10 f).

The Israelite had a concern for the past, but he did not look exclusively to the past. His was a religion primarily of hope in events to come. He could endure life in virtue of a deliverance that was sure to happen in the future. The night of the Passover with its remembrance of liberation from Egypt, in a series of events long behind the pious Jew, was but token of a full and future liberation. "Tomorrow shall the iniquity of the earth be abolished, and the Savior of the world—Yahweh—shall reign over us."

In his work, *Homo Viator,* Gabriel Marcel speaks of hope as establishing a relationship between the soul and time. Hope always establishes an extremely logical connection between a return to the past (*nostos*) and something completely new (*kainon ti*). The aspiration can be expressed in the simple and seemingly contradictory words, "as before, but differently and better than before." Liberation, for the Jew and the Christian, is never a simple return to the *status quo;* it is that, and much more, and even the contrary of that: an undreamed of promotion, a transfiguration.

In what sense is it true that the kingdom of God is close at hand, that "the glory of the Lord shall be revealed, and all flesh shall see the salvation of our God" (Isaia 40, 5)?

What is the reality described when we speak of "the deliverance from the perils that threaten us by reason of our sins?" (Collect, IV Sunday of Advent). How will the Lord Himself be stationed at the rampart of the city wall of Zion, the mountains, hills, and every woodland tree paying Him tribute by singing a song of praise? Even a little serious reflection by the believer, Jew or Christian, yields an answer to these questions.

He will come. Surely He will come and save. But in between there is the uncertainty, the longing. "Is it your coming that was foretold, or look we for another" (Magnificat Antiphon, II Sunday of Advent)? They put the question to Jesus, but it is one that would have been put to many in that age of anguished expectation.

. . . say to those whose hearts are frightened: Be strong, fear not! Here is your God, he comes with vindication; with divine recompense he comes to save you. Then will the eyes of the blind be opened, the ears of the deaf be cleared; then will the lame man leap like a stag, then the tongue of the dumb will sing. Streams will burst forth in the desert, and rivers in the steppe. . . . A highway will be there, called the holy way; no one unclean may pass over it, nor fools go astray on it. No lion will be there, nor beast of prey go up to be met upon it. It is for those with a journey to make, and on it the redeemed will walk. Those whom the Lord has ransomed will return and enter Sion singing, crowned with everlasting joy; they will meet with joy and gladness, sorrow and mourning will flee.—Isaia 35, 4–10

There was not much more, really, that a poet of Israel could say about the days of deliverance. How could he praise the God of his fathers better than to say that in the days of Messiah the dispersed captives would throng the city of Jerusalem once more and fill the air with their pious shouts? The Lord Himself would come and save. In that day all the woes that plagued a mystified near-East would be no more: the withered limbs, the deafness, the eyes sightless from birth, the all-pervading thirst. Surely the Lord would destroy them in the last days. How could He show Himself the vindicator of His people—their *go'el*, the ransomer, or bail bondsman, who was one of their blood—if He did not wipe the tear from every eye, if His people could not "draw water with

joy from the springs of salvation" (Isaia 12, 3), pure water flowing from the temple, "for the cleansing of sin and uncleanness"
(Zacharia 13, 1)?

Israel's prophets used to dream about what the messianic age
would be like. The Spirit of the Lord would pour out streams of
water on the dry earth; the new Israel in that day would be a
spring "whose waters never fail" (Isaia 58, 11). Like the four
rivers of Eden, like the sweet waters of Mara near the springs
of Elim, a garden fountain from Lebanon would make the desert
bloom in that era; and the lame would walk, the halt would
cavort with joy. Indeed, all this was fitting since the Lord Himself
would come on a straight path and a high road.

It was not a fiction, as we know, not a flight of Oriental fancy.
For when He came in the person of Jesus, as the Christian holds
—Lord and Messiah in one, surely not His only coming in the
flesh or His last—He came on the filled valleys, the hills made
low, the straightened ways of a few hearts prepared. He came unto
Zion, the holy mountain, and He spoke to the men of Israel, in
their city and their temple, of the signs that meant fulfillment.
And some believed that Jesus came from God and some did not.
Later, Gamaliel put the meaning of Jesus to a pragmatic test.
"For if this plan or work is of men it will be overthrown; but if
it is of God, you will not be able to overthrow it. Else perhaps
you might find yourselves fighting even against God" (Acts 5,
38 f).

Why does God speak? Why does the one God give utterance?
Surely to hear a response, in love, from His own people—from
his creature Adam, man whom He sent in love to rule the earth
through serving Him alone.

But Adam is no longer one as God made Him in love. Like
a potter's vessel, he has fallen to the earth and has shattered
into a thousand pieces. A thousand? Yes, but chiefly into two
pieces. He is an elder brother and a younger, a son long faithful
and a brash young wastrel. Adam is Sem and he is Chanaan; he

is Isaac and he is Ishmael; he is Jacob and he is Esau; he is Juda and his brothers, and he is the Gentile; he is the Jew and the Christian; he is two who are not one, except to their Father for whom they will ever be one as He is one.

Speaking from the side of the Christian brother, we have not had enough trust in our Father to believe that. In proposing the test of Gamaliel, we have proposed that it be put only in one way or in such a way as to achieve but a single result. We Christians have told the Jews what they ought to be, religiously, and have not bothered to learn that they do not remotely fit our specifications. We have said, "You ought not to be Jews at all; but, since you are, you had better be Orthodox. That's the good kind." But when Jews became Conservative and Reformed and when some of them began to eat pork and everything else (saying that in those matters the Scriptures are not to be interpreted literally), we said they had lost all faith. What we forgot was that we, centuries earlier, had declared our own freedom from those prescriptions of the Law and any such view of the Scriptures. We Christians assumed that our Sacred Scriptures continued to be theirs, ignoring the fact that the quality of the traditions of the ancients with the books of the Bible had been claimed as far back as Jesus' day. Our learned Christian men quote Isaiah and Jeremiah for the instruction of the Jews (a trap I have here not escaped), while their sages are frequently concerned with Talmudic Lore, something we Christians have not bothered to master.

We declared Judaism static, lifeless, a vestigial thing which exists not by divine right, but, if anything, by a terrifying act of disobedience. Yet Judaism, seemingly unconscious of the ban, has developed and found new expression continuously. All this while, we ourselves have been doing a perilous thing, though we say that the Spirit of God keeps us from doing ultimate harm to our faith. As a people, we have forgotten our roots; we have neglected our Scriptures. Oh, we Christians can still name the great patriarchs and prophets and recite their lives in outline, but we tend to make one great leap from Adam to Christ. Of the Lord Jesus and Mary, His mother, we still affirm proudly that they were Jews. However, what all of this should mean to us, we Christians have largely forgotten. The Jewish antecedents of our faith remain a fact, but a fact without much meaning to us. Yet we may not forgot that what we call the New Law—another perilous term, for it has about it the ring of God's unfaithfulness to His promise—was impossible without the Old, that religion meant to Jesus what it meant to Abraham, Moses, David, the prophets. Each of the two religious cultures, Judaism and Christianity, has gone its own path of development with the result that the fact of common ancestry according to the spirit seems far-off and, in a sense, unimportant.

May I propose a way back, at least from the Christian side, to the ramparts leading to that bridge to the Father which for us is Christ? It may seem so trivial as scarcely to deserve attention.

You remember, perhaps, what the elders of the Jews said when they went to Jesus and urged Him strongly to heal the centurion's slave? "He deserves to have you do this for him, for he loves our nation, and it was he who built us our synagogue" (Luke 7, 5). In other words, he loves our people; now make what you will of that, they said to Jesus.

How we come to love Jews, as people, is of no special consequence; but *that* we must love them—this is imperative. We may see in them signs of a divine mystery, "the one indisputable proof of the existence of God," as Barth says. We need not be so metaphysical or so ultimate about it, however. To see in the Jew our estranged brother whom, above all men, we are called to love and, much more importantly, to like, this is enough. In any case, if we Christians fail, we may be sure that we have earned our Father's wrath.

If the Catholic is thoroughly filled with the Bible and his own liturgy—these two undying monuments of Hebrew thought—he has made the best remote preparation to embrace the Jew as a brother. He has done very little by way of immediate preparation, however, because, if for no other reason, most Jews do not know their Scriptures any better than does the Catholic at the present moment. Such Jews can be no more offended by the claims of an incarnation or by Paul's teaching on conditional reprobation than if a Hottentot were to press these claims. For, in the main, these people know that they are Jews and that there is a kind of natural protection afforded them if they remain Jews. They are afraid to step out of the circle and lose all.

This leads to some perhaps unattractive conclusions for the Catholic. He must learn Jewish Judaism, not Catholic Judaism; he must know something about a Simchas Torah, the ordinary Friday night service, the modern dietary observances; he must give outward signs—heartfelt signs—that Jewishness is a thoroughly acceptable human condition and that the Jewish religion is a way to serve God in reverence and love; he must even try to comprehend the United Jewish Appeal and the case for the State of Israel.

This process of understanding is a conversion of the self, and all conversion is painful. It ceases to be a question, as it now is, of how much the Jew will have to change to be one with the Catholic if the Catholic has first changed to become one with him. For as Paul wrote long ago (Ephesians 2, 14), Christ has broken down the wall that was there between Catholic and Jew. While that may be true in some radical cosmic sense, it is not true in fact. Christians have seen to that by their lack of faith in what God has accomplished in Jesus, though they do keep talking about it.

I conclude by holding out the hope that Catholic education— and not necessarily our school education only—is currently in a tentative state of reform. The stirrings of Vatican II, so often unsatisfactory even to us Catholics, are those of a giant waking from sleep. He has almost forgotten how to walk. He is capable of being a bully, like all giants, and one is right to fear him. But if he can learn to walk in gentleness, and brotherhood, and absolute trust in God, there is everything to hope for.

We must leave ourselves open to what of God is at work among us. What do you and I mean to the legions of black Africa, to teeming India, and to China in the design of God? Surely they are His sons, too. And surely our behavior borders on the frivolous if we do not come to see who we are to each other and stop acting out that oldest of human archetypes: brothers who are so far separated because they are called to be so close.

RABBI JACOB B. AGUS

The Concept of Israel

RABBI JACOB B. AGUS *has been Rabbi of Beth El Congregation, Balti-more, Maryland, since 1950. Ordained in 1935 at the Issac Elchanan Yeshivah in New York, he received his Ph.D. in 1939 from Harvard University in the Division of History and Philosophy of Religion. Author of several scholarly volumes dealing with the evolution of Jewish thought and modern philosophies of Judaism, Rabbi Agus' most recent book is in two volumes:* The Meaning of Jewish History *(Abelard-Schuman, 1964). Our contributor is a consulting editor of the* Encyclopedia Britannica, *and his collaboration with Arnold Toynbee was acknowledged in Toynbee's* Reconsiderations. *He is a member of the Rabbinical Assembly of America.*

Israel is at once the name of a people, a State, a religious community, and an ethereal ideal. A certain ambiguity characterized the term, Israel, from the very beginning. Jacob's name was changed to Israel in order to indicate his elevation to a high cosmic status. He was now on a par with angels, "for thou hast struggled with gods and men, and has prevailed."[1] Philo interprets Israel to mean, "he who sees God," that is, the man of divine visions.[2] Certain it is that from the moment of its historic genesis, the people of Israel considered itself to be "covenanted" unto the Lord. A covenant is more than a love affair, no matter

229

how impassioned, since it cannot conceivably be terminated at
the whim of either partner. It is rather like a marriage, as marriage was originally intended to be: exclusive, enduring, indeed
eternal.[3] Accordingly, the people of Israel are also called "sons of
the living God," or "the first-born son," or the treasure-people.[4]

It is not possible, in any case, to speak of the historic community of Israel without taking note of its special relation to the
God who was different from all other gods, a Being unique and
alone (meaning of Ehod). A people that is lifted out of the mass
of struggling humanity by the one God, set apart from all other
nations and given a unique cosmic status cannot but deem itself
radically different. When the elders suggest to the prophet Ezekiel
that it might be wise for "the house of Israel to become like all
the nations," he storms at them, "it shall not be."[5] The very
thought is absurd. The children of Israel are not at liberty to
mold their own destiny. They are committed. They "belong" to
God who will rule over them as their "King," with "wrath out-
poured" whether they will it or not.

This feeling of *radical difference* from the Gentiles became a
powerful historical force. It affected the policy of the last Kings
of Israel. So Hezekiah resisted Sennacherib, pinning his faith
on the one God for whose sake he inaugurated a reformation.
Josiah carried forward that spiritual revolution and centralized
all sacrificial worship in the Holy Temple of Jerusalem. Though
he died on the battlefield, his reform was not undone.[6] In time,
the feeling of being radically different penetrated into the depths
of the national psyche. Jeremiah phrases in Aramaic the message
that the exiles were to bring to Babylonia: "so shall you say to
them, 'the gods that did not make heaven and earth will pass
away from the face of the earth.' "[7]

In this formula, Jeremiah articulated the uniqueness of the
One God of Israel. He is not merely one, but He stands above
and beyond the whole of creation as its master. He transcends
the battles between the diverse gods and the empires that wor-

ship them. But this God, who is Alone, is not simply the God of the universe that all can find and worship in their own way. He, too, is committed, covenanted, bound by His spoken word. He is wedded to Israel, as it were; He had sworn an oath to the Patriarchs; He had spoken to all the Israelites at Sinai; He had revealed to them His Torah. Thus was the import of Israel's message given a more personal tone and a cutting edge: "It is *our* God, the God of Israel, who is the One God of the universe."

It is this double message that demonstrates the two-sidedness of the concept of Israel. The self-image of the historical community reached up to the universal realm of metaphysical entities. It "corresponded" to a heavenly reality.[8] But this self-image also contained a written history of a living people, its poignant memories, its agonizing anxieties, its bread-and-butter needs, its flesh-and-blood desires and hopes.

The two-sided character of the Jewish self-image and its resultant sense of radical difference from all other nations evoked a corresponding reaction among the non-Jewish population. How could they help but react with an extra measure of hostility to a people that considered itself especially set apart from all others, separated by a distinction that ranks far and beyond the usual differences that separate all human groups? If they acknowledged the unique status of Israel and its message in an affirmative way, they became either converts, semi-converts, or sympathetic hangers-on.[9] If they reacted against either the cogency of the message or the claim of Israel's election, they came to regard the Jews as "the most odious race of mankind." Here was a people that insulted and assaulted their gods and arrogated to itself an exalted cosmic rank. In many cases, admiration and scorn were combined in a puzzling complex of hate. Thus, classical anti-semitism emerged as one of the responses of the pagan world to the twin challenges of Israel and its monotheism. In their turn, the Jewish people felt the loneliness of their situation to be a direct consequence of their covenanted status.[10] If God had chosen to make them "different," their destiny in history must also be "different." When the nations are uplifted, they are degraded; when the others are defeated "in the end of days," then Israel's turn will come.

In periods of bitter rivalry and persecution, the notion of being chosen as *against* the rest of humanity tends to take the place of the feeling of being chosen *for the sake* of humanity. The eschatological vision becomes zealot, narrow and exclusive, a vindication of Israel rather than the triumph of its teaching.[11] Thus, the actual situation of Jewish people at any one time helped to shape the outlines of their collective self-image. Their earthly misery and their cosmic power, their martyrdom in the present and their messianic glory in the future lent vitality and vividness to one or another aspect of the traditional concept of Israel.

The Triad

One trinity of ideas remained unbroken throughout the long history of the Jewish people down to the emergence of our secular age: the presumed unity of the conceptions of Israel, Torah, and God. Israel was convenanted to the Lord, and Torah was the bond that united them—the contract which stipulated the terms and conditions of a union, that could be cruelly stretched, but never entirely severed. It is in the Zohar that this unity is formulated in the most incisive way: "Israel, the Torah and the Holy One, blessed be He, are one."[12]

The Qabbalistic author assumed that each of the three entities in this triad was a cosmic current that attended all the way from this lowly earth to the highest heaven. The Glory of God fills the world, but in His essence the Lord is infinite, transcending all humanly conceivable categories. The designation, "the Holy One, blessed be He," corresponds to the aspect of the Divine Being that is directly concerned with the administration of earthly affairs.[13] In a similar way, the Torah is in this earthly life a body of laws, principles, and narratives; but up in the heavens it is an ethereal essence, "written in black fire or white fire," and consisting of an articulation of the Names of the Lord.[14] So, too, the people of Israel "correspond" to heavenly essence that merges at its source into the effulgence of the Divine Being.[15]

This mystical concept of Israel illustrates the extent to which the collective self-image of the Jews was an integral part of the prevailing theology. Its contours varied in accord with one's philosophic approach. Accordingly, we may best describe the concept by filling in the details in the several self-images as they appear at the rationalistic pole of thought and at the mystical pole. It will then be possible to indicate the degree to which one or another concept predominated in the minds of the legalistic authorities, who steered generally a middle course between the two extremes.

The Mystical Pole

Already in the Talmud and Midrashim the mystical character of Israel is suggested. "The image of Jacob is carved into the throne of Glory,"[16] we are assured, and, when the patriarch enjoyed his famous dream, the angels went up and down on the heavenly ladder, comparing the upper image with the lower one.[17] The Throne of Glory symbolizes the aspects of Divine Power that relate to the administration of mundane affairs. We are told that this Throne of Glory "hovered over the deep" before the creation of the Cosmos.[18] The souls of the righteous are kept there, after death, until the messianic redemption, the resurrection, and the world to come.[19] Another passage tells us that "the Patriarchs—they are the Divine Chariot"[20]—that is, they are part of the mediating channel of divine grace. Abraham, in particular, had a continuing function in heaven. His prayers and that of the other patriarchs keep the scales of mercy weighted

against those of justice.[21] Also, he stands at the gates of hell in
order to prevent those who are circumcised from being thrown
into its yawning abyss.[22]

The close mystical association between Israel and the Divine
Being is adumbrated in the concept of the *Shechinah,* the Divine
Presence. In one sense, the *Shechinah* is found where love, compassion and devotion abide.[23] In yet another sense, "ten persons
who steadily engage in the study of Torah, the *Shechinah* rests
with them . . . even five . . . even three . . . even one . . ."[24] In a
more potent, more openly manifest way, the *Shechinah* was found
in certain synagogues in Babylonia.[25] But, in a special and more
immediate sense, it dwelt in the Holy Temple, and it departed
thence prior to the destruction of its abode, although, according
to some authorities, "the Schechinah did not move away from the
western wall."[26]

The Holy Temple "corresponded" to the Sanctuary in one of
the heavens, and the Archangel Michael offered "lambs of fire"
on the heavenly altar, matching the sacrifices of the High Priest.
Now that the Holy Temple is in ruins, Michael continues to
sacrifice on his altar the souls of the saints.[27]

The Sanctuary in the wilderness and later the two Temples
were visible manifestations of the Divine Presence, but even when
these were destroyed, the *Shechinah* did not depart from Israel.
"Wherever the Israelites were exiled, there the Shechinah too
went into exile."[28]

Indeed, Moses was assured that the *Shechinah* will be associated with Israel, and Israel only. "Said Rabbi Yohanan in the
name of Rabbi Yose': Three things did Moses ask of the Holy
One, blessed be He, and He granted them to him—that the
Shechinah shall abide in Israel . . . that it shall not abide on
the 'worshippers of stars,' and that he might know the ways of
Providence . . ."[29]

Explaining the superiority of the pure-blooded Israelite in regard to the capacity to intuit the Divine Presence, the philosopher, Halevi, writes:

The Shechinah which is visible to our eyes is presently lacking, for it is revealed only to the prophet or to the people generally only in the selected place, and this is the meaning of our prayer for the return of the Lord to Zion, "and may our eyes behold when Thou returnest unto Zion."

But the hidden, spiritual Shechinah dwells with every born Israelite, who is also a believer in the true faith, whose deeds are pure, whose heart is true, whose soul is attuned to the God of Israel.[30]

This association was so commonly accepted that to be converted was described as "entering under the wings of the Shechinah."[31] In the course of the discussion concerning the non-Jewish identity of Job, some rabbis in the Talmud argue that he could not have lived after the death of Moses: "after Moses died, did the Schechinah abide on worshippers of stars?" (that is, non-Jews)[32]

The bond between Israel and the *Shechinah* was so close that every worshipper was "to feel as if the Shechinah were opposite him."[33] So deep was this awareness that some rabbis considered it sinful to walk erect or with head uncovered: "it pushes the legs of the Shechinah."[34] This mystical consciousness of the Divine Presence heightened the tone of Jewish piety: "He who commits a sin in secret, it is as if he pushed the legs of the Shechinah."[35] The Divine Presence was a comforting reality to the downhearted: "The Shechinah rests on the heads of the sick";[36] "when a person is troubled, how does the Shechinah speak—'my head hurts, my arm hurts.' If the Holy One, blessed be He, is so pained by the blood of the wicked, how much the more so by the spilled blood of the righteous."[37]

In their prayers, Jews were admonished to think of "the exile of the Shechinah" or of the "Anguish of the Shechinah," rather than of their own troubles.

After detailing the mystical effects of evil deeds in closing the channels of mercy, an Orthodox pietist of the nineteenth century describes the function of prayer.

Though the law of the Talmud permits a person to bring to mind his own troubles when he prays, the core of his intention must not be the petition to assuage his own sorrows, since it is through suffering that his sins are purged . . . But the essence of his intention must be the need on high, for there might be an involvement of his Name, if the honor of Israel is involved . . . But even if there be no desecration of the Name, the Divine Presence feels his pain, and if the worshipper forgets his own pain in his intense concentration on the anguish of the Lord, then indeed his sins are forgiven . . .[38]

The Ideal Congregation

The ideal "congregation of Israel" (*Keneset Yisroel*) is often treated in Talmud and the Midrashim as an interlocutor with the Deity. It presents the case of the empirical people to the Lord and the demands of the Lord to the people. So any one who partakes of the pleasures of life, without a prior offer of thanks (*berocho*), "it is as if he robbed the Holy One and *Keneset Yisroel*."[39] The benedictions were formulated and instituted by the rabbis, acting in the Name of God. So *Keneset Yisroel* is the heavenly counterpart of the sacred tradition.

"Said *Keneset Yisroel* to the Holy One, blessed be He—acknowledge this as my favor to Thee, that I made Thee known to the mighty in the world [that is, in the discussion, to the Jewish people]."[40]

Here, too, the ideal congregation is regarded as distinguished from the actual, living people of Israel. Referring to the symbolism of the Song of Songs, which portrays the Lord and Israel as a lover and his bride, a Talmudic Sage says, "I am a wall, that is Keneset Yisroel, 'and my breasts are like towers,' these are the Synagogues and houses of study."[41]

Naturally, even in the first centuries of our era some Jewish people frequented the circuses and theatres of their cities more than the synagogues. Yet, the ideal congregation is imagined to speak as follows: " 'I did not sit among players.'[42] Said Keneset

Yisroel, 'Master of the Universe,' I have never gone to theaters and circuses of the nations of the world, and played with them."[43]

To the mystics the revealed Torah was only an earthly shadow of the heavenly entity.[44] Since the Written and Oral Laws refer almost exclusively to the people of Israel, an intimate association had to be assumed between the Divine Being and the ideal congregation of Israel. We have already referred to the unity of the triad—God, Torah, and Israel.[45] At times, Torah is left out, and a dual unity is asserted: "The Holy One, blessed be He, and *Keneset Yisroel* are called one."[46] The image of a lighted candle is often used: "Israel is the wick, Torah is the oil, the Divine Presence is the flame."[47]

The pre-existence of the heavenly Torah was a widespread assumption in the literature of the Midrash. From this belief it followed almost inevitably that the congregation of Israel, its acceptance of the earthly Torah, its destiny and its eventual redemption through the Messiah, were also previsioned. "If the Holy One, blessed be He, had not foreseen that after twenty-six generations the people of Israel will accept the Torah, he would not have written in it—'Command the children of Israel.' "[48]

The Torah was the goal of creation, since it represented the will of God, while all creation was merely the work of God. Hence, the Midrash asserts that the Torah furnished the design for all creation, and the "Holy One, blessed be He, looked in the Torah as He created the world."[49]

It follows that Israel, the people of Torah, occupies a central role in the administration of this world, not merely in the world to come. On its account, the sun shines, the rains come down to bless the soil, and the golden harvest ripens at summer's end. By the same token, however, the failure of the empirical people to abide by the precepts of the Law causes the order of nature to be disturbed, with dire consequences for all mankind. If the nations had only known of this relationship, "they would have appointed two policemen for every Jew," to make certain that he observed the entire Law.[50] All earthly gains are due to the merits of Israel; "even boats that travel from Gaul to Spain are blessed only for the sake of Israel."[51] On the other hand, the catastrophes of nature and history are also due to Israel: "No disaster comes to the world, save for the sake of Israel."[52] While the constellations of the stars and the ministering angels usually and largely control the affairs of "the nations of the world," the people of Israel are lifted above this natural order and governed directly by God. "There is no *mazal* [determination of stars] for Israel."[53] For, they are "beloved more than the ministering angels."[54]

Even while they glorified the congregation of Israel as an ethereal "City of God," the mystics allowed that not all living Jews were equally exalted. The Talmud asserts that "all Israelites have a share in the World to Come" and "will not see the face of hell."[55] Yet, the Zohar, which concentrates and magnifies the mystical streams in the ancient tradition, declares, "Not all Israelites are alike, for some of them are princes, deriving from the Holy Kingdom (*Shechinah*), and some of them are slaves, deriving from the side of the slave (Satan)."[56] Also, "Israel is called man and beasts; if they merit, they are man, fashioned after the one above; if they do not merit, they are called beasts."[57]

The notion that the people of Israel contain a vital core of saints who are closely associated with the divine administration of the world is rooted in Talmudic literature, though it was left for the Hasidic movement of the eighteenth century to provide concrete institutionalization of this belief.

So we read in the Talmud that "the Holy One, blessed be He, decrees, but the Saint repudiates it;" that also, "the Saint decrees and the Holy One, blessed be He, abides by this decision." These saints suffer for the sins of their people, and their anguish is accepted as a sacrifice of atonement for their contemporaries. Since the order of the world depends upon these saints, "no Saint perishes until a Saint of equal stature is created."[58] While the world may exist even for the sake of one saint, it was widely believed "that there are never fewer than thirty-six saints who confront the *Shechinah* every day."[59]

The Qabbalists deepened the gulf between the pneumatic saints and the ordinary scholars.[60] The power of the saints is felt even after their death, when their souls enter into hell in order to redeem the wicked who were attached to them in some way.[61]

The Hasidic movement created many saint-centered societies on the supposition that each saint was an embodiment of the redeemed world. In him, the evil desire and the impulses of material nature had been transmuted into forces of holiness. Even the occasional sin of the saint is due to a holy impulse. "The Holy One, blessed be He, in his Mercy impels the Saint to sin, so that he might fall from his high level and descend to that of the public; then, later, when the Saint raises himself to his holy height, he uplifts the people along with himself."[62]

The emphasis on the ideal of sainthood did not lead, in the Hasidic movement, to the weakening of the ethnic element in Jewish piety. The saint was never thought of in isolation, but as the living center of "all Israel." His prayer is focused on the "exile of the Shechinah," and in behalf of all Israel.

In the mystical stream of thought, the Jewish people were a unique metaphysical creation; hence, they were biologically different from the rest of mankind. So we read in the Talmud: "Why are the worshippers of stars unclean?—Because they did not stand at Mount Sinai. Because when the serpent cohabited with Eve, he threw uncleanliness into her. The Israelites had their uncleanliness removed at Sinai. The worshippers of stars, not having been at Sinai, their uncleanliness was not removed."[63]

We have here a version of original sin, which is purely racistic, assuming that Jews are free by birth from the corruption which is the lot of humanity. Yet, this racist emphasis was contradicted by the law which admits Gentile converts into the holy community. The Talmud assumes that, in the case of converts, "though they were not present at Sinai, their *mazal* was there."[64] This means that they were included in the Holy Community, but in a category of their own ("under the wings of the Shechinah," as against "over the wings of the Shechinah").[65]

The romantic philosopher, Halevi, assumes that even in the Messianic era, the descendants of converts will be distinguished from those of pure Israelitic lineage in this, that only the latter will be endowed with the gift of prophecy: "Whoever clings to this way, will participate along with his descendants in our nearness to God. But the convert will not have equal standing with the Israelite by birth, since only the Israelites by descent are suited for prophecy . . ."[66]

In the Talmud, the gift of prophecy is further restricted, even in the future, only to those whose line of descent is completely unblemished: "The Lord causes His Shechinah to rest only on the pedigreed families in Israel."[67]

The racist dogma permeates the mystical stream in Judaism down to the present day, even in the case of such thinkers as Halevi who admitted the worth of the other monotheistic faiths.

We deny to no man the reward for his good deeds, no matter which creed he belongs to, but we see the perfect good which comes to the people that are close to Him, in their lifetime . . .

But our destiny it is to cleave to the divine quality in prophecy and in states of mind that are close to it . . .[68]

The belief in the dogma of Jewish centrality and supremacy in the divine scheme of creation became more deeply rooted in the popular mind in the late Middle Ages as a result of the decline of rationalism and the growing influence of Qabbalah. In fact, the medieval era continued for the Jewish masses of Central Europe down to the twentieth century. So we find the most extravagant formulations of the holy character of Israel in the last few centuries. Israel should properly be "the portion of the

Lord," because "the Perfect One should have the perfect."[69] A sixteenth-century pietist wonders why the physical appearance of Jews is so much like that of non-Jews, seeing that their souls are drawn from radically different heavenly realms. The founder of the Liubavich dynasty of Hassidim asserts that of the two souls of every Israelite, one is a divine portion of the Lord Himself, and the other derives from the shell of *Nagah* (radiance), which is both good and bad, while the souls of the other nations are formed "out of the unclean shells, which have no good at all."[70]

A nineteenth-century Hassidic author writes:

Every nation has a certain holy spark, even as it possesses vicious qualities, since "Thou givest life to them all," and this is the purpose of the Jewish exile, to absorb these sparks . . .

As the root of *Keneset Yisroel* is the love of the Israelites for God, so the root of all the nations is their love for the pleasures of this world . . .[71]

So deeply rooted is this dogma in the tradition, that even some of the modernist reformers of the nineteenth century could not resist its impact. Thus, Geiger, the architect of Reform Judaism, spoke of a Jewish "genius" in religion.

In Talmud and Midrash

The mystical temper predominated in Jewish life only in the darkest periods of political oppression and cultural stagnation. Whenever the warm winds of enlightenment mellowed the hostility of their neighbors, the Jewish spirit regained an equilibrium between the insular mentality of self-glorifying myths and the open horizons of theistic humanism. In such open cultures as those of the Hellenistic era, of the Moslem Renaissance, of Christian Humanism, and the Age of Enlightenment, the rationalistic threads in the web of tradition came to light.

Contrary to a widespread impression, the Talmud contains significant components of a moral-rational approach to the understanding of the Jewish character and destiny. A broad definition of what it means to be a Jew is offered on a purely intellectual plane: "Every one who denies idolatry is called a Jew."[72]

"Said Rabbi Elazar, The Holy One, blessed be He, exiled Israel among the nations for the sole purpose of adding converts to their number. So, it is said 'and I shall sow it in the ground.'[73] Doesn't a person sow one measure only in order to harvest many more?"[74]

According to this view, the dispersal of Israel was not due to an outburst of divine wrath, but, on the contrary, to His concern for the redemption of mankind. The "chosenness" of Israel was, therefore, to be interpreted not as an exclusive privilege, setting Israel apart from the nations, but as a task, to bring hosts of men and women to the service of the Lord. Israel is "the first born," but not the only child. In the Torah, "the first born" cannot lay claim to the whole inheritance, but only to a portion double that of his brothers. Israel's vocation is to be an example, not an exception, to the other nations. It is not set apart, but set ahead, and ordered to work for and with other peoples.

Elaborating on Israel's task to "witness" unto the nations, the Midrash applies the law in regard to those who withhold testimony from judges: " 'if he does not tell, he shall bear his sin'— if you will not explain my Divinity to the nations of the world, I shall punish you . . ."[75] This missionary task was imposed upon Israel from the very beginning: "The Holy One, blessed be He, gave the Torah to Israel in order that they might bestow its merit upon all the nations."[76]

Naturally, the people of Israel are not alone in this task. The wise and the pious, wherever they may be, are allies of Israel. They are "priests," so to speak, individually, as the people of Israel were designed to be "a people of priests": "The Holy One, blessed be He, will grant to the pious among the nations a share in the life of the World to Come . . . because they are priests to the Holy One, blessed be He . . ."[77]

The duty to "bring people under the wings of the Shechinah" is treated as a supreme *mizvah*. Said the leading Sage of third-century Palestine, R. Yohanan: "Why was Abraham our father punished and his children were enslaved in Egypt for two hundred and ten years, because he separated people from entering under the wings of the *Shechinah*. As it is said, the king of Sodom said to Abraham: "give me the souls, while you take the property (and Abraham returned the captives, without converting them)."

For this reason, it was mandatory for masters to convert their slaves; they, in turn, were then obliged to observe the practices which were obligatory on Israelite women. Upon liberation, these slaves would become full-fledged Israelites, qualifying to be counted in the prayer-quorum of the synagogue.

The interpretation of a Biblical verse offered the great Rabbi Yohanan ben Zakai an opportunity to illustrate and to condemn the chauvinism of his disciples.[78] In Proverbs 14, 34 (usually rendered, "Righteousness exalts a nation, but sin is a reproach to any people") the Hebrew original puts the last two words in the plural—"the nations"—and it seems to draw the line between the one people—Israel—and all other nations. The zealous disciples vied with one another in finding an interpretation that would exalt Israel and scorn the Gentiles, namely, "even the charitable deeds of the nations are imputed to them as a sin, because of the impurity of their motives or their arrogance."[79] Then the aged Master points out the true meaning of the verse: "as the sin-offering would bring forgiveness to Israel, so does charity bring forgiveness to the nations of the world."[80] This interpretation is the one favored by Abraham Iben Ezra, in his commentary.[81]

We may assume that this discussion took place after the burning of the Temple, when the Israelites, too, could count only on deeds of charity, along with prayer and repentance, for the expiation of their sins. Jew and Greek became one in their need for forgiveness. So that, when the same rabbi was apprised of the burning of the Temple, he said, "We have a nobler means of atonement-righteousness and charity."[82]

The tension between the moral-rational and the romantic-mystical interpretations of the difference between Israel and the nations can be recognized in the many debates in the Talmud in regard to such issues as to whether Torah should be taught to slaves or not;[83] whether those who accepted Judaism and were baptized, but did not undergo circumcision, were to be considered full-fledged members of the community;[84] whether the laws of the Torah, barring inter-marriage with the neighboring nations were to apply to their descendants at all times, or possibly even be extended to all Gentiles, as Ezra and Nehemiah inferred, or whether those laws were no longer valid, "because Sennacharib had come and had mixed up the nations."[85]

There was also the theological question of "exclusive salvation," that is, whether the Gentile who accepts "the Seven Principles of Noah" and is classified as a *Ger Toshav*, must do so in the presence of three learned Israelites and on the basis of a dogmatic acceptance of the Torah of Moses.[86] Finally, we encounter the well-known dispute as to whether or not "the pious of the nations have a share in the world to come."[87]

The lines of demarcation are frequently blurred, particularly since dialecticians always endeavor to impose systematic consistency upon ancient controversies. The same Midrashic work might contain views that are in diametric opposition to one another. So, in an honored Midrash we encounter a dramatic affirmation of the equality of all men in the sight of God:

> I call heaven and earth to witness that a Gentile or an Israelite, a man or a woman, a slave or a servant-girl—the Holy Spirit rests upon him only according to his deeds. . . .[88]

Is it conceivable that the Lord will discriminate between a Gentile and a Jew, between a man and a woman, between a slave and a servant-girl? No, whatever *mizvah* one does necessarily brings its reward, for it is said, "and Thy righteousness is like the mighty mountains."[89]

But we also find the assumption that, in point of fact, only Israelites are "God's children," and they alone are due to share in the glories of the world to come:

> Though everything is His, and all are His creatures, He does not delight in all, but only in the seed of Abraham. . . .[90]
>
> Once, as I was going from place to place, I met an old man. Said he to me, "Will the nations of the world exist in the days of the Messiah?"—I said to him, "All the nations of the world that tortured Israel and oppressed Israel will come and behold its joy, then return to dust and not ever be revived. But all the nations and peoples that did not oppress or torment the Israelites will become the peasants and vineyard-keepers for the Israelites . . ." But, this is only the days of the Messiah, not the world to come . . .[91]

We need add only that the zealous author discriminated among Israelites as well. He praises the Lord for choosing the Sages and their disciples "to the end of all the generations," assigning to the "sinners in Israel" the dubious distinction of being destined to be burned within "the Great Synagogue and the Great Academy of the Future."[92]

While the *Aggadic* material of the Talmud varies greatly, containing even crude insertions by vulgar hands, the *Halachic* material is more organized and consistent. In Talmudic law, Ezra's insistence on "the Holy Seed" is definitely repudiated. Converts are warmly welcomed after due warning of the hardships they may expect to encounter.

> When a person comes to be converted, we say to him, "Why do you wish to convert? Don't you know that Israel is at this time driven, distressed and troubled?"—If he says, "I know, and I am not worthy to join them," he is immediately accepted. He is then told the roots of

the faith—the unity of God and the prohibition of idolatry, elaborating on the meaning of these principles. Then, he should be told of the *mizvot*, the light and the awesome ones . . .

And he should be told that by means of those *mizvot* he will merit the life of the World to Come, and that there is no complete Saint, except for the wise who know and observe these *mizvot*. He should be addressed as follows:

Be it known to you that the World to Come is kept only for the saints, and they are Israel. The circumstance that in this world Israel is troubled is really a favor to them, for they cannot receive an excess of favors in this world, like the worshippers of stars, lest they become arrogant and err, losing the reward of the World to Come. But, the Lord does not punish them too severely, that they might not disappear. For all the nations will perish, but they will endure.[93]

In the eyes of the Law it was a *mizvah* to induce a person to accept the Jewish faith. "Whoever brings one person under the wings of the *Schechinah*, it is accounted to him as if he had fashioned and brought a person into the world."[94] To be sure, some of the converts reverted to their pagan ways, causing all Israel to be guilty of sin in accordance with the principle that "all Israelites are responsible for one another."[95] Some of the rabbis protested for this reason against "those who accept converts."[96] Still, the legal authorities considered that all the nations will be converted in the time to come.[97] Once converted, a person has the same privileges as those who were born Jewish, except that they may not be judges or kings over Israel.[98] He is expected to think of Abraham, Isaac, and Jacob as his ancestors, for "Abraham has been called 'the father of a multitude of nations.' "[99]

Hellenistic Judaism

Hellenistic Judaism, to judge from the writings of Philo, was conspicuously liberal in its interpretation of the concept of Israel as the vanguard of humanity. Although Philo speaks of the Jewish people as "sons of God," he maintains that all who have knowledge of the universal Father are "children of God."[100] The people of Israel represent symbolically "those who have a vision of God."[101] Prophecy (in the highest or dogmatic sense), resulting in laws, was reserved for the Israelites of the Biblical period, but the message of the Scriptures is universal. Indeed, Philo identifies Plato's "philosophic frenzy" with one of the phases of prophecy. "For what the disciples of the most approved philosophy gains from its teaching, the Jews gain from their law and customs, that is, to know the highest and the most ancient cause of all things."[102] Out of Abraham "there issued a whole people, and it is of all nations the most beloved by God, for, as it seems to me, to them priesthood and prophecy were given for the benefit of the entire human race."[103]

Philo describes proselytes as being related to Jews "by kinships of greater dignity and sanctity than those of blood."[104] Praising the proselyte "who comes to God of his own accord," he adds, in order that all men who behold this example may be corrected by it, learning that God receives gladly virtue which grows out of ignoble birth, utterly disregarding its original roots."[105]

The semi-proselytes, or the "spiritual proselytes" (to use Wolfson's term), are included in the Mosaic polity of the "sons of God." They are the philosophers and the righteous men who share the monotheistic philosophy of life. Thus Philo speaks of "the blameless life of pious men who follow nature and her ordinances" and of "all who practice wisdom either in Grecian or Barbarian lands and live a blameless and irreproachable life" as belonging to the ideal community.

The Torah itself was, to Philo, not a mystical entity and a supreme source of values, but an educational instrument conveying the saving truths that God had built into human nature. The Sabbath is a covenant between God and mankind, not merely between God and Israel. It is a call for men to share in the divine activity of contemplation. In his listing of ten festivals, Philo leaves out Hannukkah and Purim, possibly because he regarded them as national observances. He listed "every day," if it is lived as a holy day. In Philo's judgment, Passover was not so much a festival of national freedom as a perennial call on all men to "pass over" from a life of passion to the life of yearning for God. Similarly, Sukkot was not a symbol of divine concern for the Israelites, but, rather, a symbol of the equality of all men and of the duty of cultivating the virtue of gratitude.

For Philo, therefore, the empirical community of Israel was still the most beloved community, but ideally its boundaries shaded into a twilight zone, embracing those who in various degrees dedicated themselves to the love of God. Philo, too, looked forward to a Messianic era when Israel would triumph, but then all other nations would merge with it: "I think that each nation would abandon its peculiar ways and, throwing overboard their ancestral customs, turn to honoring our laws alone, for when the brightness is accompanied by national prosperity, it will darken the light of others as the risen sun darkens the stars."[106]

Medieval Rationalism

The rationalistic and mystical streams in Judaism diverged more decisively in the Middle Ages than they did in the Talmudic and early Gaonic periods. For a century the Jewish world was torn by a long and bitter controversy between the followers of Maimonides and the anti-rationalists. Both schools included in their category of Israelites the "righteous proselytes," that is, those who were fully converted to Judaism. However, regarding those who worshipped the one God in purity of thought and in ethical action, the romanticists and the legalists hesitated to make use even of the category of *ger toshav*, the "semi-proselytes" of the Talmud.[107] As was earlier noted, some maintained that the *ger toshav* is one who accepts only the "seven *mizvot* of the sons of Noah" on the basis of Mosaic revelation and by way of a formal declaration in the presence of three learned men. Others added that this category applied only "at the time when the Jubilee institution was in effect." In this school, even the "so-called pious of the nations" were merely peripheral to the only bearers of salvation, the empirical people of Israel.

On the other hand, the rationalistic school in non-legalistic works projected the concept of a spiritual "elite," who, apart from any rites and ceremonies, advance ever closer to the Divine Being through the service of mind and heart. For them, the empirical people of Israel were significant only in so far as they were likely to produce a greater number of such philosophical saints.[109] The "Torah-Society" was so designed and ordered as to stimulate the emergence of men and women who love God and ceaselessly meditate on the wonders of His creation. But it is not the *mizvot* in themselves that generate holiness, or "nearness of God," but their presumed effect upon the moral character of the individual and the peaceful order of society. This effect is by no means certain or even likely in the case of the majority of the people. Saintly philosophers may arise among all nations, and only a few Jews may qualify for the honor. The living people of Israel were, therefore, in Maimonides' view, by no means co-eval with the spiritual elite, those who approach most closely to the Divine Being. It was a good school, indeed the best possible school, designed by the Lord Himself. But even in the best schools some students will be no wiser on their graduation than on their initiation. And students of poor schools have been known to excel. Salvation or fulfillment is an individual achievement.

R. Isaac Arame, whose work, *Akedat Yizhak,* was long a popular source book for preachers, manages to combine the view of individual judgment, on the one hand, and the collective salvation of Israel, on the other. He maintains "that one is truly designated as *Yisroel* (an Israelite) only if he is a saint (*zaddik*),"

for an Israelite and a saint are synonymous in respect of their
tasks. " 'All Israelites' (that are assumed to have a share in the
World to Come) means those who fulfill the obligations imposed
upon an Israelite." And the Torah, according to Arame, is so
designed as to lead all its devotees to salvation. Writing in the
last decade of the fifteenth century, Arame saw hope only for
"the remnant" of the nations that will accept the Torah.

> For he scattered and subordinated Israel among them, in order that
> they [that is, the nations] should be encouraged to learn to know the
> Israelites, their customs and the ways of their Torah, so that they will
> desire and accept it [the Torah]. In this way, Israel will cause a
> remnant of the nations to be saved, that they might call on the Name
> of God. But they see and do not take it to heart . . . interpreting the
> verses of Scriptures as they desire . . .[110]

Maimonides maintained that only "true ideas" lead to God, but
those ideas are accessible to the human mind and are readily
deducible from first principles. They comprise the doctrines of
God's unity and incorporeality, the first two of the Ten Commandments. All the other *mizvot* are principles of training for
the individual and of a properly ordered society. He summarizes
his view of the various categories of religious people in a famous
passage.

> I will begin the subject of this chapter with a simile. A king is in
> his palace, and all his subjects are partly in the country and partly
> abroad. Of the former, some have their backs turned toward the king's
> palace, and their faces in another direction; and some are desirous and
> zealous to go to the palace, seeking "to inquire in his temple," and
> to minister before him, but have not yet seen even the face of the
> wall of the house.
> Of those that desire to go to the palace, some reach it, and go round
> about in search of the entrance gate; others have passed through the
> gate, and walk about in the ante-chamber; and others have succeeded
> in entering into the inner part of the palace and being in the same

room with the king in the royal palace. But even the latter do not immediately on entering the palace see the king or speak to him; for after having entered the inner part of the palace, another effort is required before they can stand before the king—at a distance or close by—hear his words, or speak to him.

I will now explain the simile which I have made. The people who are abroad are all those that have no religion, neither one based on speculation nor one received by tradition . . .

Those who are in the country, but have their backs turned toward the king's palace, are those who possess religion, belief and thought, but happen to hold false doctrines . . . Because of these doctrines they recede more and more from the royal palace, the more they seem to proceed . . .

Those who desire to arrive at the palace, and to enter it, but have never yet seen it, are the mass of religious people, the multitude that observe the Divine commandments, but are ignorant.

Those who arrive at the palace, but go round about it, are those who devote themselves exclusively to the study of the practical law; they believe traditionally in true principles of faith, and learn the practical worship of God, but are not trained in philosophical treatment of the principles of the Law, and do not endeavor to establish the truth of their faith by proof.

Those who undertake to investigate the principles of religion have come into the ante-chamber; and there is no doubt that these too can also be divided into different grades.

But those who have succeeded in finding a proof for everything that can be proved, who have a true knowledge of God, in so far as a true knowledge can be obtained, and are near the truth, wherever an approach to truth is possible, they have reached the goal, and are in the palace in which the king lives.[111]

In Maimonides' gradation, the philosophers of the nation who seek God are far ahead of the masses of the empirical people of Israel, coming nearer to God than the zealous Talmudists who only go round and round the palace of the king. A commentator expressed the views of many shocked pietists when he wrote,

"Many of the wise rabbis said that this chapter was not written by the master [Moses Maimonides]. And if he wrote it, it should be hidden or, better, burned. For how could he say that those who contemplate the laws of nature are on a higher level than those who busy themselves with the duties of religion?"[112] Maimonides did not list the belief in the Chosen People among his principles of faith. He welcomed genuine converts most warmly, writing in a famous letter to a convert: "You may say, 'our God and God of our fathers,' for Abraham is your father. Since you have entered under the wings of the Shechinah, there is no difference between us and you . . . Let not your pedigree be light in your eyes . . . If we trace our descent to Abraham, Isaac and Jacob, you trace it to Him who spoke and the world came into being."[113]

However, in his popular and legal works Maimonides employs the imagery and rhetoric of the people in the belief that the maintenance of the Torah-society requires that certain popular opinions be stated by the philosophers as if they were true. In his letter to the Jews of Yemen, he asserts that those who leave the fold are not descended from ancestors who stood at Sinai. These "necessary truths," as he calls them,[114] help to bridge the gap between the philosophers and the populace, creating an enduring, vital community, in which the few guard the many from gross errors, and the many help the few to attain human fulfillment.

Divine Providence, in the judgment of Maimonides, was not focused on the people of Israel except in so far as the Messianic Age was predetermined, but normally the degree of divine guidance depended on the extent of attachment to the Divine Being by single individuals. However, to placate his opponents, Maimonides reintroduced the belief in the Resurrection and in the World to Come as predestined events at the end of history.

The radical intellectualism of Maimonides was repudiated by many of his successors. Arame postulates a special miraculous form of divine providence that is distinctive for Israel as a people.

In turn, there are several levels of divine providence in Israel, depending upon degrees of piety.[115] Some felt that "nearness to God" was more a matter of love, or of faith, or of divine grace than of sustained reflection. But the axiom that the way to holiness is infinite and that it is reached by inward meditation and self-scrutiny was accepted by many popular preachers and pietists.

The axiom that the pathway to God is through the intentions of the heart and the further realization that this pathway is infinite could, in theory at least, blur the distinction between "the people of Torah" and those without the Covenant. It is this emphasis on inwardness that, in the Hassidic movement, served to elevate the dignity of the unlearned masses. The application of the same principle to non-Jews was already foreshadowed by Rabbi Judah the Prince, editor of the *Mishnah,* who, upon being told of a Gentile who offered his life for God, wept and cried out, "Indeed, it is possible for a person to acquire his world in one hour." Albo added the principle that the Lord may well give different Torahs to various peoples. "Even when the Torah of Moses was valid for the Israelites, there was the Torah of the sons of Noah for all the other nations. There is no doubt that people would attain through it their fulfillment as human beings, since it was Divine, though it was not of the same degree of attainment as the Israelites could obtain through the Torah . . . So we see that it is possible to have two Divine Torahs at one time, but for different people."[116] Since the "chosenness" of Israel was effected by the Torah, specifying the terms of the Covenant, it could no longer be regarded as an exceptional phenomenon. To be sure, in Albo's view, the merit of the Mosaic Torah consisted in the fact that "human perfection could be attained by means of even one of the *mizvot* . . ."[117]

Unity of People and Faith

All through the Middle Ages the intimate association between ethnic feeling and religious loyalty in the concept of Israel was not questioned. The rationalists might recognize the relative holiness of other faiths, but only for non-Jewish groups. They might interpret the purpose of Israel's existence in terms of the education and ultimate redemption of all mankind.

For indeed the earth belongs to Me, and the pious of the nations are precious to Me, without a doubt. "But, ye shall be unto Me a kingdom of priests." In this respect, you will be My treasure—you will be a kingdom of priests to instruct and to guide the entire human race, that they might all call on the Name of God and serve Him together, shoulder to shoulder, as Israel will be so transformed in the future.[118]

Even the mystics thought of Israel as the vanguard of the redeemed portion of humanity in that it is the Jewish function to gather "the Holy sparks" that have become imprisoned by the "shells of uncleanliness" throughout the world. These holy sparks "must be rescued before the appearance of the Redeemer. The messianic redemption of Israel would justify the divine intention in the creation of man; through Israel's triumph, the human race would come into its own and attain fulfillment.

For Christian theologians as for Jewish thinkers, the ethnic separateness of the Jewish people was axiomatic. The place of the Jew in the medieval world was determined by the fact that he was of the "stock of Abraham." Socially, too, the Jews were nearly a self-governing enclave. They were outside the feudal system, not as individuals, but as a corporate body. Taxes were nearly always levied upon the community as a whole, and it was up to the Jewish authorities to distribute them. In the Spanish communities, Jewish authorities had the right to impose severe corporal punishments. In the German and Slavic areas, similar, though unofficial, means of discipline were frequently available. Furthermore, the semi-autonomous Jewish communities had in common the same basic laws and religious literature. The local variations, considerable as they might be—especially those between the monogamous society of Ashekenazic Jewry and the polygamous society of Sephardic and Oriental Jewry—did not prevent the rabbinic authorities from moving freely throughout the Diaspora and speaking in the name of a common sacred tradition.

Those in Moslem or Christian lands who left the Jewish faith might still be considered members of the Jewish community in the first generation on the ground that they were irrevocably committed by the oath that their souls took at Sinai.

Once Israel was chosen to be God's people, no Israelite can become a member of another nation. They belong to God's people, even against their will and even if they leave the fold of their religion. Therefore, said the prophet, "When thou passest through the waters, I will be with thee." This is an allusion to the angry waters of baptism through which pass all those who accept their religion [i.e., Christianity].[119]

The travail of the Marrano families in both Christian and Moslem lands is well known, but in the course of time they disappeared from the Jewish community. Even the Frankist Jews who joined the Catholic Church *en masse* in 1759, with the intention of retaining their own collective identity, did not leave more than a nostalgic memory in the first half of the nineteenth century, when Adam Mickiewitz, the poet laureate of Poland, was their most illustrious descendant.

It was through the changes in their religious convictions as well as outside pressure that some Jews left the fold. Their rationalist views might lead them to feel that the various monotheistic religions are so many social expressions of one philosophy, so that a change from Judaism to Catholicism is not very different from the change of one language to another. In their view, those differences which were left were not worth the cost of lifelong martyrdom.

On the other hand, Jewish pietists might be led by the impetus of the mystical tradition to feel that the Christian faith was the logical development of Biblical Judaism. Abner of Burgos, Spain, who was converted in 1321, was a famous and ardent convert, and he addressed many books and pamphlets to his former co-religionists, calling upon them to emulate his example. His arguments were directed chiefly against the rationalists.

"Abner began with a critique of the rationalist interpretation of Judaism, cultivated by the Jewish intellectuals who were his friends—and for this he found ample support in cabbalistic doctrine—and moved ultimately to a position of complete identification with the Christian ideology."[120] The majority, however, retained a balanced faith, rejecting the extremes of both rationalism and mysticism.

Liberalism and the Jewish Self-Image

The modern period opened with the dawn of the Age of Reason. The intelligentsia began to glory in the balancing of religious tradition by rational and moral enlightenment. At the same time, the feudal age with its corporate bodies began to evolve into the modern State, which consists of individual citizens.

The new ideals and circumstances confronted the Jewish people with the task of reorienting their own self-image to suit the new categories of social thought. Spinoza met this challenge by calling for the complete dissolution of the Jewish community. Reducing the core of Jewish faith to a few principles, which could be applied in diverse historical religions, Spinoza maintained that the vast body of Jewish law applied only to a self-governing community, living in its own land. He did not rule out the possibility of the emergence of a Jewish state in Palestine, but, in so far as the Diaspora was concerned, he declared that only the essential principles of faith in Judaism were valid. As to the people of Israel, they were no more "chosen" than any other nation that accepts its lot with gratitude and seeks to make the most of its heritage for the benefit of mankind. ". . . we have shown that the divine law, which renders man truly blessed, and teaches him the true life, is universal to all men . . . ingrained in the human mind."[121]

Although Spinoza lived as a lonely Titan on the border of the Jewish community, his philosophy exerted enormous influence on the Jewish intellectuals who remained within the community. Yet his contention that the State had the right to regulate all the actions of its citizens, as distinct from thoughts and feelings, ran counter to the emerging liberal philosophy of government.

For a century Jewish statesmen in the West allied themselves with the dominant ideology of liberalism. Religion and State must be separated; the State should abolish the corporations and estates of feudalism and base itself on a free and equal citizenry; all institutions, including those of religion, should be subjected to the scrutiny of reason. The concept of Israel, argued Moses Mendelssohn, should not be taken as an example of the ideal unity of religion and civil government. For ancient Israel was a unique creation, intended for the meta-historical, especially chosen people of the Biblical period, and reserved also for the meta-historical period of the messianic era in the future. In historical times, the laws of reason, common to all men, must govern human society. Religion, consisting of the free interaction of the divine mind and the human heart, cannot be subject to the coercion of the State. Also, in historical times, the Jews are simply a religious community, with the hope for a return to Zion being merely a transworldly, pious dogma, affirming an action on the part of God, not on the part of the empirical community. "This state existed only once in the world. Call it the Mosaic society by its proper name. It has already disappeared from the earth. Only God knows in which people and at which time we shall again see a similar situation."[122]

Mendelssohn agreed with Spinoza that the Torah was a revealed law of action intended for a specific community, but he maintained that the Jews of his day were still individually obligated to abide by the Torah in so far as a personal observance of ritual laws was concerned. Mendelssohn also agreed that the ideas necessary for salvation were placed by God in the hearts and minds of all peoples, that they are in no sense, therefore, a monopoly of Israel. The loyalty of Jews to their Law is due to the impetus of the past. They were born into the Torah-community, but the salvation of mankind does not depend upon them. All men are judged by God as individuals, and as individuals the Jews should enter the State. The concept of Israel, for Moses Mendelssohn, was dual in nature: total separateness and a metaphysical dimension in the distant past and in the mythical future, but social integration, in all ways except religion, in this mundane realm.

Mendelssohn's concept of Israel was a logical development of the rationalist stream in Jewish thought; it implied a complete repudiation of the romantic-mystical currents which removed the empirical community of Israel as well as the ancient and eschatological ones from the common course of human events. His viewpoint was certainly shared by the upper circles of Jewry in western Europe, but in the long belt of Jewish mass-settlements, extending from the Baltic to the Black Sea, the influence of Qabbalah was reinforced by the rise of Hassidism. The wall between East and West, established by the division of Poland and the policy of the Czarist Empire, was supplemented by a cultural-religious schism between the rationalist philosophy of western Jewry and the mystical isolationalism of eastern Jewry. Although this wall was constantly breached by the flow of immigrants from East to West and by the return of young men from the universities of the West, it nevertheless remained an obdurate social factor down to our own generation.

In the West, the exponents of Judaism were aware that the ancient Covenant of Israel with the Lord needed to be complemented by a second covenant between Israel and the nations.

The new covenant would be far more than a business transaction. But, like the ancient one, it would involve a total re-orientation of heart and mind. For, unlike the various agreements of the Middle Ages, the new society called for the attainment of "fraternity" with the host-nations. No longer was the Jewish status to be that of an alien enclave, tolerated by the sovereign under certain conditions; the Jews were to become members of one unit —the Nation State—which, on the surface, was a legal-rational entity and, below the surface, an idealized fellowship which reached down to the dark, bedrock sentiments of a blood-brotherhood. So it was that the Grand Sanhedrin of Paris was asked whether the Jews would regard Frenchmen as their brothers.

Because the rationalists had already subscribed to a concept of Israel which included the fellowship of the right-thinking, it was but a small step for them to identify the fellowship of the right-thinking with the society of the Enlightened in the eighteenth century, with German *Kultur* in the nineteenth, with the French homeland of liberalism, and with the architects of a free society in England and America. Although they could not join a blood-brotherhood without physical assimilation, they could become part of the new cultural fellowship as well as its political expression, excepting only religion.[123] "The Freedom of the Jews," noted a French-Jewish author, "has put an end to our exile."[123a]

This trend of thought within western Judaism was reinforced by the rising tide of liberalism in Europe which aimed to separate the Church from the State, that is, the fellowship of culture and politics from the traditional institutions of religion. The liberal world was based upon the association of individuals, sharing cultural values as well as political loyalties. The Jewish individual could become part of this new fellowship, since his specifically Jewish loyalties were restricted to the transworldly realm, the mythical past, and the eschatological future.

Romanticism and the Meta-Myth

But the liberals within Judaism, as well as similarly minded men and women in the Catholic and Protestant worlds, were pulled back by the residual romantic-mystical forces in their respective traditions. The European nations of nineteenth-century Europe were Janus-faced, now turned toward the liberal vision of an open society, now facing back to the older plan of a closed society associated with one or another religious tradition, and going back through the mists of prehistoric time to the primitive, yet potent, feelings of blood-brotherhood. The religious romanticists, who called for a Catholic France, a Protestant Germany, a Greek Orthodox Russia, were allied psychologically with the ethnic romanticists, who idealized the Slavic or the Russian soul, the Teutonic character or the Gallic spirit.[124] Both kinds of collective romanticism were engaged in fighting the same, all-pervasive enemy, the rational spirit in philosophy, the egalitarian spirit in politics, the progressive élan in culture and in social legislation. Soon enough the emancipated Jew became the symbol of the hated age of liberalism to the romantic lovers of the good old days. To the protosocialists and economic romanticists the Jew symbolized the rising industrial era, with all its vulgarity and corruption, causing the coarse and uncultured *nouveau riche* to usurp the leadership of the well-born and the well-bred.[125] To the ethnic romanticists, the ideal age antedated the historic era when an alien Christianity and a citified culture were imposed upon the guileless, noble savages whose innate culture was too inward and too refined to be noticed by the earliest chroniclers with their monkish minds. To the religious romanticists the emancipated Jew was also the symbol of the passing of an idealized age, the great Middle Ages when religion dominated the private as well as the public life of the country, separating the faithful flock from the goats who would not so believe, and putting the latter in their proper places.

In each of these three phases of romanticism, a distorted image of the Jew was constructed around a grain of truth. Jews were predominantly an urban people, participating actively in the creation, first, of a commercial and, later, of an industrial society. They were long the one and only tolerated religious minority. Their ethnic roots went deeper into the past and farther into distant lands than did those of their neighbors. Moreover— and on this point the three kinds of romanticism concurred again, though, on the whole, they were mutually contradictory —the Jew was a child of mystery, doomed by a dark destiny to dwell apart from and in opposition to the rest of humanity.

Thus, the "meta-myth" of modern anti-Semitism was born— the mythological notion of the Jew as being metaphysically set apart from the rest of mankind. Between the Jew and the rest of the nations of Europe the gulf was cosmic, eternal, and unbridgeable. This myth, deriving from both Jewish and Christian dogmatism, was now set up in three dimensions: religious romanticism, ethnic culture, and the economic sphere.

In Europe of the post-Enlightenment age, religion was rooted in "feeling" rather than in supernatural revelation. Thus the dogmatic image of the Jew was transposed into the language of "feeling"; his "Semitic" nature could not possibly appreciate the noble sentiments of Christianity. In this view, the Jewish non-acceptance of the Christian faith was now transposed from theology to biology. In the realm of politics the same myth implied that the Jew could enter only into superficial alliances with the host-nations, since, in moments of national crisis, the Jew would listen to the voice of his blood. He belongs to a unique species of mankind, a mystical category that is *sui generis,* an international nation.

In the dimension of economic life this myth projected two images which reflected the same animus, although they were mutually contradictory. In the literature of proletarian rebellion and anti-bourgeois propaganda, the Jews took on, collectively, the lineaments of Shylock, that caricature of the heartless capital-ist.[126] In the reactionary literature of those who struggled against the exploding age of industry, the Jew was the economic radical, the new messianic enthusiast who had no roots in or love for the ancient virtues of aristocracy.

The one "meta-myth" combined the feelings of traditional religion, the "pooled pride" of ethnicism, the resentments of the military aristocracy, and the militant malice of the new pro-letarian radicals. It is easy to see that these diverse elements could be given a spurious façade of unity through the "meta-myth" of anti-Semitism, though this development did not appear until the rise of the Nazi movement.

Echoes of the "meta-myth" abounded in the Jewish world since writers in the western as well as the eastern world were exposed to the same influences which produced the romantic reaction to the liberal revolution. Samson Raphael Hirsch re-asserted the claims of Orthodoxy along the romantic-mystical lines of Judah Halevi. His vision of a *Yisroel-Mensch* imposed the luminosity of humanism upon the image of a unique ethnic group segregated supernaturally from the Gentile world. Even Geiger, the rationalist, taught that the Jews were endowed with an ethnic genius for religion. Krochmal wove a new pattern of Jewish history around the ancient dogma that, while the Gentiles worshipped certain angels, the people Israel were alone dedicated to the one God. A'had Ha'am asserted that in the domain of ethics the Jewish national soul was at work. And it was unique, incomparable, unlike that of all other nations.[127]

Even the Jewish writers who left the fold shared in some of the manifestations of the myth that was torn from its Judaeo-Chris-tian context. Disraeli viewed the Jews as not merely another ethnic group but a messianic race, bearing the seeds of universal salvation.[128] To Marx, the Jew was the capitalist par excellence, the class enemy that had to be overcome. Moses Hess, the one-time socialist, projected the vision of a Jewish utopia in Jerusalem reborn. Even to Leon Blum the Jew was uniquely disposed to bring into realization the glorious utopia of socialism.[129]

Jewish secularism, however, did not appear as a world-wide movement until the year 1897 when the World Zionist Organization came into being in Geneva and the nucleus of the Jewish socialist movement was formed in Vilna. From that time to the present, the variety of Jewish self-images did not change drastically. The revolutionary events of the past two generations—the transfer of the center of gravity of the Diaspora from the Old World to the New, the replacement of Czarist oppression by Communist repression, the annihilation of Central European Jewry, the rise of Israel, and the virtual liquidation of the Diaspora in Moslem lands—all these developments have been fitted into the following spectrum of shades and nuances, marking the contemporary concept of Israel.

Contemporary Orthodoxy

Going from right to left, we have, first, the ultra-Orthodox movement which is small in numbers, but intense, even feverish, in devotion. Theirs is an airtight world which rejects the viewpoint of categories of the secular age and employs the ancient axioms of the romantic-mystical school of medieval Judaism. They regard the State of Israel not as a messianic-eschatological event, but as simply another framework within which the people of Torah may live or not, as they choose.[130] While they agree that it is a *misvah* to live in the Holy Land, they insist on viewing this *misvah* with the perspective of the ancient commentaries, as if there were no State and no ingathering. Indeed, in their view, the Jewishness of the secularists and the socialists who control the Government of Israel is so woefully attenuated as to border on the meaningless. For the Torah—and the Torah alone—is the sole yardstick of belonging to the "people of God." The messianic-eschatological State is one in which the Torah is the constitution, the Holy Temple is brought down from heaven or built up, the Sanhedrin is reconstituted with the help of the Holy Spirit, and the Messiah is revealed. All else belongs to the historical world where the loyal remnant of the meta-historical people must make do, waiting for the coming of the Promised One.

The moderate Orthodox (*Mizrahi,* or Religious National Party, or the modern Orthdox in the Diaspora) assume that the concept of Israel is bipolar, national, and secular as well as religious and fundamentalist. They participate in the Government of Israel, recognizing the Jewishness of all ethnic Jews who have not broken away from the fold officially and flagrantly. They regard the State of Israel as "the beginning of the growth of our redemption." They look upon the present situation as the twilight between the night of exile and the day of messianic redemption, the borderland between history and meta-history. They have not given up the hope for the fullness of redemption, but they feel that its course must be plotted in advance.[131] Hence it is the duty of all Jews to work for the upbuilding of the land, the ingathering of the exiles, and the sovereignty of Torah within the limits of a modern State. They waver between the teaching that it is a meritorious deed for a Jew to settle in Israel and the doctrine that it is the bounden duty of a Jew to live in the land of Israel. This indecision is due only in part to practical considerations; essentially, it is a reflection of the feelings of tension between the compulsions of our temporal existence and the claims of the meta-historical realm that is even now taking shape. Were not the excesses of twentieth-century anti-Semitism, culminating in the Nazi "final solution," precisely "the pains of the Messiah" that the ancient tradition foretold? Was not the flight of the Arabs from Israel in 1948 a miracle that made possible the ingathering of the exiles? Do we not live in a world where the light of redemption and the night of exile are commingled? If so, how is one to tell whether any issue is to be seen in the sober perspective of everyday existence or in the wondrous mirror of the days of the Messiah? For the present, there is no answer to this question.

The ideology of the national-religious movement in Israel was expressed most profoundly by the great Orthodox mystic, Rabbi Abraham Isaac Kuk. While he esteemed all forms of nationalism to be fragmentary and partial expressions of the holy dimension, he considered Jewish nationalism to be clearly and fully divine, "the foundation and essence of Judaism."[132] "Torah and Zion are two sanctities that supplement and imply each other."[133]

The divine quality of "the congregation of Israel" is not due to any achievements of the empirical people, but to the free act of God.[134] But the living people can bring its divine endowment to fruition only when it is healthy, physically as well as spiritually. "The wisdom of holiness shines only in the land of Israel. Whatever is envisaged in the Diaspora is nothing but the corollaries of the understanding and its branches. . . . In the land of Israel, the spiritual fountain of the inwardness of holiness, which is the light of the life of the soul of the congregation of Israel, flows spontaneously."[135]

In the mind of Kuk, the yearning to live in the land of Israel is itself proof of the activity of the Holy Spirit which functions primarily only in the Holy Land.

The Holy Spirit received in Palestine continues to function, even if the recipient should by chance go to the Diaspora, either through an error or for some compelling reason . . . The more difficult it is to bear the atmosphere of the Diaspora, the more one feels the spirit of un-cleanliness of the unclean soil, the more true it is that the soul has inwardly assimilated the holiness of the land of Israel and that the grace of the Lord did not desert it . . .[136]

Yet, Kuk believed that the redemption of Israel would bring salvation to all mankind, since there was an inner correspondence between the spirit of Israel and that of humanity. "Original Jewish creativity, in thought and in the practical achievements of life, is not possible for Israel, save in the land of Israel . . . and this is a great boon for Israel and the world . . . Judaism of the Holy Land is salvation itself."[137]

This last statement is a neo-qabbalist doctrine, equating "the secrets of Torah" with the course of redemption.

Secularists in Israel

In Israel there is no organized religious ideology apart from the Orthodox and the Ultra-Orthodox. The secularists fall into two categories—the romanticists who continue to use the traditional categories of thought, albeit with new meaning (for example, substituting "the Rock of Israel" for "the God of Israel"), and the humanists or leftist socialists who seek to build a State that will in no way differ from other progressive countries. The romanticists intend to retain the bond between the Synagogue and the Government of Israel, because they consider the Jewish religion to be the matrix of Jewish culture and inseparable from the life of Jews. For them, too, a Jew who converts to another faith cannot be designated as a Jew. They do not necessarily believe in a God who chooses, but they do affirm with impassioned zeal that the Jews are the Chosen People, somehow separated from all the nations, set apart and charged with a messianic vocation. They sound the tocsin for the ingathering of the exiles, specifically for the immigration of American Jews, partly because they feel so insecure and partly because they can see no future life for Jews in the Diaspora. Thinking in nationalistic terms, they consider the Hebrew language to be the key to the tradition, and the mark of assimilation to be the non-use of Hebrew.

Yet nationalism does not exhaust their concept of Israel since their national awareness is forged in the crucible of the "meta-myth." By itself, the national ethos does not inspire a process of global concentration; the Irish do not leave the "fleshpots" of America; the Italians are not deserting the sidewalks of New York; and even the French Canadians with all their bitterness against the English and the Protestants show no signs of emigrating en masse to *la Patrie*. It is nationalism plus the protean cloud of myth and mystery that extends to the heavens, appearing as a "pillar of flame" by day and a "pillar of smoke" by night. So the Jew feels, in the light of his history, that his is a special glory; but he also feels that he is dogged by a massive Satanic hate which can never be overcome. Even after Israel has been established, the Jew is still not among the nations, but unique, as against them all. Certain it is that if the gates of Russia were opened, many thousands would flock to Israel and to the West in order to be able to affirm their unity with the millenial stream of Jewish history. And this in spite of the fact that the present generation of Russian Jews received hardly any religious or even Hebraic instruction.

Romantic secularist nationalism is a real factor in the life of Jewish people today, even if it seems irrational to liberals and humanists. It enshrines the feelings of identity that were nourished by the religious tradition, though it negates the central faith of the heritage. It is a reaction to, or the Jewish counterpart of, the "meta-myth" in the Christian world. It is the equal and opposite reaction to the nationalist frenzy in the twentieth century. Finally, it reflects the awareness of Jewish history which throws a vast shadow on our age. Three thousand years cast a strange spell, like a heaven-piercing pyramid so massive that it seems to be part of the inner structure of the universe.

Humanism in Israel

Romantic nationalism is Israel is balanced by the ideals of humanism and socialism which European Jewry embraced so heartily. It is these ideals which impel the Government of Israel to undertake a program of foreign aid that is far out of proportion to its size and resources. More than fifty new and underdeveloped nations are being assisted by technicians and scientists sent out of this small State of barely 2,500,000 people. Scholarships by the hundreds are made available to students from Asian and African nations. The *Histadrut* (Organization of Workers) maintains a year-round institute for the training of African industrial managers and secretaries of cooperatives. Toward the Arabs in Israel, the *Histadrut* directs a number of projects with the purpose of developing the skills of these people and of furthering their integration into the economy of the land.

The lamentable rift between Israel and the Arabs was not due to the absence of a humanist approach in the ideology of Zionism. On the contrary, the vision of Zion (rebuilt in the writings of Herzl, A'had Ha'am, Lilienbloom, and Borohov) included the native Arabs of Palestine in the idyllic picture of a non-competitive, non-exploitative, non-aggressive utopia. The "exiles" would go back to awaken the East as returning natives armed with the technical skills of the West. They would embrace the Arabs as long-lost "brothers," descendants of Abraham, laying the foundation for a joint renaissance of the two kindred nations.

That the Arab phase of the Zionist ideology went so tragically awry was due to a number of factors. The returning Jews were actually Europeans, in the cultural sense, and "Semites" only in their own dreams and in the eyes of anti-Semites. The rhythm of their life was centuries away from that of the Arab masses, while the Arab leaders could gain standing in the eyes of the mandatory Government only as nationalist agitators and revolutionaries. So, a generation later, to sit for a few months in an English jail was a prerequisite for any would-be savior of his country. Again, the contending ideals of romantic nationalism and liberal humanism did not move on the same plane. For the former aimed at making the life of Israel possible, while the latter detailed that which the life of Israel would make possible. As Herbert Spencer pointed out long ago: in a crisis the necessities of life will always prevail over its ideals. And the rebuilding of Israel was effected by way of an uninterrupted series of crises.

Buber's Concept

The renowned religious thinker, Martin Buber, traces the mystical dimension of the Zionist idea from the dim beginnings of Biblical history to the present day. A modernist and an antitraditionalist in the field of ritual, Buber is essentially a mystic, though with reservations. He does not aspire to achieve unity with God or to overcome "selfhood," but he is perpetually aware of a Divine Presence, a Divine Call that may address us in diverse ways. While his mystical or existentialist philosophy is shared by few people, his interpretation of the Zionist ideal is resonant with the undertones and overtones of Jewish history.

He speaks of Zionism as an age-old religious and popular reality, adapted to the universal form of the national movements of the nineteenth century. This reality was the holy matrimony of a "holy" people with a "holy" land, the local point of which was the name of Zion.

In other respects the people of Israel may be regarded as one of the many peoples on earth, and the land of Israel as one land among other lands; but in their mutual relationships and in their common task they are unique and incomparable. And, in spite of all the names and historical events that have come down to us, what has come to pass, what is coming and shall come to pass between them, is and remains a mystery. From generation to generation, the Jewish people have never ceased to meditate on this mystery.[138]

Buber regards this "mystery" as an obpective phenomenon, by no means comparable to the similar illusions of other nations. In the case of Israel, the "mystery" was embraced in authentic faith. It was given by the Divine Commander.

The essential point is that Israel heard the will of the Lord of the world at the beginning of its expedition to Canaan and conquered the land in the perfect and well-founded faith that it was accomplishing His Will . . . at all times there have been peoples who have given divine labels to their passions and interpreted the acts of violence born of their own greed for possessions, power and destruction as commanded by these divinities . . . but, so far as we are able to judge from the record, no other people has ever heard and accepted the command from heaven as did the people of Israel. So long as it sincerely carried out the command, it was in the right and is in the right in so far as it still carries it out. Its unique relationship to its land must be seen in this light. Only in the realm of perfect faith is it the land of this people . . . Where a command and a faith are present, in certain historical situations conquest need not be robbery.[139]

Coming down to modern Zionism, Buber shows how "the love of Zion" steered the quest of Jewish leaders for a haven of refuge toward Palestine, regardless of rational and pragmatic considerations that pointed to other territories. Such westernized intellectuals as Pinsker and Herzl wavered, but the instinct of the masses was sure and firm. A'had Ha'am, rationalist though he was, recognized the mystical dimension of the land of Israel and projected the ideal of a cultural center. Yet A'had Ha'am did no go far enough when he wrote "of the power of the historical feeling that unites the people and the land." For Buber, the bond between the people and the land was not merely subjective feeling. "The decisive question is the objective reality which is mirrored in the historical feeling." He asks, "Is it merely a historical reality, transient like all merely historical things, capable of being annulled by new historical facts like all merely historical things? Or is what has befallen this people in its encounter with this land, and this land in its encounter with this people, the token and expression of a supra-historical relationship?"[140]

For Buber, there is no question that a "supra-historical" reality is incarnate in the Zionist enterprise. He quotes approvingly from the writings of A. D. Gordon, the revered *halutz* and mystic. " 'It seems as if the whole nature of the plenitude from on high that is poured from all worlds into the soul of man, but especially into the soul of the Jew, is entirely different from what it is in the lands of the Diaspora.' "

Gordon was a mystical poet, but not religious in a formal sense. He apotheosizes the spirit of the land of Israel because of its intimate union with the people of Israel. "David's harp can only regain its power here in the land of Israel." And the land speaks, as it were, to the people. "It is not we, it is our land that speaks to the people. We have merely to express and intimate the words spoken by the land, and we say to you, to the whole people: 'the land is waiting for you.' "[141]

Buber's ascription of a mystical dimension to the people Israel and to its bond with the land of Israel is based upon two sources: the romantic folkism of his youth and the testimony of the Hebrew Bible. Though he has disavowed the mystical racism of his early writings, he has continued to glorify the primitive sense of direct communion with God, nature, and folk. Once "feeling" is the guide, there is no way for mankind to keep from repeating the bloody errors of the past. The elimination of the context of rational culture from the quest of reality puts all ethical considerations on a secondary plane. To reassert Biblical nationalism as unique, because the Israelite conquest was kept within the framework of a divine command, is to open the floodgates to similar feelings and similar consequences.[142]

Buber does not believe in the literal revelation of the divine will in the Hebrew Bible. It is the light of meaning which a person experiences when he studies the Scriptures that is divine. Like Spinoza, Buber regards the entire Law as invalid, but unlike the great rationalist, he looks to the feelings of devotion for guidance, and he esteems the "mystery" of Israel as a "spiritual reality" that is objective and normative.

The mystical concept of Israel, in all its variations from the

Qabbalists to Buber, contains several dynamic tendencies that might lead to the self-transcendence of the individual and the nation. First, the emphasis on inwardness in the service of God.[143] In comparison with the supreme significance of the intention of the individual, the boundaries between the various systems of serving the Lord lose some of their dogmatic rigidity. If the whistle of a shepherd boy could open the heavens, why not the Gregorian chant or the cry of the muezzin? So, there is an undercurrent of anti-nominalism in any upsurge of mysticism. Second, the projection of an infinite dimension in the cultivation of religious feeling reduces the finite variations among diverse sects to insignificance. Third, the awareness of an ever-present mystery militates against the need of dogmatists to direct the events of history by their own power and do God's work for Him, as it were. The overtones of skepticism toward the affairs of this world introduce a healthy detachment from the plausible panaceas of the moment.

Rationalist Nationalism

As we move from the romantic-mystical side of the spectrum to the rational and humanistic views, the concept of Israel tends to break along the line between religion and nationalism.

The nationalists, like Dubnow and A'had Ha'am, regard the Jewish religion as one of the historical expressions of national culture. While there are no radical breaks in history, the creative energies of the people may be expected to seek new expressions, in keeping with the spirit of the times. Both Dubnow and A'had Ha'am were convinced that the age of religion had ended. The Jewish people that had formerly lived within the protective walls of the "inner ghetto" of law and myth must now rearrange its life in order to be a "cultural," or "spiritual," people. A'had Ha'am saw the future Jewish world-community as one organic body, with its heart in Israel and its scattered limbs in the

Diaspora. He maintained that this "center and periphery" arrangement would sustain the Jewish sense of being radically different (the "meta-myth" in our analysis) and would halt the "normal" processes of assimilation.

Dubnow portrayed the entire panorama of Jewish history as of "a spiritual nation," a people that learned long ago to confine the drives of nationalism to the domain of culture and self-government. He fought for the principles of autonomy for all minority-nationalists. In the interim between the two world wars, Dubnow's philosophy became the basis of the minority clauses at the Versailles Treaty as well as of the organization of the Jewish communities in eastern Europe. Long before the final blow, the currents of life had ebbed away from the secularist communities and all their agencies. The community organizations of the large Polish cities were torn between the two irreconcilables—the Bundists and the Orthodox. In the Soviet Union, the Yiddish organizations lacked popular support, with most Jewish parents preferring Russian schools and cultural fare. It was not the language that appealed to them in the first instance, but the ideal and sentiments of the literature—ideals which the Communists did their best to undermine. The impassioned will to live as a Jew falters and fades away in the atmosphere of secularism.

In America, the philosophies of A'had Ha'am and Dubnow were brought up to date and revised in the Reconstructionist movement, founded by Prof. Mordecai M. Kaplan. Religion is not a temporary, dispensable "garment" of the enduring genius of the people, but it is the crown and glory of every civilization. So, religion is the "first-fruits" of the evolving civilization of the Jewish people.[144] It should change in accord with the changing patterns of Jewish life, reflecting its collective hopes and ideals. Organizationally, Israel should be constituted as a world-community, centered in the Holy Land where its civilization is dominant and extending into the Diaspora where Jews will live in "two civilizations." Liberal in religion, Reconstructionism is romantic in its concept of "the organic community." But, unlike A'had Ha'am, Kaplan disavows the "chosenness" and the uniqueness of the Jewish people. The meta-historical phase of the concept of Israel belongs to a supernaturalist world view which should give way to a naturalist philosophy of religion, and to a concept of Israel which reintegrates it into the evolving society of mankind.

From Rationalism to Existentialism

At the extreme end of the nationalist spectrum, the attempt was made to remove the ethnic plane entirely from the concept of Israel. The Jewish community was simply a religious community —nothing more. This view emerged with some hesitation, even in the ranks of the classical Reformers. Abraham Geiger still postulated a Jewish racial genius in the domain of religion. At the turn of the century, classical Reform was radically opposed to the Zionist view of Israel as a nation. The Jews ought to take on the national character and the specific culture of the nations among whom they live, retaining only their own distinctive faith. And their mission to humanity consists in the promotion of "ethical monotheism."

Perhaps the most profound thinker among the ideologists of this school was Hermann Cohen, who thought of Israel as the vanguard of humanity. Its religion consists of the glorification and sanctification of pure ethics. Its collective purpose is to help establish "the kingdom of heaven," the perfect society of universal justice for all mankind. Its destiny is to be "the suffering servant" of humanity, since all chauvinists and zealots, sensing in the Jew the harbinger of the time to come, vent their fury upon him.[145]

Cohen combatted the Zionist ideal not on the ground of its impracticality or its utopianism, but because it was a deliberate attempt to reject the noble role of martyrdom. "They do want to be happy," he complained of the Zionists.

Cohen's disciple, Franz Rosenzweig, veered sharply from rationalism to existentialism. He believed in the revealed religion of Judaism, not in a "religion of reason," and he thought of the people of Israel as a community formed by Divine Will and lifted out of the course of history—a meta-historical people. But Rosenzweig's view was remarkable in that, for him, the Christian community was engaged in fulfilling Israel's mission. The people Israel was like the sun; the Christian community was the effulgence of divine rays, permeating the nations with the spirit of monotheism. The boundary line between Judaism and Christianity was not along the plane of intellectual thought, since the Divine Being could be caught only figuratively or symbolically within the meshes of human reason. Existence is prior to thought in the life of the community as in the experience of the individual. Our role is determined by our place within the unfolding charade of world history. Now specific functions were assigned by Providence to each community: the cultures of India, Greece and China to prepare the ground; the people of Israel to preserve the heavenly fire; the Christian community to convert the pagan world. Both communities are the agencies of divine redemption, since "salvation is from the Jews."

Rosenzweig bases his conception upon the assertions of both Halevi and Maimonides that Christianity and Islam are "preparations" for the coming of the Messiah and the ultimate triumph of Judaism. Yet his view is a distinct advance, for they operated within the context of a literalist faith. Hence, the deviations from the "pure" faith were grave sins. At the same time, Rosenzweig moved within the thought-world of modern Judaism where diverse religions are so many pathways to the one goal. For him, the Being of God was the ultimate truth, and deviations were only distractions which are unavoidable in any case.

Rosenzweig saw the course of revelation in the actual processes of history, inverting Hegel's dictum, "the rational is the real." For him, "the actual is the way to Truth." Thus anti-Semitism, embodying Christian resentment of the metaphysical character of the Jews, was, in the view of Rosenzweig, part of the divine revelation as was the defiant stubbornness of the Jew, his indomitable pride in possessing the fullness of truth and standing at the goal toward which others only stumble and fumble—a self-assurance which exasperates and offends.[146]

Rosenzweig felt that Judaism was both "more and less" than nationality and also "more and less" than a religious denomination. It was unique, meta-historical in the present because of its meta-historical roots in the past and the persistent incursions of divine grace within the stream of history. He conceived of the Zionist enterprise as being in the same relation to Judaism as socialism is to Christianity. Both social movements operate on the basis of opposing ideologies, but historically they fulfill the real purpose of religion: the establishment of a just society here on earth.[147]

Ideology and History

The position of classical Reform is still maintained by some ideologists, but it is now largely defunct, chiefly because the course of events had rendered it academic. The Jews of the western countries could not shed their nationality in one century when the eastern Jews were so obviously reasserting their ethnic character and their determination to reconstitute themselves as a nation. The triumph of racist anti-Semitism in Germany made all theories worthless. For a while, at least, the vision of one humanity had turned into a cruel mirage.

Yet, in spite of his temporary successes and his slaughter of six million Jews, Hitler failed after all. And his downfall had served to clear the air and to usher in an era, rich in hope and boundless in promise. The apostles of hate have retreated into the shadows, and concerted efforts are made in many parts of the world to overcome the dragon's teeth of bigotry still embedded in the soil of contemporary culture.

No concept can be understood apart from the historical context in which it is placed. In the past generation, the Nazis provided an object lesson of the powerful momentum of ancient hatreds. At the same time, the rapid realignments in the post-War world, projecting the vision of a Europe united, demonstrated the range of freedom in human affairs. It is not written in the stars that France and Germany must forever fight against each other. Nor is it written that the Jews must be forever homeless wanderers. The rise of Israel through the voluntary effort of individuals in the course of two generations is perhaps the greatest demonstration of the range of freedom in the history of mankind. Its foundations were laid by individuals from many parts of the world, and they received their inspiration from books; they labored for several decades to realize a vision which appeared to be hopeless, but which was, for them, the quintessence of spiritual rebirth—a blend of hope, faith and love.

Projections and Warnings

If we should now proceed to project the concept of Israel into the future, we must take note of the following considerations.

First, the continuity of trends in Jewish history. As a community that is constituted by reverence for a sacred literature, we cannot ever dismiss any of the major movements of antiquity. We may expect that there will always be fringe-groups, and by no means only in isolated communities, that will cherish ancient myths and legends, however antiquated they may seem to those who are in the mainstream. We do not have an authoritative body to define the faith for all Jews. We may regret many passages in the Talmud, and we might want to edit some of its discussion. But, as a collection of notes and a record of ancient disputes, it belongs to the past. To the Conservative and Reform it is a literary monument of the past, to be studied with ardor and devotion, but not as a guide for our times. Still there will always be some pietists who will insulate their minds from all contemporary winds of doctrine and force their living souls into the frozen molds of ancient times.

For this reason, the entire spectrum of opinions from the past looms as a perpetual pageant of potentialities for the future.

Second, the gradational character of the concept of Israel. Whether Israel be defined primarily in ethnic or in religious terms, allowance must be made for those who will associate themselves with it partially or marginally. In the domain of religion we run the gamut from ultra-Orthodoxy to total skepticism, stopping short only at the lines of express atheism. In the domain of ethnic loyalty we have the "Canaanites" of Israel at one end, and the Councilites of America at the other. Ethnic assimilation can be as gradational and near-total as an asymptotic line.

Third, the interaction of the concept and the complexities of life. The equilibrium of tensions within the Jewish community is naturally responsive to the changing forces in the general society. Every flareup of anti-Semitism is likely to frustrate the liberals and to strengthen the isolationists. Every intellectual movement in philosophy as in statecraft will challenge either the religious or the ethnic phase of the concept of Israel and evoke a corresponding response. The self-image of the Jew is too intimately enmeshed in the texture of life to be kept pure and inviolate, "unspotted of the world."

Fourth, the diversity of views within Israel is too great to permit any kind of meaningful communal unity. Jews will agree that anti-Semitism is evil and that a united effort to combat it is possible. They will also respond to campaigns for refugees and for the relief of whatever branch of Jewry is sorely threatened at the moment. But short of the necessity to combat the physical threat of annihilation, Jews are unlikely to act in concert or even to share a vision of the future. On the other hand, a persistent threat, maintained for a long time, might well call into being an association of organizations representing world Jewry, a quasi-community that might continue to exist for years, by the impetus of sheer momentum, after the emergency has passed.

Fifth, we took note of several tendencies that might eventuate in the expansion of the scope of the "invisible Synagogue" and the identification of Israel with the moral-spiritual vanguard of humanity. The strong component of rationalism within Judaism focuses attention on the moral-spiritual core of faith, "the religion of reason"; in this view, the diverse faiths of our time incorporate this core in varying degrees.

The rites and ceremonies of the different denominations are only so many varying instruments. And it is not the instruments, but the manner in which they are used that matters.

The mystical trend also favors the view of a greater Israel, in so far as it deprecates the criteria of ritualistic conformity, and it points to the infinite dimension of religious intention and enthusiasm. The "inter-subjectivity" of the realm of feeling corresponds to the objective standards of the rationalistic philosophers.

On the ethnic plane, the secular version of messianism implies an active commitment to the task of building the "kingdom of heaven" here on earth. This goal may well go hand in hand with the warning that emerges out of so many pages in our tradition— the warning against the varied seductions of pseudo-messianism. Jewish messianists are cautioned by their history against the assumption that any project, or plan, or person represents the final hope of mankind. The Messiah is up in heaven; He is a vision, a goal, a hope; in historic times, He is not here and now.

The secularized version of Jewish messianism was embodied in the past century in three movements, each promising redemption for the Jew and claiming to be the final form of Judaism "in the end of days."

The first ideal which appeared in this light was that of individualistic liberalism. All men were to be torn out of their historic context and left to float in splendid isolation within the ethereal realm of absolute law. The Jews in France and western Europe were indeed emancipated by the upsurge of liberalism. As we have seen, to many of our nineteenth-century philosophers, "the religion of reason" was indeed the soul and substance of Judaism.

The second ideal to acquire the deep pathos and ringing resonance of messianism was the vision of socialism. It was represented as a contemporary "scientific" version of the prophetic quest of righteousness, of the "kingdom of heaven" on earth. At the same time, it would liberate the Jews from the historic hates of anti-Semitism which—so it was proven again and again—derived from the "inner contradictions" of capitalist society.

The third ideal which appeared to be the light of the Messiah was that of Zionism. The Jew would be redeemed from the crushing burdens of hate, and his faith would be revitalized in the land of its birth.

We can now say without fear of contradiction that these three secular versions of messianism represented different colors in the ideal spectrum, but that none of them constituted the final revelation. Each movement achieved fulfillment in the modern world, but each also eventuated in certain frustrations of its own.

Here, then, we have concrete illustrations of the dangers of pseudo-messianism.

Two major events are likely to intensify the attraction of the movements at the two ends of the spectrum. First, the rise and rapid growth of the State of Israel is likely to dramatize and reinvigorate the ethnic base of Israel. Secondly, the growth of the ecumenical movement is likely to strengthen the humanist trend in the concept of Israel, transforming it into the vision of the invisible fellowship of all who seek the Lord with heart and soul. This development is likely to gather additional momentum if Moslem intellectuals should fall into line. We may expect some deep and sustained soul-searching among Jews, and this will result in according full recognition to the latent universalism within the Jewish faith.

Will the universalist trend be opposed by the resurgent national loyalties centered on the young and fragile State? The State of Israel is dominated by secularists, though the Synagogue is not separated from the Government. To the preponderant majority of Israeli, the concept of Israel is largely that of a nationality, united by sentiments of affection and concern with the nuclear center in Israel—largely, but not entirely. For the bond between nationality and religion has been hammered out by the forces of history. So the non-religious will concur in a law prohibiting the raising of pigs or disqualifying the "Jewishness" of a Brother Daniel.

The secularists may embrace their religious heritage in one of two ways. They may esteem the Jewish faith to be an asset and instrument of the national ethos, in which case they will stress the doctrines and customs that confer a mystical aura upon the national being. Consciously or not, they would seek to revive and glorify the "meta-myth." On the other hand, they may spurn the manipulative and cynical approach toward the Jewish religion and, in their earnest search for spiritual roots, discover and make their own the prophetic core of Judaism, the eternal quest of the soul for truth and holiness. In that case, they would strengthen the unifying thread between their historic past, their vision of the future, and their bold social experiments that are designed to follow the narrow pathway between messianism and pseudo-messianism.

In sum, the "Chosenness" of Israel remains a tantalizing challenge to Jewish people, whether they be secularist or religious. For the dogma derives not only from the many-sided tradition that we have analyzed, but from two sources that are perennially replenished: the wonder of Jewish history and the personal experience of the Divine.

Within the complex course of history the role of the Jew has been particularly conspicuous. His past appears to be unique as the agent of monotheism, as the target of hate, as an object of mystery, as a pioneer, and as a pariah. So, many secularist Jews will find in the experiences of their own day subjective confirmations of the "meta-myth" which they will articulate in the literary-cultural terms of their day. Strange as it may sound, the secularist mentality has had no difficulty in accepting the status of "chosenness" while rejecting belief in a God who chooses. The resources of the mythological imagination are endless. It would be easy to cite abundant evidence from contemporary "mystics of Jewish history," who reassert the metaphysical uniqueness of Israel, though in all other respects they are realists and pragmatists.

At the same time, "chosenness" is a phase of the individual's experience of grace. As we move in thought and feeling away from the outward appearance of things and yearn for "the nearness of God," we do get on occasion that flash of illumination which is the basic quantum of religion. It is at once a feeling of surrender and of assurance. As we yield in trust, we feel the upwelling of the Divine within us. We are accepted, we are loved, we are anointed, we are commissioned—these are various ways in which our grateful reception of divine favor is expressed. And this sense of possession that accompanies all religious experience is so close to the notion of "chosenness" as to merge with it. To be sure, religious experience also leaves us with the feeling of privation—we know that we do not know. Hence, its inexhaustible dynamism.

Thus, personal religious experience in the case of Jews is likely to seek confirmation in the rhetoric of the Jewish tradition and in the collective experience of the Jewish people. In turn, the ancient doctrine in all its variations acquires the fresh resonance of contemporary experience from the mystical fervor of deeply religious people.

Rooted in the sacred tradition, in history and in religious

experience, the "Chosenness" of Israel, however it is interpreted, will long continue to intrigue the imagination of Jews and non-Jews alike.

NOTES

1 Genesis 32, 29.

2 *De Congressu Eruditorum Causa*, 10.

3 The school of Shammai maintained that divorce was permissible only in the event of the woman's adultery. Their attitude was similar to that of Jesus (Sanhedrin 90a).

4 Hosea 2, 1; Exodus 4, 22; Exodus 19, 5.

5 Ezekiel 20, 32.

6 2 Kings 19, 15–31; 2 Kings 23, 25–27.

7 Jeremiah 10, 11.

8 The notion of "correspondence," which was developed extensively in Qabbalah and in the medieval commentaries was probably contained in the Torah. The vessels of the Sanctuary were modeled after heavenly patterns (Exodus 25, 9). In the higher reaches of pagan thought, the same assumption was axiomatic—the ritual on earth affected a corresponding reality in the invisible world.

Abraham Ibn Ezra (Exodus 25, 40, *Commentary*) lays down a general principle: "We know that His Glory fills the world; still, there are places where His Power is more manifest than in others, either because the recipient is more adapted, or because of the higher Power supervening above a certain area. Therefore, the place of the Holy Temple was chosen. And if the Lord put wisdom in your heart, you will understand the Ark, the Cover, the Cherubim that spread out their wings . . . These are the Glory of the Lord."

9 Isaiah 56, 3; Esther 9, 27; Zechariah 2, 15; Daniel 11, 34.

10 Thus the Hellenizers are described as eager "to conclude a *covenant* with the nations around us." The Covenant of Israel with God interposed an obstacle to their fraternity with their neighbors (I Maccabees 1, 11).

11 On the other hand, in times of peace, the concept of Israel was expanded generously to include "those who seek the Lord," or "those who fear the Lord" (Psalms 69, 33; Psalms 34, 11; Psalms 118, 4; Psalms 135, 20).

12 This much-quoted passage occurs in various forms. A more careful formulation is this: "Three series of levels are bound together: the Holy One, blessed be He, Torah and Israel." *Zohar*, Vayikro, 73; also *Zohar*, Vayikro, 93.

13 *Zohar*, Beshalah, II, 64b. R. Shimeon asks how the generation of the desert could doubt if the Lord was among them, seeing that the clouds of

Glory were around them. He answers that they sought to know the relation between "the Ancient One, the Hidden of Hidden," and the "Miniature Face *(Zeir Anpin)* that is called YHVH."

14 "The Commandments of the Torah are all limbs and fragments that add up to one mystery . . . He who removes even one of the Commandments, it is as if he diminished the image of the faith . . . for they all add up to the pattern of Man . . . For this reason, Israel is called one people . . ." *(Zohar,* Teruma, 162b). Nahmanides in the introduction to his commentary on the Pentateuch: "We have a true tradition that the entire Torah consists of the Names of the Holy One, blessed be He . . . that the Torah written with black fire on white fire was to be so construed . . ."

15 "And when the Holy One, blessed be He, decided to destroy His House below and the Holy Land below, He first removed the Holy Land above *(Shechinah)* and lowered it from the level where it drew from the Holy heavens *(Tiferet)*, and only then did He destroy the earth below" *(Zohar II,* 175a). This action was in keeping with the general principle, "The Lord does not cause a nation to fall, before He casts down its prince above." (Shemot, Rabba. 21a)

16 Hullin 91b; Bereshit Rabba 82.

17 Rashi, in Hullin 91b: the image of Jacob was that of the man in the Divine Chariot.

18 Rashi, Genesis 1, 2.

19 Shabbat 152b.

20 Bereshit Rabba 47.

21 Baba Mezia 85b.

22 Bereshit Rabba 51.

23 Sota 17a.

24 Abot III, 7.

25 Megillah 29a. The commentary of the *Mahavsha* distinguishes between the *Shechinah,* as such, and *giluy shechinah,* the revelation of the Divine Presence.

26 Rosh Hashono 31a; Shemot Rabba 2, 2.

27 Menahot 110a. In time to come, the altar that is above will descend to earth. Midrash Aseret Hadibrot, 1.

28 Megillah 29a.

29 Berochot, 7a.

30 *Kusari,* V, 23.

31 Shabbat 31a. Sanhedrin 96a.

32 Baba Bathra 15b.

33 Baba Bathra 9.

34 Berochot 43a; Kiddushin 31a.

35 Hagigah 16a.

36 Shabbat 12b.

37 Hagigah 15b.

38 *Nefesh Hahayim,* by R. Hayim Volozhin II, 11

39 Berochot 35b.

40 Menahot 53a.

41 Pesahim 87a.

42 Jeremiah 15.

43 Lamentations, Rabba.

44 "Woe is to the wicked who say that the Torah is only the narrative, for they look at the garment only . . . The narratives are the garment of Torah . . ." (*Zohar,* Bamidbar 152).

45 *Zohar,* Vayikro 73.

46 *Zohar,* Vayikro 93.

47 *Tikkunai Zohar,* 21.

48 Bereshit Rabba, 1.

49 *Ibid.*

50 Tanhuma, Behukotai 2.

51 Yebamot 63a.

52 Yebamot 63a.

53 Shabbat 156a.

54 Hullin 91a.

55 Sanhedrin 90a.

56 *Zohar,* Bamidbar 244.

57 *Zohar,* Bamidbar 147.

58 Yomah 38b.

59 Sukka 45b.

60 Raya Mehemna, Deuteronomy, Tetse.

61 *Tikkunai Zohar,* 32, p. 72b. *Shaarai Zohar,* by R. Margolis. Jerusalem 1956, Berochot 15b.

62 *Noam Elimelech,* by R. Elimelech of Lizhensk, Vayehi.

63 Shabbat 146a.

64 *Ibid.*

65 See *Shaari Zohar,* by R. Margolis, in reference to Yebamot 49a and Shabbat 146a.

66 *Kusari* I, 115

67 Kiddushin, 70b

68 *Kusari* I, 109

69 *Kitvai Maharal MiPrag* (Vol. I, p. 127).

70 *Tanya,* chaps. 1, 2.

71 *Zidkat HaZadik,* 256, 257, by R. Zadok HaKohen of Lublin.

72 Megillah, 13a.

73 Hosea 2; 25

74 Pesahim, 87a.

75 Vayikra Rabba 6, 8.

76 Tanhuma, Deuteronomy, 52.

77 Yalkut, II Kings, 296.

[78] Nedarim, 32a.

[79] Yebamot, 48b.

[80] Baba Bathra, 10b.

[81] See note by W. Bacher, *Agadot Tanaim Veamoraim*, Vol. I, p. 26.

[82] J. Berochot 2, 1, *Standard Prayer Book for Rosh Hashono and Yom Kippur*: "Repentance, prayer, and charity avert the severe decree." Also, Berochot 17a and 26a.

[83] Yoma 87a.

[84] Yebamot, 57a.

[85] Yadaim 4, 4.

[86] Avoda Zara 64b.

[87] Tosefto, Sanhedrin 13.

[88] *Tana dibai Eliyahu*, ed. Ish Sholom, chap. 45.

[89] *Ibid.*, chap. 135.

[90] Seder Eliyahu Raba, 2.

[91] *Ibid.*, p. 121.

[92] *Ibid.*, p. 14.

[93] *Shulhan Aruch*, Yore Dea, 268.

[94] Horayot 13a.

[95] Shevuot 39a.

[96] Yebamot 109b.

[97] Aboda Zara 3b.

[98] Yebamot 102a.

[99] Jer. Bikkurim 1, 4.

[100] *De Confusione Linguarum*, M. I. 426.

[101] *De Congressu Eruditionis Gratia*.

[102] *De Virtutibus*.

[103] *De Abrahamo*, M., 1, 15.

[104] Wolfson, *Philo*, II, p. 401, Note 25.

[105] Praem. 26, 152.

[106] *Moses* II, 7, 44. Wolfson, in Note 100 of *Philo* (II, p. 417), equates the opinion of Philo with that of the Talmud, citing as reference, Aboda Zara 24a. But the term, *gerim gerurim*, connotes contempt and a lower status than that of righteous proselytes, let alone Israelites. That term is still compatible with another reference in the Talmud that in the Messianic Age all Gentiles will become "slaves of Israel." Airuvin 43b.

Rashi explains the term, *gerim gerurim*, "dragged converts," as meaning that "they will convert of their own accord, but we shall not receive them, because their motivation is the triumph of Israel." This interpretation is in accord with the oft-quoted principle: "We do not receive converts in the days of the Messiah. So, too, converts were not accepted in the days of Kings David and Solomon." Cf. Yebamot 24a. In the Talmudic text the implication is that the Lord will delight in humiliating them. Cf. Aboda Zara 3b.

[107] See Tossafot on Avoda Zara 2a.

[108] Maimonides, *Yad*, Hilchot Issurai Bia, 14.7.

[109] The distinction between Maimonides' legalistic and philosophic works has been the subject of heated debates. Philosophy deals with principles, not laws. In the long night of exile and dispersion the medieval rabbis felt powerless to amend the law and to bring it into conformity with their principles. Cf. Mainonides, *Yad,* Hilchot Issurai B in, 14.7.

[110] I. Arame, *Akedat Yizhak,* 60.

[111] *Guide of the Perplexed,* III, 51.

[112] R. Shem Tov ben Joseph, ad hoc.

[113] Teshuvot HoRambam.

[114] *Guide of the Perplexed,* III, 28 and 36.

[115] *Akedat Yizhak,* Gates 15; 31; 38; 56.

[116] J. Albo, *Safer HaIkkarim,* I, 25.

[117] *Ibid.,* 23.

[118] Seforno, *Commentary on the Pentateuch,* Exodus XIX, 6.

[119] I. Abravanel, *Mashmia Yeshuah,* Saloniki, 1526; Amsterdam, 1644.

[120] I. Baer, *A History of the Jews in Spain,* Philadelphia 1961, p. 335, Note, p. 446.

[121] *Tractutus Theologica Politicus,"* translated by R. H. M. Elwes, London, 1909, chap. 5.

[122] *Jerusalem,* Part II.

[123] Rabbi Ishmael of Modena (1723–1811), a leading Halachic authority, wrote as follows in answer to Napoleon's inquiry about "fraternity": "Though the term brotherhood implies natural kinship, there is a unity of faith between the Frenchmen, or the other peoples of Europe, and the Jews. Since these nations serve the One God, each in their own way, they are now accounted in the eyes of the children of Israel as brothers, for we are obligated to deal with them in fraternity and love, in friendship and peace, and the Holy Torah commands us to help their needy." Cf. J. B. Agus, *The Meaning of Jewish History,* Vol. II, p. 330.

[123a] J. B. Agus, *The Meaning of Jewish History,* Vol. II, p. 338.

[124] About Fichte's opposition to Jewish emancipation and his concept of the eternal struggle between the people of Vernunft and the people of Verstand, see Agus, *The Meaning of Jewish History,* Vol. II, pp. 333–342.

[125] Toussenel, a notorious socialist, in *Jews, the Kings of the Epoch,* wrote: "Like the masses of the people, I apply the odious name of Jew to all the people who lived by the manipulation of money, to all the exploiting parasites who live by the sweat of others."

[126] The pre-Marxist socialists of France were generally anti-Semitic. So were Fourier, Toussenel, and Leroux. Even Karl Marx, in his youthful articles on the question of Jewish emancipation, maintained that the real problem was emancipation from Jewry. He identified Jewry with the capitalists. It is only in the latter two decades of the nineteenth century that the socialists of Europe realized that anti-Semitism, as the "socialism of fools," was a tool of the reactionary forces. Cf. Agus, *op. cit.,* Vol. II, pp. 334–344.

[127] "But every true Jew, be he orthodox or liberal, feels in the depths of

his being that there is something in the spirit of our people—though we do not know what it is—which has prevented us from following the rest of the world along the beaten path, has led to our producing this Judaism of ours, and has kept us and our Judaism 'in a corner' to this day, because we cannot abandon the distinctive outlook on which Judaism is based. Let those who still have this feeling remain within the fold; let those who have lost it go elsewhere. There is no room for compromise."

This excerpt from A'had Ha'am's reply to Montefiore reveals the pathetic contradiction between his "sovereignty of reason" in matters of faith and his surrender to what may be called "the sovereignty of feeling" in urging the authority of a sense of radical difference. Cf. Leon Simon, *A'had Ha'am*, p. 127.

128 Cf. *Coningsby*, by B. Disraeli: "The Jews, independently of the capital qualities for citizenship which they possess, are a race essentially monarchical, deeply religious and essentially Tories. The fact is, you cannot crush a pure race of Caucasian organization."

129 Cf. Louise Elliott Dalby, *Leon Blum, The Evolution of a Socialist,* New York, 1963. Blum is quoted as believing that the Jew would take an active part in the building of a socialist State because of "the national law of their race." For Blum, the Jewish religion was only a tissue of ceremonies, but the real faith of the Jew was justice. "If Christ preached charity, Jehovah wanted justice," or "it is not an oversight of Providence that Marx and Lassalle were Jews." Blum felt that "the essence of Jewish thought is, perhaps, the gift for ideal reconstruction of the world."

130 By the term, "ultra-Orthodox," I refer here to the members of the *Agudat Yisroel,* not to the still more zealous pietists such as the Grand Rabbi of Satmar (Rabbi Joel Taitelbaum). This group holds it is a sin to participate in the government of Israel to the extent of voting in the elections to the *Keneset*. Their main reason is the statement in the Talmud that the Israelites took an oath not to come out from exile, by collective effort and "not to force the End" (cf. Kethubot, 111a).

Referring to the decimation of world Jewry in our day, this Rabbi writes: "Now in our generation it is not necessary to go searching for hidden reasons, since the sin which brought this catastrophe upon us is clearly stated in the words of our Sages who, in turn, learned it from the Holy Writ—not to end the exile by a united effort and not to force the End, 'lest I make your flesh free for all like that of the deer and the antelope'" (*Vayoel Moshe,* Brooklyn, 1959, p. 5).

And he thinks of redemption as occurring only through repentance and the works of piety: "For the Holy Temple above is constructed through the labors of the saints and their good deeds. And when it is completed, our righteous Messiah will come, but the wicked cause the destruction of that which the Saints build up" (*ibid.,* p. 11).

The first task of the Messiah, who will bring back the *Urim Vethumim,* is to compel Israel to return to the ways of Torah (*ibid.,* p. 134). The first group of those resurrected from the dead will precede the Messiah or accompany Him when He is revealed (*ibid.*, p. 135).

[131] The Maharal of Prague, favorite author of Chief Rabbi A. I. Kuk: It is impossible for redemption, that is, an exalted form of existence, to come all at once." Cf. *Kol Kitvai Maharal*, Vol. II, p. 347.

[132] J. B. Agus, *Banner of Jerusalem*, by J. B. Agus, New York, 1946, p. 61.

[133] *Azkarah*, Vol. V, p. 364.

[134] Introduction, *Shabbat Haaretz*, second edition, p. 7.

[135] A. J. Kuk, *Orot Hakodesh*, pp. 133, 134.

[136] *Banner of Jerusalem*, p. 215.

[137] *Loc. cit.*

[138] Buber, *Israel and Palestine* (London, 1952), Introduction.

[139] *Ibid.*, p. 49.

[140] *Ibid.*, p. 147.

[141] *Ibid.*, pp. 160, 161.

[142] *Philosophic Interrogations*, edited by Sidney and Beatrice Rome, New York, 1964. Buber replies to my question on pp. 77, 78.

[143] The elaboration of the infinite pathway of the "duties of the heart" was the meeting ground of the philosophical and Qabbalist schools, as well as the preoccupation of the popular preachers. Cf. Bahya Ivn Pakuda, *Duties of the Heart*, Introduction.

[144] Mordecai M. Kaplan, *Judaism As a Civilization*.

[145] J. B. Agus, *Modern Philosophies of Judaism*, New York, 1941.

[146] *Briefe*, Berlin, 1935, p. 670.

[147] *Ibid.*, p. 580.

7

❋ Afterword: Next Steps

RABBI ARTHUR GILBERT

Next Steps in the Jewish-Catholic Dialogue

RABBI ARTHUR GILBERT *has been Staff Consultant to the project, Religious Freedom and Public Affairs of the National Conference of Christians and Jews since 1961. Ordained at the Jewish Institute of Religion in New York in 1951, he pursued his graduate studies in counseling at the National Psychological Association for Psychoanalysis and is registered as a psychiatric social worker with the New York State Department of Health. Rabbi Gilbert served for seven years as Director of the National Department of Inter-Religious Cooperation of the Anti-Defamation League of B'nai B'rith where he was editor of the* Christian Friends Bulletin. *He is coauthor of the book* Your Neighbor Celebrates *and has contributed to such volumes as* American Catholics, a Protestant-Jewish Viewpoint *(Sheed and Ward, 1959),* Meet the American Jew *(Broadman Press, 1963), and was awarded a prize in 1961 by the Catholic Press Association for the best nonfiction article. He is a member of the Board of Directors and Editorial Committee of the Institute of Church and State of the Villanova University School of Law and serves on the Editorial Board of the* Reconstructionist *and the* CCAR *Journal. He is a member of the Central Conference of American Rabbis.*

THE BACKGROUND OF THE COLLOQUY

It is not without some joy and relief, too, that the four-day theological colloquy between twenty-six Jewish and Catholic scholars is brought to a close with these summary remarks. For in the light of history there was every good reason to doubt that it would even be possible for Jews and Catholics to engage each other in a conversation on matters of faith. In the past, Jews had been compelled by Catholics to enter the disputations and to listen to Catholic preachments intended to deprecate Judaism and to convert Jews.

Despite the clearing of the air by the recent actions at the Ecumenical Council, the question was legitimately asked at the very beginning of this colloquy, "Can we trust you?" One of the rabbis wanted to know whether the change in the Church was genuine. Was the new attitude expressed in Church pronouncements an indication of genuine conviction or was it merely a reaction to the external pressures of a world in revolution only to change again once the situation stabilized?

I think it fair to say after these four days of frank and honest talk with each other that such question need not be raised again. If anything at all occurred within these four days it was a growth in trust. Of course we realize that much conversation is still necessary merely in order to get to know one another. The bitterness of the past, the illiteracy that comes from the wideness of our breach, the harsh distortions created by the psychology of the attack and defense are all deterrent to any true objective or sympathetic understanding of that which we share together and that which divides us. In these four days, stereotypic conceptions were tested by the light of experience, and misinformation gave way to new knowledge.

The idea for such a colloquy first took root more than four years ago when it was decided that the Secretariat for Promoting Christian Unity would encompass the Jews within their concern and that a statement on anti-Semitism was to be prepared for the Vatican Council. It was my pleasure then to spend several days as the guest of Abbott Leo Rudloff, O.S.B., Abbot of The Church of Dormition on Mount Zion in Jerusalem, at his priory in Weston, Vermont. The Abbott and I had grown to respect and to trust each other in the course of my several visits to Israel. Now we dared share together the hope that an effective statement on the part of the Ecumenical Council would serve a healing and reconciling purpose in the relations between Jews and Catholics.

Abbott Rudloff and I considered the possibility of a small Jewish-Catholic scholarly conversation at his priory in Vermont. Action at the Vatican Council on the Resolution on the Jews however was delayed from session to session, and it soon became evident that any meeting between Jews and Catholics was open to every possible misunderstanding. The colloquy was necessarily postponed.

As the situation in Rome became more hopeful, Father Colman Barry, O.S.B., now president of St. John's College in Collegeville, Minnesota, took up the burden. With the help and assistance of Archabbot Rembert Weakland, O.S.B., of the St. Vincent Archabbey and with the support of the Most Reverend William Connare, Bishop of Greensburg, Pennsylvania, we at last decided that the time had come to conduct such a theological conversation. We recognized, of course, that all of us would have to come to such a meeting with no thought of proselytizing or conversion in our minds. As Bishop Connare put it so admirably in his word of greeting at the opening session: "A probing of our common roots and an inquiry into the relevancy of the Jewish-Catholic faith for the problems of the modern age" was to characterize our deliberations.

Since we wanted the conversation to plumb depths and to evoke honest exchange, we decided to keep the participation limited. A small group of Bible scholars, theologians, historians and social-action executives were called together. The American Benedictine Academy and the National Conference of Christians and Jews assumed responsibility for the administrative arrangements.

I regret that only one Orthodox rabbi accepted our invitation.

It is the conviction of the Orthodox rabbinate, based on theological grounds but motivated, I believe, much more by an
understandable defensiveness and fear, that conversations on
matters of faith are futile and that the Jews must, of necessity,
be disadvantaged in such encounters. Instead, the Orthodox are
ready to engage in any conversation designed to apply religious
insight to a mutually significant problem in the social order.
I suspect that it was similarly difficult for the Catholics to have
all points of view within Catholicism represented. If only these
fearful had been able to witness the graciousness, the honesty,
and the concern for human dignity that embraced every exchange,
then they would have realized how important and valuable such
a colloquy can be! I regret their failure to be present because
in honesty we needed their viewpoint as a corrective and as an
enrichment to those views so well articulated in the four days
of study and conversation.

The magnificent provisions made by the Archabbey for Kosher
food, brought some forty miles each day from Pittsburgh, symbolized the spirit of mutual esteem and the sincere desire for
growth and understanding that motivated the Catholics at this
conversation. The Benedictines, in fact, were most sensitive to
every need of the Jewish participants. I jokingly told one of the
priests before we had our first meal, "After four days of this
Kosher food, you'll understand why there is a Reform Judaism."
But I must now confess that the food was so good that the course
of Reform Judaism has been set back fifty years.

Some of the rabbis voluntarily asked permission to observe
the monks at prayer. Three of them arose for the morning service at 5:00 A.M., recognized in the Latin many of the very same
Psalms used in the Jewish morning worship, and then they engaged in their own prayer service.

Several other rabbis attended the celebration of the Mass
in the vernacular, and I am told that the observations and crit-
icisms made by the rabbis were found helpful by the priests who
are still involved in adjusting to their new liturgy.

Finally, I must explain that there was no intent at discrimination in limiting this conversation to Jews and Catholics. Certainly there were many occasions when a Protestant Christian insight would have been helpful, but it is clear that there are issues that emerge out of the distinctiveness of our past histories that require a separate Jewish-Catholic conversation, just as there is need for Catholics and Protestants to hold theological conversation with each other on occasion without Jews present. Of course, we must never forget that we cannot be satisfied merely with the development of the Jewish-Catholic rapprochment. Together we must also confront the world. Thus, at the last session of the Colloquy, visitors from the greater Pittsburgh community, including Protestant clergy and lay civic leaders of the Jewish, Protestant and Catholic faiths, were invited to the discussion.

Each of the papers presented at the Colloquy is rich in implication. Only if we study these papers carefully can we begin to understand fully the significance of this historic exchange. What I can do, however, is to communicate something of the flavor of the conversations and the discussion. These were off the record and no transcript was made. Frequently the questions put to the speaker and his answers were more clarifying than the paper itself. Often the emotional overtones in exchange between rabbi and rabbi and priest and priest carried more meaning than the written word ever could communicate. What I hope to do is recall that agenda of topics for future consideration that emerged from the Colloquy. These, then, are the issues that the participants recognized as demanding further study and our mutual collaboration.

ISSUES FOR FUTURE CONSIDERATION

History

At the session dealing with the historic past in Jewish-Catholic relations, disagreement erupted over the role of the Gospels in contributing to the growth of a Christian anti-Semitism. It was agreed, however, that a fruitful joint undertaking would be a study as to when and how distorted teachings concerning the Jews entered into Christian thought.

One rabbi suggested the need for interpretive material to accompany the Gospels. These would explain and put into context harsh references to the Jews in the New Testament and particularly those passages where the word "Jew" seems to signify "the enemy."

A priest pointed out that the recent renewal of Old Testament studies in the Church served "as an antidote to the de-evaluation of Judaism in Christianity."

Both rabbis and priests recognize that not only in Bible studies but in the study of history, as well, it is incumbent upon all of us to face the bitterness of the past rather than to repress it. The past has influenced our present. Only as we know that past and work through it together in trust and respect can we create a future. There is guilt to be acknowledged, but that guilt can also be used constructively in order to cement a firmer and wiser foundation of relationship.

The Meaning of Israel

Certainly the most difficult, provocative and enriching of the sessions at the Colloquy were those devoted to an effort at defining the meaning of Israel. To begin with, both Jews and Catholics each conceive of themselves as Israel, as the Chosen of God. Are these definitions mutually exclusive? Can Jews and Catholics allow for each other? How? And in what ways? What does it mean to be Israel? Added to the difficulty of explaining ourselves to the other was the fact, soon made dramatically evident by the conflict that emerged among the rabbis and then among the priests, that there are significant differences within each of our faiths. Catholics are struggling to define for themselves the nature of the Church and the identity of the People of God just as Jews remain divided on the meaning of the election, chosenness and nature of Israel.

One Catholic acknowledged that the Church does not yet know how to define its relation to contemporary Israel. He said, "The Church can define its relationship and indebtedness to the Jews of old, but our failure to deal with the contemporary significance of Israel jeopardizes the value of the assertion of this partial truth." Then he added: "The call to the Jews partakes a quality of *firstness* not only in the past, but also in the future. It is an understanding of exactly what this means that continues to raise a problem for the Church."

It was agreed that a worthy line of inquiry could be directed to understanding the significance of the survival and the existence of the Jews, contrasting old answers once given by churchmen with those that are now offered. In the past, for example, the existence of the Jews was seen as a sign of the curse and the punishment meted out by God to a stiffnecked and rebellious people who had failed to accept the Savior. Today some Christians would answer that the survival of the Jews is a sign of assurance of God's love and fidelity.

The Catholics, on their part, found it difficult to understand what it is that makes a Jew who denies his faith and religion still a Jew, and in what way such a Jew is to be considered a part of Israel. Pointing to the large number of secularized, non-practicing, non-religious Jews, one Catholic, in as gracious a way as possible, asked how much grace and faith still abides in contemporary Israel and whether it was sufficient to offer a promise of salvation for the Jews and for others as well.

Inevitably, there was discussion of the eschatological hope held by Jews and Catholics for the conversion of the world. What do we believe is our responsibility to evangelize, to proselytize, or to witness, and particularly in our relation to each other? Are Catholics satisfied just to leave the issue of the conversion of the Jews to God—to the far-off eschatological future—without any action on their own part? Can one distinguish between an organized campaign of "proselytization" and an active "witness," or, in different words, is there not even in the longed-for hope of conversion a judgment made on the integrity and value of the unregenerate "other" that itself is a deterrent to understanding.

It was pointed out that Jews once before, particularly at a time when they were under severe spiritual and physical coercion from the Church, had developed theological judgments providing a status for Christians and Moslems. What does Judaism now teach concerning the claims of the Church? In light of Jewish eschatological aspirations, what is the role and the significance of Christianity?

It was apparent that neither Jews nor Catholics have worked out a clear conception of the role or the vocation assigned by God to all other major religions in our universe.

The rabbis questioned whether past papal opposition to the establishment of the present State of Israel and the present failure of the Church to recognize the existence of the State testified alone to prudential and political factors or, rather, whether it did not suggest that the emergence of the State was a challenge to Christian theology.

Liturgy

After discussions of such an emotionally charged nature a change of pace was required; the session on liturgy was such a delight and pleasure. Rabbis and priests found themselves agreeing that liturgy provides the occasion for the community to confront the Living God. Exploring the common roots of the prayer tradition, the participants discovered each other as pastors sharing a common concern! What is it that we can learn from each other as to how to relate the liturgy to character formation and to the development of a communal sensitivity to issues of social justice?

The Church is only now beginning its liturgical renewal. In the Synagogue the renewal has taken place many times. Sagely, therefore, a Reform rabbi warned the Catholic confrères not to expect too much from revision of one liturgical form or another. "Renewal," he said, "is a constant and continual effort."

The priests praised the Jewish pattern of religious home ceremonials, but the Reform rabbis pointed out that they had moved many of these ceremonials into the synagogue and now they were regretful. Together, therefore, the priests and rabbis explored the ways that men's lives could be enriched by private, familial, and corporate worship.

Freedom of Conscience

Although there was much criticism of Rabbi Gordis' suggestion that the concept of religious freedom was a product of the secular enlightenment rather than a contribution of religion to the Western world, it was admitted that neither Jews nor Catholics have worked out as adequately as they should a theology that would explain the relation of Church and State and provide meaning to the concept of freedom of religion. It was agreed that much of our conflict with each other on Church-State issues and on matters of public policy have reflected historic circumstance and the sociology of our communal existence rather than the imperatives of faith commitment.

These particular Jewish and Catholic scholars found themselves closer together in their concerns on this issue than appears to be the case in the larger community. For example, Catholics expressed vigorously their fear over entangling alliances between Church and State. As one priest put it, "Power corrupts. State power corrupts absolutely, and religious power corrupts spiritually." The rabbis revealed an anxiety lest too rigid a separation between Church and State tip the scales in favor of a secularistic, State-supported faith of "Americanism" that would tend to rob us of our religious distinctiveness and would also relegate to religion only a minor role in the shaping of the public order. To the surprise of the Catholics, several of the rabbis revealed that while they would zealously oppose any State-supported religious ritual in public education, they were not adverse to the State's providing financial support for child benefits, such as textbooks and bus transportation for all children including those in parochial schools.

It was proposed that Jews and Catholics, individually and together, engage in a theological examination on the meaning of religious freedom and the relation betwen Church and State, hopeful that such a study would enable us to develop creative and new approaches to our differences on this issue.

Bible Scholarship

The discussion at this session was vigorous. The differences were not between rabbi and priest; rather it extended beyond the boundaries of faith community. At issue was the scholarly question: Can we ever discover the "pristine," or original, meaning of the Sacred Word? Or, in other words, have we not evolved, each of us in his own way, such a rich interpretation of "overmeaning" that we cannot find an original Biblical text. Bringing Faith to the Word, we can no longer hear Scripture in exactly the same way.

It would have been valuable, particularly at this point, to have had in our midst a Protestant Bible scholar, for it is the Protestants, particularly, who have labored so vigorously to discover the Biblical Word in its original context. This issue was never resolved. However, we could and did agree that there was value in encouraging Jewish and Christian Bible scholars to continue their investigations into the pristine meaning of the original text.

The observation was also made that we needed to know much more about how each of us, starting from one text, had developed over the centuries such widely different interpretations. The ecumenical posture would suggest that we ought now not label the other's interpretation "error," but seek rather to understand how, and why, and in what ways the other evolved his understanding and came to believe that it represented a fulfillment of the Biblical promise.

The priests were surprised when one rabbi opined that "Biblical literature was undoubtedly superior to rabbinic literature, but rabbinic religion was by far superior to Biblical religion." After some of the rabbis described how Jewish Biblical concepts had evolved during the rabbinic period, the Catholics insisted that the rabbis provide them with reading lists and reference titles. The exchange of bits of scholarly knowledge and footnote anecdotes that trailed off into the late evening suggested that there is no end to the need for such scholarly exchange.

Social Action

The concluding subject was that of social action. It was readily apparent that we were capable of joining forces together to engage in the quest for social justice with less difficulty than we shall face in pursuing many of the prior theological issues. Nevertheless, even here significant questions were put to the speakers for which neither they nor the participants could find easy answers. For example, what are the theological justifications for the involvement of the corporate Church in influencing the public order? In what ways are Church and Synagogue to exercise their power? Are the limitations that we would put on Church involvement a result of theological conviction or rather prudential judgment based on certain convictions concerning the nature of the democratic process?

To be specific, if the Church can lobby vigorously for the enactment of the Civil Rights Act, why not for a measure that would curb pornography, to cite the example given by Rabbi Tanenbaum? If Synagogue leaders can threaten congressmen with the loss of votes on an issue that concerns the welfare of the State of Israel or the economic interest of the Sabbath-observer, is it wrong for a bishop to exercise that same threat on the issue of the bus transportation of parochial-school students or the revision of the divorce law?

What is the rightful area and responsibility of the State and Church, together and separately, in the effort to achieve and maintain standards of private and public morality? What is the particular role of the corporate Church and Synagogue, as against that of the individual clergyman and in contrast to that of the layman, as we seek to make religion a significant force in life? How can the Church wield its power and yet maintain respect for those of other faiths who differ, as well as for those within the faith who differ with the Church on political issues which have spiritual or religious significance? Where does the political and moral meet and separate?

A priest called for the more vigorous participation of his laity in the work of social action; a rabbi, on the other hand, protested the recent insistence of Jewish religious leaders that only they were the proper spokesmen for the Jews in inter-religious social action endeavors.

Recapitulation

This summary indicates that there is a tremendous agenda of issues for future consideration that have emerged from these four days of conversation. Even before we concluded, the participants began to speak of "next time." I have no doubt that a fertile field was plowed and good seed planted. Present at the Colloquy were seminarians and scholars who by their individual studies will demonstrate the fruit of this exchange. There are some who can marshal the resources of their institutions in order to engage in further conversation. Already the American Benedictine Academy is exploring possible approaches for another such colloquy.

My own feelings about this meeting were summarized in a report I have made to the local press which was allowed to interview us only at the conclusion of the event. I said in that report: "Now that this meeting is concluded, we are enheartened that God has enabled us to confront each other as brothers. By this encounter each of us has been strengthened in our own faith and enriched by a glimpse of the Divine as held by the other. We are convinced that there is much merit in such conversation and hope that similar studies on matters of faith will continue."